(FIRST PERSON)²

(FIRST PERSON)²

A Study of Co-authoring in the Academy

KAMI DAY
MICHELE EODICE

UTAH STATE
UNIVERSITY PRESS
Logan, Utah

This book is dedicated to

PATRICK M. HARTWELL
February 10, 1937 – October 4, 2000

Manufactured in the United States of America.
Cover design by Tom Child, Mazyne, Inc.

Library of Congress Cataloging-in-Publication Data
Day, Kami, 1950-
 (First person)² : a study of co-authoring in the academy / Kami Day,
Michele Eodice.
     p. cm.
Includes bibliographical references and index.
 ISBN 0-87421-448-3 (pbk. : alk. paper) — ISBN 0-87421-458-0 (e-book)
 1. Academic writing. 2. Authorship—Collaboration. 3. Group work in
education. I. Title: (First person)two. II. Eodice, Michele, 1957-
III. Title.
 LB2369 .D38 2001
 808'.02—dc21
 2001003523

CONTENTS

ACKNOWLEDGMENTS

If we were to name every person, living and dead, who has contributed to this book, we would need to write at least a chapter of acknowledgments. So, we will limit ourselves to those with whom we have developed relationships, those who have been part of our lives and our work. First of all, we want to thank the co-authors who generously volunteered their time to talk with us, and, in many cases, to review transcripts and offer further guidance and encouragement. We could not ask for better mentors and models for our professional and personal lives, and we are happy to call many of these co-authors our friends as a result of our communication with them. We would also like to thank others who gave us permission to use their words—from email messages, conversations, and the 2000 Conference on College Composition and Communication workshop on co-authoring.

Several people read the manuscript of our book, or part of it, and gave us thoughtful input which helped shape our revisions: Rebecca Moore Howard, Derek Owens, Frank Farmer, and of course our editor, Michael Spooner. Our relationship with him has been truly collaborative as he demonstrated his respect for our work with his productive and challenging feedback.

We must acknowledge Carol Lacque, a co-author of a dissertation in 1975; this dissertation was the precedent we hoped would make our co-authored dissertation easier to sell to our graduate school. Speaking with her on the telephone was a pleasure, and she sent us several volumes of her poetry after our conversation. Toni Knott and Lynne Valek, who recently completed a collaborative dissertation, have been soul sisters to us—thanks.

Back when we wrote our very first paper together, our friends in graduate school were eager to see us succeed, and they continue to be some of our very favorite people and strongest supporters. Our colleagues at the University of Kansas and Johnson County Community College have been welcome cheerleaders. And our friends and family, in places near and far, have been patient, curious, and supportive. They will all no doubt be glad to see this work finally published!

Before we embarked on this project, we were taught and encouraged by several good teachers, including Mary and Larry Shanahan, Thomas J. Reigstad,

Donald McAndrew, C. Mark Hurlbert, Lynne Alvine, and Patrick Hartwell. This book is dedicated to Pat, who died in October 2000 and was our most influential mentor and a dear friend. He taught us that we learn about writing, and really about everything, from "little stories about teaching and little stories about learning." We think this book is full of little stories—ours and many others—that contribute to the big story: we are the relationships we have.

Finally, as we write this together, we decide to thank each other for the gifts we bring to our work and to each other's lives.

If I could let you know—
two women together is a work
nothing in civilization has made simple,
two people together is a work
heroic in its ordinariness,
the slow-picked, halting traverse of a pitch
where the fiercest attention becomes routine
—look at the faces of those who have chosen it.

Adrienne Rich

1 HOW WE CAME TO WRITE THIS BOOK

BACKGROUND

We are co-authors who study co-authors. We observe them as they write, but our primary focus has been the stories they tell about their work together. The research we've compiled here is bookended by an attempt to write a collaborative dissertation in 1997 and by a College Composition and Communication Conference 2000 workshop involving experienced academic co-authors. Occupying the central position is a study involving in-depth interviews with ten successful academic writing teams, representing a range of disciplines, experiences, and expertises. This book features particularly the voices of these interviewees but also includes those of the participants in the CCCC workshop and the voices of students and other co-authors we have encountered in classrooms, online, and even in casual conversations. We seem to find co-authors wherever we go, and as we have collected and analyzed more and more of their stories, we have come to understand that the integral components to successful co-authoring include more than productive material practices and publishable products.

Our work has led to a book with two authors' names on the cover, but those two names represent more than the final result of a scholarly project. Behind them, as behind the names of Ede and Lunsford, Hurlbert and Blitz, Roen and Brown, Spooner and Yancey—and numerous other co-authors in the field of composition and outside of it—are the stories of their work together. These are the stories we wish to tell, and we will begin with our own. What Mary Ann Cain observes about her own researcher role as "both participant in the construction of this story [*Revisioning Writers' Talk*] and observer of that construction" goes double for us: especially as co-authors, our story "should not be excluded in constructing the meanings of the contexts in which [the] writers [in our study] talk about their work" (1995, 111).

In the spring of 1997, we began writing a proposal for a co-authored dissertation. We realized the task we had taken on: challenging the traditions of the research and academic communities, attempting to contribute something new to the theory and practice of collaboration, and especially investigating the ways we weave our very different voices and writing styles into a voice we called "(first person) ^{2}." We proposed to continue this process, writing collaboratively sentence by sentence, with the goal of building a dissertation that explored what happens when people write together.

This project was a result of synchronicity. We met in the doctoral Rhetoric and Linguistics program at a mid-sized northeastern university as graduate students in a department that fosters collaborative efforts among its students and is exemplified by collaborative faculty projects. We were in a group of composition teachers learning about teaching writing at a time when the field was benefitting from the work of theorists who were recognizing the social dimensions of learning. Our first co-authoring effort was in our very first class, a course in research methods. We found that, unlike other times in which we had just "worked with" others, we were engaging equally and productively from the initial idea stage through the research to the writing of the final sentence. We did not think at the time about why our collaboration worked because it seemed to happen so naturally, but upon reflection, we realize the design of our graduate program promoted cooperation over competition. In this rich, intense learning environment, we forged supportive relationships rapidly and bonded over our work.

In our search for stories about how collaborative relationships formed in our program, we contacted several graduates. In an email message (May 27, 1997), Beth Boquet echoed our experiences. Like we were, she was a member of a unique cohort that formed as a result of entering this intensive academic environment:

> Friendships that I had with people [in the program] were particularly close . . . and unusual. I think you will have a difficult time getting at why that is though—seems pretty intangible to me. But we had women's dinners, we had Blue Moon parties, we spent evenings together on the dock at Two Lick Reservoir. We were very involved in each other's lives. When I've talked to people from other programs, they're usually amazed. "You had a good time in graduate school?!" is the pretty typical response.

We, like Beth, saw that while this emotionally supportive atmosphere carried over into the classroom, the intangible nature of our wanting to work with others stemmed from the program's pedagogical influences as well—the reading, the talking, the modeling. We were always given the opportunity to work together in our courses, and we often explored the theoretical implications of collaborative classroom work for our teaching back home. Little did the faculty know (or perhaps they did know!) they were encouraging us to "set aside the conventions to create an intellectual revolution" which Duane Roen and Robert Mitten (1992) would say defines the collaborative act.

After that first summer experience, we, Michele and Kami, worked in the same way successfully on many projects and, sensing that we created something better together than we could alone, we extended this collaborative model to our classrooms. What we had not done, but felt ready to do, was examine just how our collaboration and the that of our students and others works: hence, our desire to co-author a research project. Philip Murdock (1990) confirms the need for study in this area: "Little detailed ethnographic work has explored the dynamics of collaboration in the natural setting" (iii). Eager to engage in such exploration, we planned, in a joint dissertation, to study our students, experienced writers who collaborate and publish co-authored texts, and especially ourselves as we collaborated to study collaboration! We included this last element because what better way to study collaboration than to study it collaboratively?

When we began thinking (almost simultaneously—we can't remember who brought it up first) about writing a collaborative dissertation in 1995, we knew we were probably fantasizing. Our fears about bringing this idea up at all without being laughed at had nothing to do with lack of confidence in our program or the faculty of the English department; we simply knew "it's just not done." Ironically, two other women scholars in the same Rhetoric and Linguistics program had entertained but finally abandoned the idea of a collaborative dissertation ten years earlier. Looking back on that experience, Janine Rider and Esther Broughton wrote in 1994:

> After writing a research paper together, we were encouraged to continue our work. Why not try a collaborative dissertation? Several of our professors confirmed the need for revising the concept of the dissertation, and they went on and on in class about how great it would be to see a collaborative one approved. More talk with them brought reality closer; however, getting a director in our department for a collaborative dissertation was one thing, but getting it through the university approval process was another. We would have been laughed right out of the graduate office. There was never a choice. . . . We concluded collaboration doesn't happen. (249)

We two women scholars wanted to move the concept of collaborative dissertations beyond the idea stage. We had no trouble finding a committee that was supportive of our desire to break scholarly ground; in fact, one of the members of our committee knew of a precedent.[1] So, in July of 1996, we began to build our proposal, which we knew would have to include a strong rationale for a collaborative dissertation.

As new scholars, we approached our dissertation with the understanding that we were expected to contribute something new to our field. While other researchers have studied collaborative writing from the outside, by observing writers working together, there was as yet no inside study. The only way to truly understand how collaboration works is by studying it from the inside, as it appears to collaborators themselves. In this case, those collaborators would be us. Certainly, we felt we were furthering the work of scholars and researchers we admired, those who have called for expanding the scope and depth of knowledge about collaboration in journal articles about collaboration in the writing classroom.

Unfortunately, the graduate school at our institution did not share our vision. While our advisor was more than pleased with our proposal and our committee approved our research project, the chair of the Rhetoric and Linguistics program and the dean of Graduate School and Research did not feel our dissertation, although a worthy and necessary undertaking, fit the definition of a dissertation. The dean even contacted Dr. Jules Lapidus, president of the Council of Graduate Schools, "to broaden [his] own understanding," and in a letter to us, the dean wrote he was "convinced that a jointly authored dissertation could not be considered unless the individual contributions of each student were clearly identified. In this particular case, that does not appear possible" (August 1997).² In this statement, we heard both a clear understanding of our co-authoring process and an admission that accepting this particular process was inconceivable. The program chair and the dean understood what we were trying to do, but neither man was willing to place our institution in the risky position of challenging academic tradition. After several long-distance conversations and memos involving the chair, the dean, and our advisor, we were forced to comply: we met with our committee(s) and split the dissertation into two studies. Michele's became a classroom study of students co-authoring, Kami's became a study of experienced academic co-authors, and we put the study of ourselves—what we had envisioned as the central element of our dissertation—on the back burner.³

During the weeks when the fate of our proposal was being decided, we found support for our attempt as we exchanged email messages with scholars in the field of composition to find out their views on collaborative dissertations. In an online discussion on June 3, 1997, Katherine Fischer offered us encouragement and made the following observation: "Seems there is so much chatter about collaboration in our field, but actually not so much true allegiance to it in the act of writing." When we asked Andrea Lunsford what her criteria for a collaborative dissertation would be, she said they "would be the same as any other one, since I believe that by definition all dissertations are collaborative." She saw that we might need "special" criteria though, so she added "the safest thing imaginable would be a problem/study that could not easily (if at all) be done by one single scholar" (August 2, 1997). We found her words encouraging since our study of ourselves would have certainly fit these "special" criteria. Lisa Ede was sympathetic but reminded us that "academic bureaucracies are terrifically entrenched" and that we needed to think about the "implications of a collaborative dissertation on [our] academic careers"

(August 2, 1997). When we asked Roen what he would do if two graduate students came to him with a proposal to collaborate on a dissertation, he said,

> I would do everything I could to support that proposal. I would make the case with the graduate school. Co-authored work is common in many fields, including rhetoric and composition. In my reading and in my experience . . . collaboration has led to better work, not less work. If anything, collaboration requires more work because two minds are seeing all sorts of revisions to do. (August 1, 1997)

However, according to a former administrator at the National Endowment for the Humanities, "There is little in the way of either precedent or encouragement for collaboration in the humanities; in fact, collaboration is sometimes actively discouraged. There is a tendency among humanities scholars to denigrate the significance of multiauthored works" (qtd. in Alm 1998, 136; see Borden 1992). As Lunsford told us, "If we can just get two or three precedent-setting dissertations, we will have a big breakthrough, I believe" (August 2, 1997). We had hoped to set a precedent in the humanities, but perhaps our attempt, although failed, will open the door for other innovative scholars to write dissertations collaboratively.

Since we couldn't be those scholars, we wrote two dissertations—together. We co-wrote the literature review, a chapter on collaborative dissertations, and part of the design and methodology for both studies; and we became co-researchers in each other's projects—Kami team-taught with Michele during the classroom study, and Michele took part in the interviews for Kami's study.[4] Because we live together, proximity allowed us to participate jointly in all aspects of analyzing our data. We transcribed side by side, listening from time to time to each other's tapes to provide a second interpretation of what we were hearing and to check for accuracy; after one of us had coded a section of transcript, the other often coded it again to test and expand our understanding. And we talked—as we worked, as we cooked, as we ate, as we drove, as we walked.

However, although we had the benefit of proximity, we didn't just help each other by acting as sounding boards or as trusted readers or peer reviewers. Successful co-authoring, as we've learned from our own experience and from the co-authors we studied, goes well beyond what we have formally believed constitutes collaborative writing into an ineffable realm that involves relationships based on trust, respect, and care.

The co-authors in our study taught us about these ineffable elements—as well as the material practices—of their work as they told us their stories: stories of how they came to work together; how they negotiate their different ways of learning, knowing, and writing; how they merge their voices; how they have come to value their relationships with each other over the products of their collaboration. In interviews which took place in offices, homes, hotel lobbies, hotel rooms, and restaurants, they told us these stories, and rather than distilling or summarizing their accounts, we have included substantial chunks of our conversations so readers can hear the interviewees' voices and learn more directly from them.

OUR STUDY

We chose to interview the co-authors rather than observe them writing together because we wanted to take a phenomenological approach, to create a space in which the co-authors could describe their lived experience of writing together and the meaning they make from that experience.⁵ Steinar Kvale (1996) recommends interviewing as "particularly suited for studying people's understanding of the meanings in their lived world, describing their experiences and self-understanding, and clarifying and elaborating their own perspective on their lived world" (105). In addition, we agree with Diane R. Wood (1992) that "the way teachers [all the participants in our study are teachers] experience their lives as professionals matters, and the way they interpret their work can and should be grounds for inquiry, research, and theory in education" (545). We recognize the co-authors' authority over the accounts of their own writing processes just as composition researchers have come to recognize the value of what students say about their own writing processes. Kathleen Blake Yancey (1998) provides a useful parallel in her description of a particular moment in the history of composition studies. She points out that "in crediting *students* with knowledge of what was going on inside their heads and in awarding it authority, [early composition researchers] did something very valuable and very smart. These students are the ones who have allowed the rest of us, the teachers, to investigate, to understand, *to theorize our classroom practice*" (5). Likewise, the stories we have collected allow "the rest of us"—from writing teachers to authorship theorists—"to investigate, to understand, *to theorize*" what it means to write together.

We had some questions in mind that we hoped to explore in the interviews, but we wanted to encourage discussion and hear all voices, including our own. Whether we call this kind of interview "unstructured" (Lincoln and Guba 1985) or "general interview guide" (Patton 1980) or "semi-structured" (Kvale 1996), this particular methodology falls within the feminist research paradigm. According to Shulamit Reinharz (1992), feminist researchers resist the structured paradigm: "The use of semi-structured interviews has become the *principal means* by which feminists have sought to achieve the active involvement of their respondents in the construction of data about their lives" (18).

Sandra Harding identifies three features of feminist research: "(1) it should be based on women's experiences; (2) it should examine phenomena important to women: and (3) it should involve the researcher in his/her experiences and assumptions rather than pretend objectivity through a disinterested stance" (Johanek 2000, 72). We recognize these features as present in our work (after all, we are two women researchers, composition as a field is seen to be feminized, about half of our interviewees were women, and certainly a significant number of published co-authors are women, not to mention a significant number of qualitative researchers); we see feminist research methodology as the most ethical, most inclusive, most context driven, and most compatible with our belief that the research methodology *itself* has generative power.[6] And, while Cindy Johanek's overview of research methodologies found that many consider "interviews as the best method for understanding women's communication" (71), we found that interviewing within the feminist paradigm opened possibilities for understanding the communication of *both* women and men.

THE INTERVIEWEES

The participants in our study were members of ten academic co-authoring teams. The members of all teams had written together, all but one had published together (the one exception was in the process of co-authoring a book), and all of them had plans to collaborate again. Four of the teams were male-female dyads, three teams were female-female, two were male-male, and one team consisted of two males and one female. In addition, one of the male-female pairs was a married couple. Quite a few disciplines are represented in this study: English, sociology, social work, psychology, creative studies, library science, mathematics, and education. All of the participants were teachers or teacher-administrators in higher education, with the exception of one graduate student, and they had teaching experience varying from a few years to more than twenty years.

Originally, the participants of our study were to meet these criteria: they were to be faculty or staff at a college or university and they had to have published at least one scholarly book or article they had written with each other. As we mentioned earlier, all teams but one met these criteria, and we felt the inclusion of the exception was justified since the team was writing a book together and had also collaboratively prepared and presented conference papers. We chose to limit our study to higher education because publication plays an important role in the career of an academic, because many of these people are in a position to evaluate and influence graduate education (such as policy concerning co-authored dissertations), because many of them are part of the peer review process (such as evaluating publication records of faculty), because many of them are active reviewers for academic journals (and would thus have occasion to support publication of co-authored scholarship), and because we would have easier access to co-authors in academia since we teach college classes.

We felt interviewing the team members together was important for several reasons: we wanted to observe their interaction, we wanted to observe the quality of their talk about co-authoring in a discourse with their team members, and we believed meeting with team members individually would be unethical. We were concerned that if we asked each one to meet with us separately from the other(s), we would send a different message than if we asked them to meet with us as a team. Separate interviews might have implied that we were looking for information about the co-author who wasn't there instead of perceptions about their co-authoring. They work together, and we wanted them to participate in the study together. Somehow, interviewing them separately would have felt sneaky to us. Of course, this team interviewing might be criticized as a weakness of the study—interviewees could have felt constrained to tell only about the positive aspects of their experience—but we are willing to acknowledge that weakness in the interest of a more ethical project. Besides, having met and talked with the teams, we doubt that any of them would have agreed to separate interviews, or if they did agree, we believe they would have had the same things to say about their co-authors and their collaboration. In addition, most of the teams acknowledged that the interview provided them the first opportunity to think about and talk about their co-authoring, for which they expressed appreciation. This meta-awareness was a benefit to the co-authors (and to us since it made our data richer) that would not have occurred if they had not been interviewed together.

We acknowledge that we construct meaning from the words of the co-authors, and that our construction is affected by our valuing collaboration in both teaching and human interaction. We hoped the interviewees would support collaboration, and naturally, we wanted later interviews to corroborate what we thought we were finding in earlier ones. We have also constructed meaning based on our positions as far as class, gender, race, ideology, preferences, and interests are concerned. Like feminist pedagogues Frances A. Maher and Mary Kay Thompson Tetreault, we acknowledge that we are not "distanced and objective observers" (1994, 12). Aware of our biases, we have tried to *hear* phenomenologically what the co-authors said and to base our interpretations on their words, and perhaps on a few actions we observed in the interviews, but we—along with our passions and predilections—are always "in there."

We also acknowledge it's possible the co-authors in our study were just saying what good academics would say, but we have no way of knowing if their practice is different from their words. Choosing not to take a critical approach to the interviewees' words, we have not tried to uncover what the co-authors "really feel" about co-authoring as opposed to what they say. Frankly, we chose to believe them—we had no reason not to. We choose to trust people until they give us reason to distrust them, and listening to how the co-authors interacted and what they had to say, observing their treatment of each other, and seeing their successful co-authored work provided us with evidence that they are who they say they are and that they do what they say they do. We think their enthusiasm about being interviewed and having the chance to share experiences that seem to have so much meaning to them is another indication they were not dissimulating. Yes, they could have been unconsciously, or consciously, covering up less satisfying episodes in their co-authoring, and we must consider the possibility of such collusion. In fact, collusion is necessary in all productive conversation, according to R. P. McDermott and Henry Tylbor (1983):

> Participation in any social scene, especially a conversation, requires some minimal consensus on what is getting done in the scene . . . such a consensus represents an achievement, a cumulative product of the instructions people in the scene make available to each other; and, because no consensus ever unfolds simply by predetermined means, because social scenes are always precarious, always dependent on ongoing instructions, the achievement of a consensus requires collusion. (278)

McDermott and Tylbor go on to say that "collusion refers to how members of any social order must constantly help each other to posit a particular state of affairs" (278). We can believe that the co-authors we interviewed agreed between themselves, although probably tacitly, to show us what a positive experience their co-authoring is, and that consensus led them to give each other verbal and physical instructions to help each other convey that "particular state of affairs." Not only that, but we were in collusion with them. We took pains not to tell the teams (the ones who did not already know) about our attempt to co-author a dissertation until they had given us their views on such a project, and we did not even tell them explicitly about the value we place on co-authoring in general, but we're sure our demeanor and questions revealed our bent anyway. And, of course, half the teams—Strickland and Strickland, Hurlbert and Blitz, Ede and Lunsford, Hui and Grant, and Roen and Brown—knew we had proposed a co-authored dissertation, so we cannot discount the possibility of the Hawthorne effect. They may have been not only working to present their co-authoring positively, but they were most likely offering us support and colluding to help us "posit a particular state of affairs." After all, most of these co-authors have been colluding for years; the nature of the interview event mirrors somewhat what practiced co-authors *do* in their give-and-take and co-construction of meaning.

McDermott and Tylbor acknowledge that there are certainly things "people have to arrange *not to talk about*" (294), and perhaps the interviewees made those arrangements tacitly or overtly before our conversations (or perhaps they even agree not to bring up certain topics *as* they co-author), but again, we only had their words to work with. We choose to view what our co-authors said as conversational collusion "at its cleanest . . . well tuned to people's finest hopes about what the world can be—this often despite the facts, despite a world that sometimes offers them little reason for harboring such hopes" (280). The co-authoring teams and we were all in collusion to construct a world in which co-authoring is valued, a world in which academics approach their work with a collaborative value system, and that world does, at times, seem far off.

Not only did we trust the interviewees—they trusted us. We realized how much when transcribing one of the interviews in which the co-authors told of problems with their institution's administration. In the middle of a story, one of them stopped and said, "You won't put this part in your dissertation, will you?" We assured him we wouldn't, and he continued with the story. This particular team did not return the transcript we sent them—they simply signed the consent form and gave us permission to use their real names, knowing there was information in the transcripts they would have to trust us to leave out of the dissertation. Most of the teams deleted some material from the transcript (often references to people or places), and we did not use that material. The co-authors trusted us, and we them, a mutual faith that is, after all, in harmony with our findings.

We had originally planned to include some negative cases—stories of unsuccessful or unsatisfying or failed co-authoring experiences.[7] Some of the co-authors in our study alluded to or described generally such experiences with authors outside our study, and those stories are woven into chapters four and five, but, not surprisingly, we did not find any dissatisfied or disgruntled teams willing to talk to us. For example, a female administrator, when she found out the focus of our research, declared she had vowed to never collaborate again because of a disastrous attempt at co-authoring. She expressed enthusiasm about sharing her story with us, but after several email exchanges, she decided she could not devote any time to our research. We contacted another woman who had co-authored a history of the lesbian culture in her city, and we were told that she doesn't discuss that co-authoring experience with anyone but her therapist! As we got deeper into our study, we began to see that we had so much rich data about successful co-authoring that negative stories might take away from that focus. Also, the importance of the co-authors' co-reflection became more and more evident, and most likely, we would have needed to interview members of less successful teams separately. We acknowledge that negative cases abound, but we chose to give them a minor role in this book. We were interested in why teams succeed, not why they fail.

OVERVIEW OF THE BOOK

Now that we have explained the background for our study, we will proceed in chapter two to provide an overview of current research about academic collaboration; we will try to help the reader see both the scope of existing research and the possibilities for additional study in this area. This chapter also includes a discussion of the ethical dimensions of collaboration; however, the main focus of chapter two is our position that all writing is collaborative and that the notions of authorship and co-authorship must be reconceived. Chapter three is a brief but necessary rationale for our choice of terms. Chapter four explains the framework upon which we built our analysis of the interviewees' words, a framework developed by Cynthia Sullivan Dickens and Mary Ann D. Sagaria. These researchers created four categories to describe the co-authoring of women scholars: "pedagogical collaboration: nurturance," "instrumental collaboration: pragmatism," "professional partnership collaboration: shared agenda," and "intimate collaboration: intellectual and emotional closeness." Then, using excerpts from the interviews, we show what those words reveal about who the co-authors are and how they perceive their relationships. Chapter five includes the interviewees' reflections on their material practices, such as their individual and collaborative writing processes, the ways talk is used, the importance of choice and time, and drafting and revision. In addition, we chart some of the current problems associated with co-authoring, such as forced consensus. In chapter six we describe interviewees' positions on co-authoring in an academic climate generally skeptical of co-authored texts. We explore the ways in which these writers have taken risks, their reasons for continuing to co-author, and their advocacy of co-authored scholarship (including dissertations). Finally, in chapter seven, while we deal little with pedagogical practice (this is not a "how to" chapter), we attempt to ferry our understandings of successful academic co-authoring to the other shore—our classrooms. Throughout chapters two through seven, we insert reflections about our own co-authoring—snippets of the meta-study we originally proposed as part of our dissertation.

NOTES

1.   The precedent cited by one of our committee members was written by two women in the College of Education at the University of Cincinnati. Carol Feiser Laque and Phyllis A. Sherwood co-authored "A Teaching Monograph:

Co-Designed Laboratory Approach to Writing"; each received an Ed.D. in 1975. We spoke with Laque by telephone (June 2, 1997), and one of our first questions was, "How did you come to be involved in writing a collaborative dissertation?" She told us she had earned a master's degree in English literature, but she was interested in pursuing a Ph.D. in composition before the University of Cincinnati had developed such a program. However, the College of Education at the University of Cincinnati had just approved, under the direction of Dean Sylvia Tucker, an interdisciplinary co-designed dissertation. Laque teamed with Sherwood, whose background was in education, to co-author a handbook that documented their work toward creating a writing lab at a branch campus of the University of Cincinnati, and this handbook became a blueprint for other writing labs (Laque and Sherwood 1975). The monograph was accepted for publication by the National Council of Teachers of English and was one of NCTE's top publications of 1977.

2.   Toni Knott and Lynne Valek, who wrote a collaborative dissertation (see note 9, chapter two), also contacted the Council of Graduate Schools and were discouraged to hear that "they didn't think it would be a good thing to do, but they admitted it's happened in the sciences." Yet, according to a representative of UMI (now Bell & Howell), between 1902 and 1987, out of one million dissertations, 166 have more than one name on the title page.

3.   We have taped ourselves at work, kept journals, and talked about our processes, but we have not yet conducted a full meta-study. This book, however, includes snippets of our taped conversations and our reflections.

4.   The bulk of our study took place between October 1997 and April 1998. We both participated in all interviews except two: Michele was not present for the interview with Julie Knight and Gilbert Adams because of her grandmother's funeral, nor the interview with Mark Hurlbert and Michael Blitz due to illness. However, when discussing these interviews in this book, we use the pronoun "we" as if we were both present, for continuity and ease of reading.

5.   According to Barbara Couture, "The phenomological approach does not separate one's lived experience from one's expression of it, it rather asks the author to think of his or her rhetoric as an enactment of the ongoing experience" (1998, 161). We gave the co-authors in our study the opportunity to "live through the process of validating [their] interpretations of experience, rather than to demonstrate its validity. . . . In this act, they . . . secure their own authenticity as well as validate their expression" (161).

6.   We acknowledge with Gesa E. Kirsch that although a feminist research methodology can create "greater intimacy and increased collaboration among researchers and participants [it] may inadvertently reintroduce some of the ethical dilemmas . . . potential disappointments, alienation, and exploitation of participants" (1999, 160).

7.   Our work has been criticized for presenting an "ideal" of co-authoring. In reflecting on collaborative research, Kirsch states: "I have come to realize that the ideal scenario of successful collaboration is just that: an ideal. . . . It has become abundantly clear to me that collaboration rarely unfolds in all the ways we wish" (1999, 159). And while we don't disagree with her, we believe that this ideal is possible with the right mix of co-authors and approaches.

2 WHY STUDY ACADEMIC CO-AUTHORS?

> Monologue pretends to be the ultimate word.
>
> *Mikhail Bakhtin*

TO INFORM AND ENHANCE OUR PEDAGOGY

We had several reasons for choosing to study successful, experienced co-authoring teams. First, as the view that knowledge is socially constructed has come to inform and complicate composition theory and practice, more and more instructors are incorporating collaboration into their classrooms in such forms as peer response groups, peer editing, group invention strategies, and collective text production. However, as Rebecca Moore Howard (2000) points out, "collaborative writing pedagogies seem foreign and fraught with peril" (62). She provides a useful overview of both the potential and pitfalls of collaborative writing from both student and teacher perspectives:

> When students are assigned to *write together*, a variety of problems can arise, most of them deriving from the dominant cultural model of individual authorship. . . . [N]ot only students but also teachers are accustomed to thinking of authorship in terms of the individual—and . . . the entire educational institution predicates its judgments on individual performance. . . . Yet, collaborative writing dominates the corporate workplace and many academic disciplines, and critical theory increasingly insists that all writing is collaborative. Thus, despite the perils, some teachers persevere in assigning and teaching collaborative writing. And when the perils can be averted or overcome, the benefits are impressive. (62)

It's no surprise then that educators and theorists who encourage teachers to try methods by which students learn with and from each other do so with the caveat that collaboration involves more than just putting students together; both students and teachers must be prepared (Bishop 1995; Casey 1993; Eodice 1999; Gere 1987; Hilgers 1986; Howard 2000; Spear 1988; Vermette 1998; others). Jeff Golub (1988) stresses that "it is not enough simply to decide that collaborative learning is indeed an appropriate and effective method of instruction; one must also train students to develop specific collaborative learning skills to ensure that they can work productively and harmoniously in pairs and small groups" (2).

In spite of what instructors may know about forming groups, conflict resolution, effective group knowledge-making activities, and group assessment, there seems to be some ineffable quality that makes it possible for one group to cohere, produce, and even have fun while the next group self-destructs in acrimonious name-calling, sullen silence, or apathy (and, of course, many configurations exist between those two extremes). Even those of us who have thoughtfully developed strategies for helping students to work successfully together may experience unproductive and unpleasant situations in a cooperative classroom. So, our primary reason for studying successful academic coauthors was to answer these questions: Can this ineffable quality, present in productive collaborations, be teased out? If so, can it be taught? We need to know more about what makes successful teams successful, what makes it possible for them to work harmoniously when so many others try and fail. We believed conversations with productive, effective writing teams would reveal insights that would transform the ways in which academics and our students co-author.

TO BUILD ON THE RESEARCH

Second, in addition to the need for research that will inform and enhance our pedagogy, there are lacunae in the body of research concerning collaboration in the academy: few studies examine co-authoring in academia, and even fewer are looking at co-authoring in the humanities, despite the increase in multiply authored publications. Alma Gottlieb (1995) challenges her colleagues in anthropology to explore "the unstudied practice of collaboration with spouses, colleagues, and others that characterizes much of anthropological research and writing . . . . [and] to take seriously the contemporary project of re-thinking disciplinary norms by exploring theoretical as well as pragmatic implications of . . . collaborative projects." And Mary Alm (1998), an academic who studies collaborative writing among women academics, remains "disappointed in how few scholars in composition and rhetoric turn their attention to their own writing practices or the writing practices of scholars generally" (124).

Anne E. Austin and Roger Baldwin, in their 1991 monograph *Faculty Collaboration: Enhancing the Quality of Scholarship and Teaching*, point out that an abundance of research exists concerning collaboration in the business world, but they emphasize that there is little research exploring collaboration in academia, particularly qualitative research, and even less concerning co-authoring—in spite of increased collaboration across academia.[1] They write that as part of a significant trend in our society, "collaboration in the academic professions is a growing and controversial phenomenon" (1). Reasons for this upswing in multiple authorship in such fields as social sciences, physical education, economics, health education, psychology, nursing, law, and the biomedical sciences (Burman 1982; Creamer 1999; Crase and Rosato 1992; Iammarino, O'Rourke, Pigg, and Weinberg 1989; Szenberg 1996; Woodmansee and Jaszi 1994) include pressure to publish, the complexity of large scale research, more sophisticated technology, a richer variety of expertise, the need to reduce isolation and sustain motivation, improved productivity, elevated quality of products, the security to take risks, increased creativity and support, division of labor, increased potential for publication, generation of ideas, less procrastination, access to new research networks, and increased potential for theory building. Judith Entes (1994), in her article "The Right to Write a Co-Authored Manuscript," points out that an overwhelming majority (81 percent) of published research articles in leading reading journals list multiple authors. Ray Over, in a survey of "all journals published by the American Psychological Association in 1949, 1959, 1969, and 1979, reported that during 'the 30 year period there was an increasing trend toward collaborative publications'" (qtd. in Entes, 52). In addition, during the years from 1980 through 1989, *Reading Research Quarterly* published 245 research articles, 62 percent of which were co-authored. Thirty-three percent were written by two people, 20.41 percent by three authors, 4.49 percent by four authors, and 2.45 percent by five authors (52).

Similarly, in the humanities, at least in the field of rhetoric and composition, the trend to work and publish collaboratively is increasing. Roen and Mitten (1992) surveyed nine composition journals in 1989 and were discouraged by the fact that only 22 percent of the articles were co-authored, but we found that percentage encouraging. We took a quick survey of *College English* 1990–1996 (approximately 220 articles) and found 12 instances (5 percent) of co-authored articles spread evenly over the issues. Out of approximately 140 articles in *College Composition and Communication* during the same period of time, we tabulated 33 (24 percent) collaboratively written articles. Of note, the same writing partnerships kept cropping up, which suggests to us that once people start working together, they discover, as we did, the exponential value of collaboration.

As instances of multiple authorship across the disciplines multiply, researchers are beginning to pay attention to the features of this particular form of scholarly work. For example, Mary Frank Fox and Catherine A. Faver (1984), Shirley M. Hord (1981), Joan P. Isenberg, Mary Renck Jalongo, and Karen D'Angelo Bromley (1987), and James W. Endersby (1996) have studied collaborative research and publication credit in the social sciences; Maxim Engers, Joshua S. Gans, Simon Grant, and Stephen P. King (1999) have investigated first author conditions in economics journals; Elizabeth G. Creamer (1999) interviewed academic co-authoring couples across the disciplines. A qualitative study by Nancy Allen, Dianne Atkinson, Meg Morgan, Teresa Moore, and Craig Snow (1987) looked at "shared-document collaboration" among academics and other co-authors writing in their professions. Cynthia Sullivan Dickens and Mary Ann D. Sagaria (1997) conducted a qualitative study of women academic co-authors in various disciplines, and Alm (1998) also writes about a similar study in progress. From the humanities, Murdock (1990) and John Trimbur and Lundy A. Braun (1992) studied collaborative writers in the field of biology; Ede and Lunsford (1990) surveyed writing teams in business; and Geoffrey A. Cross (1994) followed a corporate writing team through the process of composing a memo.

However, closer to home, those of us in composition studies have heard Kathleen Yancey and Michael Spooner (1998) call for "accounts of collaborative writing" because "while we know that many academic writers are composing together, we still seem to know precious little about how this joint composing is being managed, about the processes that go into collaborative writing" (46). The work of authorship theorists in composition, such as Howard, Lunsford and Ede, and Elizabeth Peck and JoAnna Mink, has sparked interest in investigating what happens when people write together, but most of the familiar and accessible studies feature students writing collaboratively (see, among others, Burnett 1994; Casey 1993; Dale 1997; Eodice 1999; Goodburn and Ina 1994; Leverenz 1994; Louth, McAllister, and McAllister 1993; Qualley and Chiseri-Strater 1994; Ritchie 1989; Rogers and Horton 1992; Spear 1988; Thralls 1992). As we mentioned earlier, several humanities scholars—especially as composition studies has emerged—have studied co-authors outside the humanities, but still, empirical studies of co-authors in the humanities are few.[2] Among studies in the field of composition are Linda Brodkey's account of a rather unsuccessful venture in her book *Academic Writing as Social Practice* (1987) and James A. Reither and Douglas Vipond's account of Vipond and Russell A. Hunt's collaboration in "Writing as Collaboration" (1989). In literature, Laura A. Brady (1988) explores the collaboration between such authors as Ford Maddox Ford and Joseph Conrad, and between Michael Dorris and Louise Erdrich; Jeffrey Masten's work (1994) uncovered collaboration among writers of Renaissance drama; Jack Stillinger's collection (1991) includes examples of literary collaborations "from Homer to Ann Beattie"; and Holly A. Laird (2000) and Bette London (1999) each studied women's literary partnerships.

In order to add to research about co-authoring, we cast a wide net, pulling in both the scholarship and the scholars from various disciplines to inform our own; we are humanities scholars studying co-authors in the humanities as well as in other fields. Ernest Boyer, in his well-known 1990 treatise *Scholarship Reconsidered: Priorities of the Professoriate*, states, "Today, more than at any time in recent memory, researchers feel the need to move beyond traditional disciplinary boundaries, communicate with colleagues in other fields, and discover patterns that connect" (20). Austin and Baldwin (1991) cite Boyer for support and stress that

> ignoring the collaborative dimension now common in academe would overlook "new realities both within the academy and beyond" (Boyer, p. 3) . . . To respond appropriately to a growing trend, colleges and universities must look carefully at the many forms of collaboration that now occupy a large portion of professors' time and energy. (3, 4).

Therefore, in later chapters of this book, we juxtapose issues emerging from our interviews—such as first authorship, ownership, ethics, shared expertise, mentoring, respect, and care—with findings from the research on academic co-authoring we have highlighted above.

TO EXPAND IDEAS OF AUTHORSHIP

The author as one and many

Third, we feel responsible to lend our shoulders to the efforts of those pushing open the door that leads to a more spacious understanding of authorship. Postmodernism's skepticism concerning the author has already expanded our notions of authorship and has created a tension between views of autonomous authorial agency and what we call the "constellated author," who can choose to act (possesses agency) but does not act alone. The drive to reconcile this tension has led us, Kami and Michele, to consider how our own sense of the existence of an individual consciousness is (or is not) compatible with our sense that one does not write alone. As we've surely demonstrated by now, we have a commitment to collaborative learning in all its forms. However, our commitment is complicated by a perplexing but undeniable sense of the author's presence. The individual author—not absent, dissipated, or dead to us—still haunts much of our sense of what Michel Foucault calls the "author-function" (1992, 143). Even Howard (1999), whose view that the author is not autonomous is clear and well-supported, admits that she has "encountered no commentator, including [herself], who articulates a unified position on either collaborative or solitary authorship" (40).

In trying to understand our own conviction that the author is both one and many, we have come to see that the fundamental manifestation of individuation is the physical body. Thus, individual writers inhabit bodies separate from other individual bodies. Johanna Meehan (2000) affirms this distinction: "Any account of individuation must recognize the extent to which the human infant is born biologically equipped with the cognitive and sensory capacities that make possible a basic experience of the self as both unified with and distinct from other things and selves" (43). A distinct body houses a consciousness influenced by the body itself (among other things), and since each body is different.[3] Our language moves through our individual bodies, and feminist theory has enabled and encouraged any and all to acknowledge, embrace, and honor this physicality. Still, even when Hélène Cixous (1992) calls for women to "write through their bodies," she ultimately invites them to join with others to "articulate the profusion of meanings that run through it [the body] in every direction—[to] make the old single-grooved mother tongue reverberate with more than one language" (315). It is this movement, this fluid thread of language, that continually and untraceably connects and reconnects individual consciousnesses.

So, for us, there is an individual consciousness but not an autonomous author. Each person combines a multitude of voices—whether they be cultural, familial, collegial, or spiritual—in a unique way, but the multitude is still there. Martin Buber's concept of the I-Thou "world of relation" (as opposed to the I-it objective "world of experience") (1987, 6) seems to support the necessity of collaboration with another in our own individual development. According to Buber,

> Little, disjointed, meaningless sounds still go out persistently into the cold. But one day, unforeseen, they will have become conversation. . . . It is simply not the case that the child first perceives an object, then, as it were, puts himself in relation with it. But the effort to establish relation comes first . . . A saying of *Thou* without words, in the state preceding the word-form. . . . In the beginning is relation—as category of being, readiness, grasping form, mould for the soul; it is the *a priori* of relation, the inborn *Thou.* (27)

And L. S. Vygotsky's theories (1978) concerning the movement from outer speech to inner speech support Buber's view that "in the beginning is relation." With Buber, both Vygotsky and Mikhail Bakhtin acknowledge the directionality of knowledge formation: "first collective activity, then culture, the ideal, sign or symbol, and finally, individual consciousness" (Bakhtin, qtd. in Davydov 1995, 16).[4] The individual author's voice is the one-made-of-many in Bakhtin's heteroglossia, the one-made-of-many discursive subject in Foucault's "order of discourse," the one-made-of-many star in the constellation. Foucault (1992) does not abandon the subject but asks that we reconsider it, "not to restore the theme of an originating subject, but to seize its functions, its intervention in discourse, and its system of dependencies." He wants us to ask not "Who is the real author?" but "What are the modes of existence of this discourse?" (148).

As Howard explains it, the author who has disappeared is the "autonomous individual of expressionism whose inner soul is possessed of truth and knowledge and who can produce unaided written drafts in which those truths are discovered and articulated" (1999, 46). That author was fictive to begin with. The author who has always been here is part of a discourse—a discourse (or discourses) defined and shaped by the context of the particular project or situation. In proposing a "practical, intersubjective rhetoric" (185) that values collaborative meaning-making, Barbara Couture (1998) characterizes the extremes of what some in our field have called "expressionism" and "social constructionism"—theories of how authors, texts, and meaning are constructed: "Rhetoric that endorses individual inquiry as the only path to credible meaning can be insidiously self-absorptive and socially alienating; rhetoric that valorizes only social ideology as the source of meaning can be hegemonic and normalizing" (43). With Couture and others, we believe that neither the concept of the autonomous author nor the concept of the author constructed solely by social and cultural influences does justice to the complex activity of creating text. And, as James Porter (1986) points out, "Even if the writer is locked into a cultural matrix and is constrained by the intertext of the discourse community, the writer has freedom within the immediate rhetorical context" and has the ability to change that discourse (41).

To put it another way, the author is unavoidably influenced by everything she has read, heard, experienced; but, though constructed, she is not reduced to what language makes her (Kanpol and McLaren 1995). Seyla Benhabib (1992), who argues that no matter how language composes us, we as individuals remain capable of rearranging "the significations of language" (216), is supported by Meehan (2000): "Language makes possible an organized, representable and sharable sense of self but it does not invent the self" (44). Instead, from a phenomenological point of view, the author's individual reflections (already stemming from an internal intersection) meet the reflections of others in a community as the members of that community make meaning together. Couture (1998) turns to Maurice Merleau-Ponty to explain that "meaning is, in a sense, acting who one is" but "understanding . . . comes about through communicative involvement with the world. My consciousness of the world is the result of my speaking [or writing] in it, and thus reaching toward it and defining myself through it" (80). Enthymematically, then, individuals act—and individuals write—but they do not act—or write—alone.

All writing is collaborative

In a special economics journal issue dedicated to collaboration (1996), Paul A. Samuelson, a 1970 Nobel laureate winner and MIT professor emeritus—

and inveterate collaborator—makes a bold statement about collaboration which lends credence to the assertion that we are always already collaborating when we write. He sees all words spoken and written, from ancient time to real time, acting as envoys of thought and language, accessible to all.

> Collaboration is wrongly measured—for anyone and especially for me—by relative number of researches jointly authored. I can genuinely say "Adam and I" about the Smith who wrote in 1776. And I can say "Black-Scholes and I" about the pair who discovered the options-price formula that I never quite arrived at. I revealed a preference to learn more (of what there was to learn) from Sir John Hicks than he cared to learn from me: who said life is symmetric? I advanced Keynes's football beyond the yardline where he left it. Why should I expect any record of mine to stand throughout time eternal? (21)

In support of Samuelson's position—and ours—many of the writers in our study voiced the notion that all writing is collaborative. However, the perception that all writing is collaborative is problematized even by some who value and practice collaborative writing but resist such a panoramic view of joint text production. For example, Yancey and Spooner (1998) challenge the willingness to let one term cover what happens when people work together on a piece of writing.

> The trouble is that the effect of an all-inclusive definition of collaboration has been to trivialize collaboration. . . . Because if our theory must call all writing collaborative, then "collaboration" becomes moot and useless as a theoretical construct. (55–56)

In an email exchange with us, Derek Owens pointed out that "if all writing is indeed collaborative, then so is all thought, all consciousness . . . [saying that all writing is collaborative] is pointing out the obvious and unavoidable." We agree with Owens, and with Yancey and Spooner, that attaching the word *collaboration* to every composing action has the potential to enervate the significance of these acts (what they call trivialization), and perhaps they, and we, resist that enervation because we experience, even savor, the act of writing together as important and meaningful to us. In other words, the concern is that if we acknowledge the collaborative nature of thought, consciousness, and writing, that emphasis will have the effect of erasing the significance of the concept of collaboration (as distinct from other modes of writing). The collaborative nature of thought, consciousness, and writing is obvious to us and others who collaborate; it's like an aquifer, always flowing underground, but the conscious, visible, dynamic action or demonstration of that source rises to the surface like a natural spring and is manifest in the act of co-authoring. It is this action and its characteristics we wish to foreground. Though the concept of collaboration may be ubiquitous, we don't want to make it transparent; rather, we hope to encourage consciousness and reflection which can highlight collaborative writing in all its diverse forms. There are productive, nurturing co-authoring experiences. There are unproductive, agonistic ones. There are productive, agonistic ones also, and the configurations go on and on. Starting with the concept that all writing is collaborative gives us opportunities to recognize the myriad embodiments of collaboration, and this recognition imbues the concept of collaboration with texture and life. We do not propose to cease to regard collaboration critically and thoughtfully, but to open up space to theorize about all the possibilities.

As we acknowledge that calling all writing collaborative risks diluting the the power of the concept, we also recognize this stance may seem counterintuitive, even execrable, to those who still privilege the solitary author. Many academics still cling ontologically to familiar binaries associated with writing: "memesis/originality . . . plagiarism/authorship . . . [and of special interest to us] collaboration/autonomy" (Howard 1999, 97). However, with Howard, we welcome some disruption of these familiar binaries. One way to begin this disruption is to think of all writing as collaborative, but convincing academics and students resistant to such a radical concept has resulted in active collaborative writers and those practicing collaboration pedagogy being labeled evangelists, missionaries, martyrs, pseudo scholars and, at the very extreme, frauds. "For all the talk about the death of the author, solo authorship is still institutionally valorized, perhaps more in English than in other fields" (Doane and Hodges 1995, 53). And Howard laments, "I have so far found it impossible to persuade all students that all writing is collaborative. Whether that 'persuasion' is undertaken directly or indirectly, many students have a lifetime of schooling that has convinced them otherwise" (41). For the most part, writers—particularly and historically white male western writers—inherit and practice a set of concepts regarding authorship which we see as constrained and constraining to a broader vision of authorship.

One pillar of support for the concept that all writing is collaborative is Bakhtin's "ideas of the dialogic and polyphonic nature of consciousness" (qtd. in Davydov 1995, 14). In the essay "Discourse and the Novel" (in Bakhtin 1981), Bakhtin claims that "language lies on the borderline between oneself and the other. The word in language is half someone else's" (293). But this recognized partiality and overlap does not connote a deficit on the part of the speaker or writer. One of the keys to understanding collaboration is to accept that it *depends* and thrives on border crossings. When we collaborate, we share, steal, borrow, and appropriate language "in a diverse social and linguistic milieu, as part of the ongoing process of 'becoming'" (Ritchie 1989, 168). Bakhtin describes what happens in this milieu:

> The word . . . enters a dialogically agitated and tension-filled environment of alien words, value-judgments and accents, weaves in and out of complex interrelationships, merges with some, recoils from others, intersects with yet a third group. (276)

When we use language, we call from and contribute to Bakhtin's "heteroglossia": "All utterances are heteroglot in that they are functions of a matrix of forces practically impossible to recoup, and therefore impossible to resolve" (1981, 428). The concept that all writing is collaborative extends from, at one end, the talk that facilitates invention; according to one of the teams in our study, 80 percent of their collaboration takes the form of talk. In fact, our study reveals that successful co-authoring is characterized by a process that includes co-invention. The collaboration moves recursively through stages of talk, co-researching, co-teaching, co-drafting, co-revising, co-analyzing, and finally to co-editing on the other end. But as Bakhtin says, the heteroglossia of this process is impossible to resolve—the forces (voices, consciousnesses, lived experiences, knowledges) are impossible to tease apart. And further, Thralls (1992), in connecting Bakhtin and collaborative writing, claims that "to speak—to write—demands collaboration with others in a communication chain" (66). We see Bakhtin's heteroglossia as a central feature of the "interpretive zone," a term we borrow from naturalistic inquiry, a field which paradigmatically honors the collective nature of knowing. Qualitative researchers and co-authors Judith Davidson Wasser and Laura Bresler (1996) define the interpretive zone as "the place where multiple viewpoints are held in dynamic tension as a group seeks to make sense of . . . issues and meanings" (6). Are Wasser and Bresler not describing the zone, a complex and rich matrix of forces, created when a writer collaborates with others proximally, virtually, historically, or spiritually?[5]

Deferring definitions

Co-authoring teams we have spoken with both as part of our study and outside of it each describe their collaborations uniquely. Their relationships and processes have some features in common, but the distinctions among them have led us to conclude that there are as many definitions for co-authoring as there are co-authoring teams—so we necessarily must define their collaborative writing polytypically. As we said earlier, we agree with Owens, and with Yancy and Spooner, that defining every act of writing as collaboration even every act which involves two or more authors—might water down the importance and uniqueness of those acts. Why study co-authoring if all situations fit into one homogeneous category? However, we believe this watering down can only occur if co-authors do not take the opportunity, or are not given the opportunity, to reflect on what they do. Institutions or individuals not engaged in this reflection break a link in the chain of utterances—effectively closing off essential dialogue. If, say, Jones and Smith, who have produced only one co-authored piece, define what they do as co-authoring, does their claim to be co-authors trivialize what Ede and Lunsford, who have written together for twenty years, do? If Jones and Smith are not invited to join the discourse about co-authoring, or if they choose not to join it, trivializing what they do becomes possible. For example, one of the teams in our study was in the process of writing their first piece for publication. They call themselves co-authors. If they are not "allowed" to appropriate the term *co-author* because we have circumscribed or quantified the theoretical construct around collaborative writing, we break the chain, cut off the discourse. An analogy might be that our students cannot enter the discourse of the academy, or the discourses of their chosen fields, if the conventions of the discourse (or our interpretations of those conventions) are too narrow and/or if the students are not invited to reflect on their writing.

In other cases co-authors have published often together, yet their co-authored work is not valued or perhaps not even recognized by their most local evaluators or even by their larger disciplines. Therefore, the locality's or discipline's definition of authoring make entering the discourse of that locality or discipline difficult. Inviting the authors to reflect on and articulate what they do makes entering the discourse possible and might even open up the discourse.

These questions involving definitions of co-authorship are not merely theoretical exercises; they pop up naturally in conversations among co-authors themselves. The participants in the in the CCCC 2000 workshop—who included Michael Blitz, Mark Hurlbert, Kathleen Yancey, Michael Spooner, Duane Roen, Keith Dorwick, and Joona Trapp—certainly worked with these issues in productive ways. Yancey kicked off the challenge to define co-authoring, and after some discussion, Blitz questioned, "What kinds of things compel us to define these different codes [for writing together]? . . . What things do we feel are urging us forward to define cooperation, collective, collaboration, et cetera? These are really interesting distinctions, but what comes next?" He wondered if the compulsion might be driven by such "professional witnessing" rituals as tenure and promotion reviews. He suggested that perhaps we "ought to be kind of" resentful of—even "bristling at"—the demand that we explain ourselves once again, and he expressed his frequent frustration at "having to prove I am who I say I am."

Yancey responded that her desires to make distinctions are practical; she felt any generalizations she might make would only hold true for "whatever it is we're talking about. I need help figuring out what the topic is . . . then I can talk about it." One thing this book might be doing is gathering distinctions made by the interviewees about their own co-authoring so we can begin to "figure out what the topic is." However, we acknowledge that any generalizations we make may apply only to the group of co-authors we studied. Having gathered all the eggs in our barn, we can show off a nice basket of eggs, but other farmers have their own chicken coops to consider: we study co-authors, we put all their stories together, and we want to tell their stories—particularly the one feature that seems to hold true for all of them—but we know what the coop down the road produces will tell a different story.[6]

So, identifying features which apply to all co-authoring may be difficult. Creamer (1999) recognizes "joint or multiple authorship of a publication [as] a convention generally used to recognize a substantial, intellectual contribution to a publication" (274). This definition, in its simplicity, may be as close as we get to a generalization about co-authoring; it allows the discourse to continue in that it embraces a wide array of collaborative writing configurations. Co-authors must become more adept at reflecting on and articulating traits that distinguish their own processes and relationships so they can participate in conversations to help create, validate, and maintain the ebullient discourse about joint text production. During the workshop, Blitz said that "one thing to say for all these constructions [of co-authoring] is that we write out of a spirit of adventure . . . to see what will happen . . . it's exciting and sometimes we get burned, but that's part of the adventure."

Terms like *adventure, excitement, fun, risk, welcome danger*, and *celebratory* popped up frequently as the participants in the workshop *played* with definitions—the terms, the processes, the outcomes—of co-authoring. As we thought and wrote about this stimulating session, Ludwig Wittgenstein's (1992) concept of "the language-game" came to mind; this game consists "of language and the actions into which it is woven" (769), a game which demonstrates the universal and profound links between language and "form[s] of life" (772). For Wittgenstein, the language-game has no fixed rules but depends on what distinctions the players wish to make and who the players (or "bearers" of the words) are; the meaning of a word is its use in the language (774). In showing that words in language do not have a common essence, but rather present a complex web of relations in which similarities allow us to see connections without the requirement that words and objects, or concepts or processes, always correspond exactly, Wittgenstein uses as an example "the proceedings that we call 'games.'" He offers a way of seeing that the meanings of words are contingent and relational.

> What is common to them all?—Don't say: "There *must* be something common, or they would not be called 'games'"—but *look and see* whether there is a anything common to all.—For if you look at them you will not see something that is common to *all*, but similarities, relationship, and a whole series of them at that . . . . One might say that the concept of "game" is a concept with blurred edges.—"But is a blurred concept a concept at all?"—Is an indistinct photograph a picture of a person at all? Is it even always an advantage to replace an indistinct picture by a sharp one? Isn't the indistinct one often exactly what we need? (778–79)

We propose that the concept of collaborative text production is a concept with blurred edges, and the CCCC workshop discussion (which Blitz described as a collaboration) illustrated this blurriness. During the exchange about definitions, Blitz told of gathering his colleagues together to write a piece (for an edited collection) about an academic program they had developed. Ironically, these people had worked hard together for a long time to create this program but, even though they were enthusiastic about the project, they chose not to sit down together to produce an article about it. Instead, they each wrote a separate piece, and Blitz's task was to stitch together the pieces. He defined this project as co-authored because each member of the group contributed to the article and all their names will be on it. Blitz explained that he sees co-authoring as the larger term which includes collaborative writing, but he felt there was no collaborative writing in this case. However, he and Hurlbert would characterize their work as co-authoring which *does* incorporate collaborative writing.

After hearing Blitz's story, Roen offered the term *co-bylining* to describe Blitz's project with his colleagues; Dorwick added the term *ghost-bylining* to describe a situation in which "a person who has nothing to do with the text appears as principal author" on the publication (in contrast to *ghost-writing* in which someone is compensated for producing text but their name does not appear as an author). Dorwick then told of a text he was trying to bring to publication: it started as transcripts of a MOO discussion involving several people. Each of the MOO participants received a copy of the transcript and was asked to add annotations. Dorwick described the contributors as "joint authors" and the piece as "co-valanced and multivoiced," and when we asked about what seemed to be his uncertainty concerning who should be listed as author, he said, "Well, it's authored."

Yancey was inclined to think of a co-authoring relationship as a *partnership*, noting that, for *her*, co-authorship extends beyond a single text, involving multiple projects, an extended time period, and a connection which goes beyond the work. She told a story of a successful project that she composed with several women, stressing that for her such a collaboration did not constitute a partnership and was therefore not co-authorship as she defines it. Kami observed that as soon as we say co-authoring must involve a long-term commitment, someone will insist that their successful one-time co-writing relationship did constitute co-authoring, and Yancey replied, "Yes, but it's not a partnership."[7]

Spooner, who is both a writer and a director at a university press, further complicated the discussion by describing the role an editor takes; he used the terms *cooperation* and *collective*, which he sees on a continuum with *collaboration* and *co-authoring*, and wondered where editing fit on the continuum: "It's not co-authoring, it's not collaboration. It may be cooperative, and surely collective. It's never the same, but somewhere along there it works." Here he had seized on Blitz's earlier tongue-in-cheek comment that we should spread rumors that everyone is collaborating, everyone is doing "collective work." But Spooner's sense of cooperation is compatible with Ted Panitz's definition of cooperation, which has to do with a directive approach structured by someone other than the participants in order to "facilitate the accomplishment of a specific end product" (2000, 3). Spooner admitted he has no trouble assuming the role of "director" in the editing process.[8] He recognizes the many different kinds of writing relationships, each with its own conventions, but sees them all fitting somehow within the rubric of writing groups.

In contrast to editing at a university press is pulling together a collection of essays on a particular topic. Yancey, who has edited such a collection, made the point, and everyone agreed, that the intention in creating such an edited text is to bring together the best writing on a subject. The editor acknowledges the need for a range of voices and expertise to fill out a broader area than could be tackled alone. While the text is a collective effort, however, it is finally known by its editor's name. We in composition are all guilty of tossing around the names of the editors of a text without acknowledging the contributors; Yancey's examples were "the Kirsch and Mortenson book" and "the Walvoord book." This kind of text is a slippery genre; we all know the work involved in editing such a collection merits recognition of editorship, but we also know of the collaborative effort for all—contributors and editor(s)—to produce such a text; yet we perpetuate the convention of single authorship when we refer to the text by the editor's name only. Of course, reciting the names of all the authors would be cumbersome; perhaps using the title would be more appropriate.

But the question of whether an edited collection—or any other piece of writing—is co-authored, co-written, collaboratively written, cooperatively written, or collectively written remains unanswered.

We could try to untangle those terms, but our point in including these stories is to illustrate the diverse ways people characterize their co-authoring. We ask, with Richard Louth, Carole McAllister and Hunter A. McAllister (1993), "How many of us can even agree on a definition of collaborative writing?"— let alone find ways to describe differences between collaborative writing and co-authoring (215). For example, Nancy Spivey (1997) sees co-authorship as overlapping with but not always equivalent to collaborative writing. Spivey problematizes the notion that all co-authors are collaborators:

> Collaborative writing and co-authorship do not overlap precisely, even though co-authors often write collaboratively and people who write collaboratively are often co-authors. Having one's name as co-author of a text does not necessarily mean that someone actually contributed directly to the drafting of the text, and participating actively in such drafting does not mean that someone will be named co-author. (139)

With these terms in mind, we found it interesting to look back at our preconceptions of co-authoring. Previous to our study, we believed that collaborative writers could not be named co-authors unless they fit *our* rather narrow definition—a definition based, of course, on our own practices and experiences. Not until we began writing this section did we see clearly how our conversion experience demonstrates one of our central points: preconceptions and misconceptions and narrow conceptions about what co-authors do limit our drive to expand notions of authorship. In an effort to unpack collaboration as it relates to writing, we want to discuss briefly the distinctions among and definitions of the terms *cooperation, collaboration, collaborative writing,* and *co-authoring* we had in mind when we conceived of this study, now that we have shown how the words of co-authors themselves complicate those distinctions and definitions.

In 1997, we thought of the word *collaborate* as the *Random House Compact Unabridged Dictionary* defines it: "to work, one with another; cooperate" (Steinmetz et al. 1996). For us, *collaboration* was a general term involving all cooperative work; we have all been, and will continue to be, collaborators as we interact with and learn from texts, and from our colleagues, children, friends, and anyone else with whom we make knowledge. However, we came to see that *cooperation* is the wider term: people who cooperate often reach consensus on some points but just as often carry on individually to reach personalized goals (Hord 1981). According to Austin and Baldwin (1991), "Collaboration is the narrower term. . . . People who collaborate work closely together and share mutual responsibility for their joint endeavor. . . . Collaboration not only involves cooperative action. It emerges from shared goals and leads to outcomes that benefit all partners" (4). In a different conception of collaboration and cooperation, Panitz, like Kenneth Bruffee, distinguishes cooperation and collaboration into two different learning paradigms: cooperation facilitates the transmission of foundational knowledge (such as a grammar rule, a math formula, a historical fact) and collaboration seems to facilitate the discovery of nonfoundational knowledge (which is derived from creative and critical thinking and is inquiry based). In pedagogical terms, cooperation defined this way looks like a teacher-centered classroom, and collaboration defined this way looks like a student-centered classroom. And to further complicate matters, Toni Knott and Lynne Valek (1999), in their co-authored dissertation of workplace collaboration, use metaphors to view collaboration as "growth and development, rhythm, power alliances, mechanical process, relationship, story, the creative act, and spiritual reality-between."[9] However, even with this seemingly comprehensive array of metaphors through which to view collaboration, they found "definitions of collaboration confusing, overlapping and inadequate."

To illustrate how we distinguished between these terms before we began our study, we'll use an example from academia. If a scholar is part of an academic department, he *cooperates* in that he meets his classes, serves on committees, turns in grades on time, and makes coffee when the carafe is empty. His actions are part of the "social grease" that keeps the department running and relationships congenial. When he *collaborates*, though, according to Austin and Baldwin (1991), he and another member (or members) of the department work together (by choice or not) toward a shared goal; they might decide to team-teach a class, present recommendations to a committee, conduct research about retention, etc. All of the activities of this collaboration would not necessarily be done together, and writing would not necessarily be involved. In fact, in our CCCC workshop, Blitz observed that "anyone who says they don't collaborate is a fraud," and Roen added that "if you ask anyone how work gets done in the academy, they'll say they do some of it sort of alone, some of it with people in the same room, some of it with people on a listserv or whatever."

To illustrate further how we viewed these terms before our study, we thought of *collaborative writing* as a still narrower term. We viewed it as an action step taken by participants and involving all aspects of collective text production; if the department member above chose (or was assigned) to write collaboratively with a partner or partners, they would together set a goal, plan, draft, revise, and edit a particular piece of writing. The work could involve a division of tasks—some sections might even be written individually and later combined—but all authors would take responsibility for the final product.

Finally, based on our own experience writing with each other, *co-authoring* carried the narrowest definition; the scholar in our example would, with his chosen writing partner, set a goal, plan, and then sit down and write face-to-face (or more likely sit together in front of a computer screen), creating text on a sentence-by-sentence, or even word-by-word, level.

However, through our study of collaboration and writing, we found that most of the researchers and learning theorists were referring to cooperative learning, collaborative learning, peer response groups, tutor-student interaction, and teacher-student writing conferences—all text-making activities—as *collaboration* or *collaborative writing*, essentially interchanging those terms. Most of them did not even discuss actually producing text together face-to-face, let alone word by word.

While we are naturally not going to elaborate on collaborative learning (the topic of a number of books already), we agreed—and still agree—with Muriel Harris (1992) that the terms *collaboration* or *collaborative writing* used so broadly are actually describing *collaborative learning about writing*. Harris makes a useful distinction between collaborative writing and collaborative learning about writing: *collaborative learning about writing* involves activities focused on peer or teacher response to individual papers; the image of the ultimately solitary writer is preserved. But Harris identifies *collaborative writing* "as involving two or more writers working together to produce a joint product. . . . Each may take responsibility for a portion of the final text, [but must take] some sort of collective responsibility for the final product" (369). Deborah Bosley's definition of collaborative writing echoes Harris's and characterizes what happens in many composition classrooms and writing partnerships: "two or more people working together to produce one written document in a situation in which a group takes responsibility for having produced the document" (qtd. in Ede and Lunsford 1990, 15). But for us, the term *collaborative writing* used in the ways described above was—and is—"problematic" (Dale 1997, x), "confusing" (Harris 1992, 369), and "far from self-evident" (Ede and Lunsford 1990, 14); it is "used to refer to cooperative planning as well as to writing separate sections of a text or to writing an entire text together" (Dale, x).

It seemed to us that these definitions describe collaborative learning about writing, not co-authoring, at least as we had more narrowly defined it. These definitions seemed compatible with the metaphor created by one of the teams we studied, who defined their co-authoring as a "seamless garment." Interestingly, though, they also admitted to a process of cutting and pasting—stitching—their individual contributions together. They described their process this way: "We've given ourselves essentially assignments . . . and come back . . . and amazingly they seem to fall into place . . . the idea about tailoring . . . the sleeves . . . the lapels . . . the body . . . the seamless garment." This group even resisted marking each other's work or writing transitions to connect the sleeves and the body. Yes, they stitched together a whole, but any garment consisting of several pieces is seamed where the parts join. (We're ashamed to say now that after this interview, we turned to each other and said, "Well, *they're* not co-authoring!")

Other teams described their work as "intertwined" or "woven" together, metaphors which seem compatible with *our* original definition of co-authoring: face-to-face, word-by-word collaborative writing. Priscilla S. Rogers and Marjorie S. Horton (1992) define "face-to-face composing" as the rare "truly multiple authorship . . . the fully collaborative enterprise involving coauthors who plan, draft, and revise a document in a face-to-face context" (122). This "melding," which Ede and Lunsford call "co-authoring" (qtd. in Harris 1992, 369), seems to go beyond what happens in most classrooms and in most professional collaborations, and we embraced this definition of co-authoring as most appropriate to describe what we believed "true" co-authors would do. For many who do sit down together (proximally or virtually) and compose sentence-by-sentence, word-by-word, collaboration *means* co-authoring.

However, as our study progressed, we found that for several of the teams we interviewed, face-to-face, word-by-word writing is not essential to their success, and that some even view it suspiciously. Furthermore—as the exchange in the CCCC 2000 workshop illustrates—there are as many definitions for *co-authoring* as there are co-authoring teams, some of which fit our original concepts of *collaboration* and *collaborative writing*. All of the teams in our study used the terms *collaboration* and *co-authoring* interchangeably to describe what they do when they work together on a piece of writing. A few used *collaborative writing* to mean the same thing. The seven teams in our study who actually sit down and produce text face-to-face included this activity in the terms *collaboration, co-authoring,* or *collaborative writing,* but one team who does not write face-to-face named that specific activity *co-writing.*

We propose that there is no one term for or definition of collaborative text production, and that the multiple definitions should be generated by intense, careful reflection and remain functions of the participants in that process. Of course, there is room for abuse at either extreme: leaving the definition so open there is no benchmark for discussion, or creating too rigid a set of criteria. We mentioned earlier Creamer's definition of a co-author (1999)—one who makes "a substantial, intellectual contribution to a publication" (274)— and defining a co-author seems to us to be a useful way of establishing criteria that could apply to many configurations of co-authoring. In a discussion of the ethics of co-authoring in biomedical scholarship, we found a statement on authorship by the International Committee of Medical Journal Editors:

> All persons designated as authors should qualify for authorship. Each author should
> have participated sufficiently in the wozrk to take public responsibility for the content.
>   Authorship credit should be based only on substantial contributions to (1) con-
> ception and design, or analysis and interpretation of data; and to (2) drafting the
> article or revising it critically for important intellectual content; and on (3) final
> approval of the version to be published. Conditions 1, 2, and 3 must all be met. (qtd.
> in Jones 2000, 13)

Although this statement was created in response to the practice of including
as co-authors those who funded research or supervised a project only (or did
not contribute at all, as in the case of "gift authorship"), these criteria describe
every co-author who has contributed to our knowledge about successful co-
authoring. These criteria seem to represent a useful common jumping off
point from which each co-authoring team can begin to describe their own
processes.

Reflection required

As Yancey said in the workshop, and as we have learned in our research, a
unique set of conventions emerges out of each co-authoring partnership, and
perhaps even out of each co-authoring occasion. We need to resist the impulse
to circumscribe the robust, protean, risky—yet productive—act that is co-
authoring. We hope the definition will remain suspended lest it become con-
cretized and reified, so narrowly defined that, say, one concept of collaborative
writing does not include or invite another. For instance, in terms of promotion
and tenure, one department might arrive at *its* set of criteria for acceptable co-
authored work. A department might limit the number of co-authored publications, assign different values to authorship positions, limit the number of
authors on a certain piece of writing, or stipulate that authors delineate their
individual contributions. However, based on what we understand now about
academic co-authoring, those criteria would necessarily inevitably exclude
some faculty member whose scholarship is co-authored. Instead, we would
admonish academic departments, when evaluating scholarship, to ask co-
authors to reflect carefully on what they do. For example, the University of
California at San Diego suggests,

> At the time of publication each investigator could be asked to specify his or her role
> in the research and records of their reports could be maintained by each department
> for review at the time of promotions. Journals could require similar statements to be
> submitted along with the copyright-transfer form. (Jones 2000, 11)

Key to the emergence of more cogent guidelines around co-authoring is the
call for making explicit not only the level of involvement but the degree of

responsibility writers are willing to take.[10] Arnold S. Relman, editor of the *New England Journal of Medicine*, outlines some criteria which focus on the responsibilities of authorship, even going so far as to suggest that co-authors sign a form attesting to their contributions. He also advises that "co-authors should be able and willing to defend the paper in public . . . be confident about the integrity of the data. . . . Co-authorship should denote . . . meaningful participation in the planning, design, and interpretation . . . and in the writing of the paper" (qtd. in Jones 2000, 9). We do agree, though by asking that co-authors ·make their contributions explicit we are not saying that their scholarship should be policed or that they should be pressured to count words and sentences; instead, co-authors should be invited to nondefensively articulate their contributions. We do not advocate trying to validate co-authorship by quantifying contributions but rather by revealing the characteristics and qualities of the interaction that led to solid research and effective writing. By the time most successful projects are completed, the co-authors most often cannot even identify individual crafting of words, sentences, or sections. But they *can* talk about intellectual contributions, what they themselves have learned from the project, and their commitment to taking their work public. They can make visible the unique processes of their co-authorship, and articulate the value of their projects beyond the published product.

TO PROBLEMATIZE THE PROBLEMS ASSOCIATED WITH CO-AUTHORING

Fourth, and finally, we must address and work through some of the doubts academics commonly have about co-authoring. In our reading of dozens of articles, books, and online exchanges, and from our many encounters with co-authoring and co-authors, we have seen and heard the litany of complaints and reservations about co-authoring. We hoped to learn why, if collaboration is supported by theory and if co-authored articles and books are appearing more frequently in academia, co-authoring is still suspect in many departments and institutions. From our observations as learners and teachers, we see people resisting, misunderstanding, and devaluing the collaborative process. In addition, it seems to us that students, writers, teachers, administrators, and others who lack experience with collaborative writing—and even co-authors who *have* had experience—do not yet understand what is involved in producing a document with more than one name on it. They worry about getting or assigning grades, getting and giving proper credit, the quality of the contributions of others, and whether all co-authors are contributing equally to the work. These concerns are real; even those who promote collaborative writing acknowledge that difficulties exist on several levels. Writing specialists Roen and Mitten (1992), commenting on their own collaboration and that of their students, admit that "collaborative work is unpopular in part because it is frightening, unfamiliar, dangerous even" (303). Long-standing cultural conceptions of individual achievement and competition, and the myriad influences that counter cooperation and encourage self-serving motivations, inform mainstream impressions of collaborative work.

We were tempted to omit this section since the problems we address here did not surface in the stories of the co-authors we studied; our study indicates that a defining element of successful co-authoring is the co-authors' engagement in an ethical project, and resistance to co-authoring is often based on a deep-seated belief that individual rights of ownership will be corrupted or compromised, posing a threat to historical markers of authorship.[11] Essentially, we've distilled the litany of perceived problems to these three: (1) plagiarism, (2) the potential for silencing voices with consensus or an unproductive drive to consensus, and (3) reconciling and recovering the self within a group; all three raise ethical questions associated with collaborative writing. Liberatory teacher and theorist Henry Giroux (1992) places all collaboration squarely in the realm of ethics when he states that "ethics becomes a practice that broadly connotes one's personal and social sense of responsibility to the Other" (74). We cannot think about collaborative writing without thinking about ethics because more than one person is always involved in some way, and we respond to the familiar doubts we listed above from our position that collaborative writing is inherently ethical and can lead to ethical projects. As we will show in the following chapters, the respect, trust, and care that are integral to successful co-authoring make anything even tangential to plagiarism, or forced consensus, or problems quantifying and attributing contributions, nonissues for the co-authors in our study; any concerns in these areas intruded from outside the co-authoring teams.

First is the plagiarism issue, one that consumes a great deal of space and time in professional journals, on listservs, in the hallways of institutions, and in deans' offices. For those who perpetuate the (mis)conception of plagiarism and use that term to cover every kind of suspect use of another's words—a conception which hinders their understanding that all writing is collaborative—co-authoring would represent a type of fraud which only they could imagine is possible. They would see co-authoring as not producing original, autonomous work. But the issue of plagiarism is easily resolved for us, and we are indebted to Howard (1999) for theorizing this complex and historically imbedded "problem." If we believe that all writing is collaborative—that all texts are intertextual, all authors are interauthorial—then plagiarism as we have thought of it traditionally is obliterated. Howard encourages us to "discard the term," and we see a parallel here between her call and ours: "the comprehensive term *plagiarism* asserts a unity among disparate textual practices" (2000, 475) in the same ways we see a single definition of co-authoring as unrepresentative. Howard argues convincingly that under the unitary label of plagiarism, "patchwriting"—or the practice by which students use the words of experts as they (the students) work to learn an unfamiliar discourse—is lumped in with fraud (outright cheating such as stealing or purchasing papers), perhaps in the same way suspicion can undermine the authority of a co-authored text. Frankly, the evidence of textual fraud—or concern about it—never emerged in our study or in the CCCC 2000 workshop, and it's a nonissue in our classrooms when our students co-author.

Second, as far as consensus is concerned, it is important for us to clarify that although we must acknowledge consensus as inevitable in producing a joint text, we can see with Trimbur (1992) that the traditional idea of consensus can be an ethical problem because it has the capacity to minimize potentially productive conflict and silence marginalized voices. By replacing consensus with dissensus, Trimbur looks at collaboration as a process of collectively identifying difference rather than "reconciling differences through an ideal conversation" (220). He calls for "replacing the 'real world' authority of consensus with a rhetoric of dissensus" that can create "a heterotopia of voices—a heterogeneity without hierarchy" (220–21). This kind of consensus is described by constructivist math teachers Jane-Jane Lo, Kelly Gaddis, and David Henderson (1996) in their study of a constructivist approach to the teaching of mathematics. They found that rather than settling on one definition of, say, a circle, the class they studied "glorified in the diversity and richness" that constructing "many possible definitions and axioms" provided—much as we are calling for a richness and diversity in definitions of co-authoring. They were "comfortable with the collection of definitions and axioms and [their] sense of connections among them . . . [which] enriched and supplemented each other and pointed out differing points of view" (39).

We often characterize collaborative interaction as dialogic, but Elizabeth Ellsworth (1994) criticizes the notion that dialogue assumes "all members have equal opportunity to speak, all members respect other members' rights to speak and feel safe to speak" (314). She goes on to say that "all voices . . . are not and cannot carry equal legitimacy, safety, and power" (316). We have certainly heard stories, and seen in our classrooms, instances in which a member of a group might not feel safe to speak, but we believe successful co-authoring invites voices that might never have been heard at all otherwise, especially less powerful voices that might have been drowned out in a hierarchy. For example, during the workshop, Yancey pointed out that "each person must be valued" in a collaborative venture. "If people don't know they have something to contribute, then you're hung up in a power differential." Roen expressed his commitment to "flattening the hierarchy." He collaborates with graduate students often, and he said that frequently "it's hard to get grad students to feel they have something to contribute." But he "doesn't think about it [their relative positions in the academy]"; rather, he persists in treating them as valued peers "until they finally lose the sense of it [the putative hierarchy]."

In addition, a collaborator might be reluctant to speak, or might "give in" to consensus, because she or he perceives conflict or disagreement to be rude. In investigating the ethics of collaboration, Rebecca E. Burnett (1994) studied a student co-authoring team that proved to be unproductive because of "their shared assumption that conflict was bad and consensus was good" (239). The writers were "excruciatingly polite to each other" and "believed that they would be most successful by hinting at disagreement rather than being explicit, by stating alternatives as hypotheticals rather than actual possibilities. . . . [T]hey saw direct disagreement as rude and demonstrating a lack of confidence in the other person (238–39).

It seems, in this case, that *both* voices were silenced as the co-authors strained to reach consensus. And one of the teams we interviewed expressed similar concerns about changing each other's words or even suggesting changes, but they did not perceive that eschewing what they saw as rudeness and lack of confidence in each other resulted in anyone's voice being silenced.

Moreover, evidence exists that the individual voice is enriched or strengthened as it "jams" with other voices. Joy Ritchie (1989) provides us with a vivid metaphor to describe this "heteroglossia," this relation and contribution of the self to the group and vice versa: "Small groups [are] like jazz combos, where a melody tossed out by one player is taken up and transformed by several other players, each of whom produces some new, unique variation" (165). Ritchie, Thralls (1992), Ede and Lunsford (1990), James Zebroski (1994), and others draw on Bakhtin to argue that although "individual utterances are never entirely original because individual consciousness and language use are socially constituted . . . the individual author can assert a voice . . . [and] has ultimate responsibility for textualizing the dialogue that takes place among collaborative partners" (Thralls, 77). As we work with others, our individual voices may be enlarged, reaccented, and modulated, but need not be lost.

Even if we embrace the possibility that individual voices can be enlarged in collaboration, we cannot ignore the "potential problems with [an] uncritical notion of community which too often emphasizes consensus and connection at the expense of conflict and difference" (Qualley and Chiseri-Strater 1994, 112) or Greg Myers's (1986) warning that "bodies of knowledge cannot be resolved into a consensus without one side losing something" (167). We admit with

Jean-Francois Lyotard (qtd. in Faigley 1992) that consensus can lead to the end of dialogue, and with Ellsworth (1994), we honor a multiplicity of knowledges. Our conviction that the individual voice (ideology, culture, gender, etc.) should not be diminished to any significant degree *does* lead us to consider the alternative—dissensus. Yet we resist with Kurt Spellmeyer (1994) the easy dichotomy of consensus versus dissensus; a discord between opposing discourses should not mean one discourse must be suspended to achieve understanding.

Shared understanding points not to consensus as terminal agreement—as the final, ultimate, desired goal of collaboration—but to acknowledgment of differences and an attempt to comprehend them in an act of collaboration distinguished by respect and genuine interest. It seems to involve substantive conflict, finding some common ground, and then creating new knowledge—a different kind of consensus. Consensus does have the potential to "throw a euphemistic blanket over real differences that remain unresolved unless agreement is deliberately deferred" (Gale and Gale 1999, 169), but Burnett maintains that in successful co-authoring, "'collaborators have the opportunity to pose alternatives and voice explicit disagreements about both context and rhetorical elements . . . . as they arrive at something like a real consensus (one that does not suppress dissent and difference)'" (qtd. in Gale and Gale, 170). Yes, consensus in successful co-authoring is necessary and inevitable, but consensus does not drive the work; the give and take, the stimulating struggle of the work process—what co-authors tell us they relish—leads to consensus or else they wouldn't be working together. We are not saying that consensus is automatic, but it does seem to be a natural outcome that is a result of a respectful, trusting relationship in which the co-authors honor each other as scholars and as people.

Buber's (1965) concept of the I-Thou relationship sheds light on the connections between the co-authors in our study: "The individual is a fact of existence in so far as he steps into a living relation with other individuals." Buber characterizes human communicative relationships as dialogic acts of "one being turning to another as another" (203). Could the conscious drive to consensus be motivated by the need to objectify the other, to "impose meaning" in what Buber calls the "I-It" relationship? Buber posits instead the "I-Thou" relationship:

> In the most powerful moments of a dialogic . . . it becomes unmistakably clear that it is not the wand of the individual or of the social, but of a third which draws the circle round the happening. . . . the narrow ridge, where *I* and *Thou* meet, . . . the realm of "between." . . . "Between" is . . . the real place and bearer of what happens between men: it has received no specific attention because, in distinction from the individual soul and its context, it does not exhibit a smooth continuity, but is ever and again re-constituted in accordance with [our] meetings with one another. (203-204)

Furthermore, Buber's reciprocal bond seems in harmony with Bakhtin's understanding that "language lies on the borderline between oneself and the other. The word in language is half someone else's" (1981, 293). Buber admits that the I-it relationship is necessary in order to organize our lives, whereas I-Thou is messy and potentially hazardous. He sees that the "solid benefits . . . of the *Thou* appear as strange lyric and dramatic episodes . . . tearing us away to dangerous extremes, loosening the well-tried context, leaving more questions than satisfaction behind them, shattering security" (1987, 34). "But," Buber adds, "all real living is meeting" (11), and "he who lives with *It* alone is not a man" (34).

In addition, Iris Marion Young's theory of "asymmetrical reciprocity," an attitude of "moral respect . . . that depends less on unity . . . and more [on] the specific differences among people" (1997, 41) provides us with one useful frame through which we will view the co-authors in our study in chapter four. The discoveries and insights—and consensus—of these co-authors came often as a result of their differences. During the CCCC workshop, Trapp told of her frustration that she and a close friend seem to have nothing to write together about since their interests and fields seem so different; the relationship is there but the topics do not seem to be. The participants in the workshop encouraged her to use the differences with her friend, to not assume they need to think the same way.[12] Yancey said, in fact, that it was the differences with her co-authors that made the work interesting. And Blitz celebrated "disparate interests":

> What happens if you put A and C together? You get a chemical reaction. Throw the two together! That's the genesis of ideas. I like this person . . . they like me . . . we like writing emails to each other . . . let's see what brews.

Co-authors reach provisional consensus, but their differences are not reduced. Those differences may be held in suspension, or they may all appear in some way in the co-authored text, but successful co-authors are able to find common ground. Not only do the co-authors in our study find consensus not undesirable—they claim to have reached it by working through and with differences but without any sense of loss whatsoever. They did express reservations about forced consensus within departments or committees, and we will elaborate on these reservations in chapter five.

The problematic issues associated with collaboration which we have discussed—those involving alleged plagiarism or suspect scholarship, and those involving consensus—remain nonissues for our co-authors primarily due to the respectful, trusting relationships they formed, a reciprocal bond. They admitted often to being unable to identify who had written or thought what, and they insisted they were not possessive about their own language. Blitz described the very real possibility that he or Hurlbert might send the other thirty pages of text, only to find the draft returned with "nothing left that is recognizable" except maybe the first sentence. And yet Hurlbert asserts that his work with Blitz is "life-affirming." The only thing that can explain what most of us would find threatening and maybe even demoralizing is the relationship between these writing partners. The ineffable and affective dimensions of the relationship, though difficult to articulate, are central to the success of all the co-authors we studied. At one point in the CCCC workshop, Hurlbert expressed that in every co-authoring relationship he enters into, he hopes for the same kind of relationship he has with Blitz. Spooner asked, "Why do you seek that model?" Spooner then read us a question he had written jokingly at the beginning of the workshop: evoking Tina Turner, he asked, "What's affect got to do, got to do with it?" Hurlbert recognized that collaboration is often necessary to get a task done, but co-authoring, as he defines it, is not so necessary in tangible terms but "in the affective realm it's absolutely essential . . . it has the capacity to bring love into our lives, to help us open up ourselves in ways we couldn't do so quickly on our own. . . . There's a spiritual and affective realm that's life-affirming and safe."

This discussion of ethics and collaboration leads us to the lens through which we came to view the words of the co-authors we studied. Feminism, with its emphasis on attention to difference and identity, connectedness, relatedness, nurturance, sensitivity to context, and nonhierarchical relationships, helps to illuminate the transcendent benefits of collaboration and the relationships of the co-authors we studied. Not only that, "feminist inquiry . . . seek(s) to transform styles of thinking, teaching, and learning rather than to reproduce stultifying traditions" (Jarratt 1998, 3). We see a confluence of our research, the approach of the co-authors we studied, and a feminist approach, and we want to make explicit connections between feminism and the ethical project of co-authoring.

In our interview with Ede and Lunsford, Ede, speaking from expertise both as a co-author and as a feminist theorist, insisted that the most important benefits of co-authoring go beyond the cognitive—well beyond, say, learning more about Lacan or post–Vietnam era economic conditions. In fact, she and Lunsford think of their collaboration as a manifestation of their feminism. Collaboration is more than merely a tool, its failure or success measured by the product. When writers collaborate, ideally they do more than pool their skills and strategies to create a better text. Karen Burke LeFevre (1987) goes so far as to say that "learning to invent in communities will do more than enable success in classrooms or careers. It is absolutely essential to achieving peace and . . . maintaining life on this planet" (129).

Can collaborative acts, acts that have the potential to enact feminine values of connection and care, resonate in ways that contribute to the ethical project, to our civic, democratic, and spiritual growth? Mary Rose O'Reilley (1993), who writes about learning to make peace, would say "yes."

> In this context the writing group [and a group can be as small as two]—as envisioned by contemporary writing theorists—functions specifically as a peacemaking strategy: it encourages us to listen to each other and figure out ways of criticizing without inflicting terminal injury, and it helps us to learn to accept criticism without rancor. The writing group forces us to stake out the terrain between our own and other people's view of reality; hence, it reinforces both personal identity and the sense of relationship to a community. It puts authority where it belongs: in whatever is compelling, whatever speaks to the heart and intelligence. I hope, in consequence, it makes for inner peace. (33)

We find feminist mathematics teacher and theorist Nel Noddings's ethic of care particularly enlightening in thinking about the ineffable benefits of collaboration. She describes this ethic as "arising out of both ancient notions of agapism and contemporary feminism," which emphasizes "caring, relation, and response" (1994, 171, 173). She also describes an ethic of care as a relational ethic, one which focuses "on the human beings involved in the situation under consideration and their relations to each other" (173). In an ethical relation, participants strive to maintain or transform the relationship into a caring one. She characterizes the relation between the "one caring" and the "one cared for" in terms of "responsibility and response" (174) but explains that caring can take place even if the cared-for does not explicitly acknowledge it; if our caring for someone affects their life in even a small way, that *caring has been completed* and the relation between us is nurtured (1984).

Another reason feminism is important to our project is that one of the central concerns of feminist theory is the breaking down of hierarchies. Evidence exists that those who work collaboratively are most often found working in the hierarchical mode, and tension arises when group members are compelled by expediency and by authority from sources outside or even inside the group. Ede and Lunsford (1990) characterize hierarchical collaboration as highly productive but conservative, conforming, and driven by a "masculine mode of discourse" (133), and they admit that even the dialogic mode, which they "longed to value as potentially liberatory and feminist—could in particular locations and situations actually resist liberatory and feminist goals" (1998, 319). For example, as Brodkey (1987) studied a professional collaboration between a male professor (a professed feminist) and a female first-year lecturer (and graduate student), she came to feel that the professor's gender and credentials

threatened "to dismantle the apparently fragile construction of their collaboration and coauthorship as a conversation between peers" (119).

But the collaborative or dialogic mode does have the *potential* to subvert that
traditional structure. Peter Mortensen and Gesa Kirsch encourage us to work
toward "a dialogic model of authority, one which infuses authority with ethics"
(qtd. in Durst and Stanforth 1996, 70). Lunsford and Ede support this model as
one in which "the creative tension [is] inherent in multivoiced and multivalent
ventures" (1990, 133). We see the dialogic mode as a feminist approach which
promises the "rejection of the conquest/conversion model of interaction and the
development of new forms of relationships which allow for wholeness in the
individual and differences among people and entities" (Gearhart 1979, 200).

Contemporary feminism insists on acknowledgment and investigation of
difference, and as we have said, the co-authors in our study appreciate and
learn from their differences. But to work successfully, they have been able to
find and cultivate patches of common ground and even experience empathy.
Barry Kanpol (1995), a multicultural theorist, moves beyond merely recognizing and appreciating difference to criticize the postmodern, left-liberal view of
multiculturalism that focuses on difference. In a refreshingly hopeful voice
(which some, we know, would call utopian), Kanpol wants us to seriously consider the concept of empathy; he believes empathy makes possible "an intersubjective consciousness that transcends dividing, cutting, and competing
differences into an arena of mutual tolerance, celebration over difference and
joy over unity, solidarity, and similarity" (180–81).

As we mentioned earlier, Young (1997) proposes the "concept of asymmetrical reciprocity" (39), which seems to us especially useful in discussing the less
concrete aspects of collaboration. Her view of communicative ethics takes issue
with Habermas's "universalizable moral norms" (39) and Seyla Benhabib's idea
that "moral respect is a relation of symmetry between self and other" (38). Young
contends that these views assume that we can "adopt the standpoint of others"
(41), that we can see from their positions, but she feels that "through dialogue
people sometimes understand each other across difference without reversing
perspectives or identifying with each other" (39). With Kanpol, Young insists
that people are not so completely different that they cannot find common
ground, and she echoes Noddings in her belief that "the ethical relation is also
asymmetrical in the sense that opening onto the other person is always a *gift*; the
trust to communicate cannot await the other person's promise to reciprocate, or
the conversation will never begin" (50). She encourages us to be open to wonder,
both at the difference and newness of the other and at our own positions (53).
Could not the kind of communicative ethic she hopes for be a desirable yet
intangible by-product of co-authoring?

❧

In naming what we do as co-authors, we borrowed from mathematics an operation that signifies exponential growth, and we then created a clever expression to represent the benefits of co-authoring—*(first person)²*. Co-authoring, a complicated set of actions and results, can hardly be reduced to such a formula, yet (first person)² represents the benefits we see in terms of products, processes, and especially relationships. In studying the relationships of other co-authors, we learned that, like us, they enact an ethic of care which requires, and leads to, a feminine approach. Our choice to employ a mathematical operation is particularly appropriate because we draw on the work of Noddings, a feminist and former mathematics teacher, who explores the potential of an ethic of care, which she calls feminine, as the means of creating a more safe, more caring, more responsible and responsive world. Through our study of what co-authors say about their material practices and their relationships, we have come to see that care is integral to what they do and who they are, and we choose to call their approach feminine.

In fact, we learned that most of the problems associated with collaboration can be mitigated, if not eliminated, when the participants take a feminine approach. Like most feminists, we hope for a better world in which everyone is valued, respected, heard, trustworthy and capable of trusting, caring and cared for; and we also believe that feminism, which we see involved in ethical actions and ways of being, is an appropriate lens through which to view the successful co-authors we studied—and co-authoring itself. Chapter three is devoted to explaining our reasons for choosing the term *feminine* to characterize the stance of the successful co-authors we studied, a stance that we believe contributes to successful co-authoring, or (first person)².

Today we revised the previous few paragraphs—deleting large chunks and writing much of it from scratch—after working for a number of weekends on the "definition of terms" sections in chapter three and deciding to ditch parts of it. Our work today started with a discussion of *(First Person)²* and what we really wanted to say in this book, and talking about this led Kami to admit her fears about the book.

I'm afraid that the importance of what we learned—and the essence of what we wanted to say—is going to be lost in academic jargon and defending our choices. We've talked before about the fact that what we learned from this study is certainly of great value to you, Michele, but it was life changing for me. I saw people connecting in a way that I knew I had never been able to do. I saw the value of that connection,

and I'm different—better—because of it, in my relationship with you,
and my relationships with my friends, my colleagues, my students, my
children, and even people I hardly know. I know that theorizing about
successful co-authoring, problematizing it, working to articulate the
ineffable, is necessary. It helped me to learn from what I was seeing
and to understand what that meant in my life and could mean in other
people's lives. I know it's not OK to just say, "Well, that's the way it is. It
just feels right," and yet sometimes that's what I want to say. Some of
the co-authors worried about analyzing what they did for fear of
destroying the almost mysterious connection they had, and that's my
concern with spending too much time in this book on theory when the
real meat is in the co-author's own words in chapters four, five, six, and
seven. You worry that members of our audience will dismiss us on the
grounds that we haven't theorized or problematized enough, or that
we have chosen to use terms they criticize as outdated or uncritical or
essentialist. I understand your concerns. I too want people to listen, to
see the value in what we have learned. I think it's important to make a
strong case for our choices. But in the long run, I don't care if some
people dismiss us. We've been dismissed before. We aren't in the habit
of taking mainstream views or perpetuating convention or caring very
much if we are in a minority.

What is really hard about writing (and not just writing
together) is constantly trying to answer the question: what
counts as evidence in our field? So my concerns go beyond just
the surface—the reader, the critic—to ask if other co-authors will
see themselves in our words. I'm asking myself—and you,
Kami—how to make this more accessible, believable, useful in
light of the current ethos around feminism and feminine. . . . I
am wondering when or if these kinds of terms become NOT
useful . . . envisioning readers . . . trying to balance our need to
say what we know from our experience with what we want
others to believe. . . . the sense of freedom (and the
responsibility that implies) is scary . . . because we have been
granted this particular forum . . . a book . . . an amazing
opportunity to speak . . . but what makes me go on confidently is
not just an intuition about our study's value, but that saying
what needs to be said in our way demonstrates a congruency
with what our study called for: uncovering and valuing multiple,
context-driven interpretations about a very particular experience

(with texts and with each other) which deserves to be heard. Our own work together on this book has embodied the (first person)² result over and over.

NOTES

1.   See, for example, Ede and Lunsford 1990.
2.   We've come to see that we were engaged in empirical research, and we find Mary Sue MacNealy, Cindy Johanek, and Patti Lather's writing on research methodologies useful. Our study fits criteria for empirical research: "research is planned in advance . . . data are collected systematically . . . data collection produces a body of evidence that can be examined by others" (MacNealy 1999, 40–41). According to Johanek, those of us in the humanities are suspicious of the term *empirical* because we associate it with "scientism or extreme positivism . . . . methods of systematic testing and observation" (2000, 24); but MacNealy sees

> studies that collect qualitative data (e.g. interviews or field notes in ethnographies and case studies) . . . provide a rich understanding of some phenomenon, person, or community. When no quantitative data are collected and no statistical procedures are used, the researcher relies on his or her experiences as a participant in the community to help in interpreting the observational data." (1999, 45)

In addition, Lather claims "feminist empirical efforts" can work within a "interpretative/phenomenological paradigm" (1995, 294). See also Hayes, Young, Hatchet, McCaffrey, Cochran, and Hajduk 1992, which Johanek identifies as useful in providing examples of empirical research in composition such as "case studies, naturalistic observation, surveys" etc. (25). See also Addison and McGee 1999, a diverse collection addressing the issues of feminist inquiry. They write: "The use of feminist inquiry within empirical research in the field of rhetoric and composition is helping us to be more reflective in general concerning the empirical research we conduct and the effects it has on our teaching and future research" (2).
3.   In discussing what constitutes the private and public, Hannah Arendt (1998) sees the connection between individuality and physicality. For her, bodily pain ultimately defines subjectivity because that extreme subjectivity renders the individual unrecognizable to the outside world: "the experience of great bodily pain [is] the most private and least communicable of all" (50–51).
4.   We have appreciated our conversations with Frank Farmer on our appropriation of Bakhtin. We want to advance Frank's position that we should "avoid

the trap of a naïve essentialism but likewise the overdetermination of a social constructionist approach to subjectivity, realizing the implicit assault on agency that the latter position entails" when calling on Bakhtin (December 18, 2000). Our goal is to "tap into Bakhtin's general orientation toward an intersubjectivity that exceeds both essentialist and constructionist formulations," a challenge for us as we are not Bakhtin scholars.

5. Knott and Valek (see note 9 below) found collaborating dyads "reported a spiritual element to their collaboration," and in our study Hurlbert and Blitz also use the term *spiritual* to describe the rewards of their writing relationship. In *Writing Double: Women's Literary Partnerships*, Bette London (1999) documents another kind of spirituality: collaborations with the spirit world practiced by women writers of the nineteenth century (such as Edith Summerville and Violet Martin, and W. B. and Georgie Yeats). In addition to earthly collaborations, much of the collaboration she describes involves "automatic writing" and paranormal communication, sometimes "with a medium as 'interpreter' and hence, 'coauthor'" (164).

6. We don't mean to imply that only hens can produce these valuable eggs; if we learned nothing else, we learned both male and female co-authors tell reflective, revealing, and even moving stories of successful co-authoring.

7. In a followup to the CCCC 2000 workshop, Yancey took the opportunity to expand on her view of partnership collaboration. Her current conception is noted here.

> Partnerships occur in many different rhetorical situations; here the focus is on writing, but they occur as well in leadership situations and in curricular projects. One person with whom I have partnered in the latter situation tells me that her view is that there is a benefit beyond the partnership that motivates the collaboration. Another friend with whom I partner says that the voluntary, non-official nature of the relationship makes it more genuine. The point—or one point worth noting—is that while composition studies acknowledges that collaboration can take many forms, it has yet to document or theorize the partnership collaboration. (Personal correspondence, Jun 2001.)

8. Stephen Farber and Marc Green (2001), in their review of a book studying Thomas Wolfe and Maxwell Perkins (his editor) and their collaboration, recognize that "there is a long-standing prejudice against any work created by two or more people" and claim that "this new volume represents one more salvo on behalf of the notion that individual creativity is the only kind that ultimately matters" (B17).

9. In 1999, Toni Knott and Lynne Valek completed a collaborative dissertation in the field of human and organizational systems at the Fielding Institute. We were in touch with them (both are women) by phone and email as they negotiated an uneven terrain; support was inconsistent, and there was even

some concern about loss of accreditation. In a recent message from Knott, she told us Lisa Ede, their external examiner, "wrote us a wonderful letter about our work and how it was done and our chair read it at graduation" and that "although Fielding may never allow another one of these, they were pleased with our process, findings, and research." She also told us they had created a circular author identifier:

WORKING AS ONE:

A Narrative Study of the Collaboration of
Male-Female Dyads in the Workplace

A dissertation submitted
by:

to
THE FIELDING INSTITUTE
in partial fulfillment of the requirements
for the degree of
Doctor of Philosophy
in
HUMAN AND ORGANIZATIONAL SYSTEMS

Interestingly, on the UMI web search, Digital Dissertations, only Toni Knott's name is listed. Lynne Valek's name did not come up *anywhere* in the database for Dissertation Abstracts International. However, when we viewed the PDF for the full dissertation online, the title page of the actual dissertation displays the "logo" above.

Along the same lines, Liora Salter and Alison Hearn have co-authored *Outside the Lines: Issues in Interdisciplinary Research*, and the front cover design of the book itself includes a circular name logo:

10. In fields where multi-author publication is more prevalent, editors and evaluators are calling for innovative ways to give credit to co-authors. Possibilities include using film credits as a model: "a *contributors* list should appear as a footnote, describing a job-driven identification of contribution. The *byline* is the list of those who 'contributed most substantially to the work' (Rennie, Yank, and Emanual 1997, 583). *Guarantors* are 'those people who have contributed substantially, but who also have made efforts to insure the integrity of the entire project'.... [This scheme] allows academic promotion committees to discern research contributions" (Horton 2000, 48). Horton also suggests what he calls "an intellectual contract" or "professional covenant between investigator and editor" (50) which deals with ethical issues up front.

11. Naomi Baron (2000) is an example of a contemporary academic who remains concerned that a proliferation of collaborative writing could make extinct our concepts of hard-won property rights, ownership, and originality. "Is authorship as we've known it, at least for the past two centuries, really breathing its last? The Romantic conceptions of authorship assumed an identified individual author. Morever, the model granted property rights—ownership—to that named individual. . . . The academic and literary worlds still continue to hold dear legal property rights of identifiable authors" (164).

12. In our communication with Trapp following the workshop, she said she found the workshop was a powerful motivator; she has contacted the friend she spoke of and they are making plans to co-author. In addition, after telling some colleagues about the workshop, she was approached by a professor from another department about writing something together.

3 WHY CALL SUCCESSFUL CO-AUTHORING "FEMININE"?

A feminine emphasis might lead to communal texts—dialogic, not monologic scores. Assemblages of documents, voices, tapes, and quotations from various sources. A range of chromatics, all circulating in the same netting; multiple voices to reflect multiple backgrounds, cultures; an impatience with the myth of a "solitary" authorial voice responsible for propagating and codifying all information.

Derek Owens

As we met with the co-authoring teams, they talked with us and each other about their individual and collaborative writing processes, their products, their strengths and weaknesses, professional issues of tenure and single authorship, pedagogy, their views on collaborative dissertations, issues of choice and time and proximity, first author concerns, and what they saw as benefits of their co-authoring; but what struck us as we listened to them and then read the transcripts was their attention to, and sometimes almost reverence for, their relationships—both professional and personal. In their collaborative dissertation study, Toni Knott and Lynne Valek (1999) found that the workplace collaborators they studied (mixed gender pairs) began their collaboration, without exception, in order to accomplish a task; not only that, they thought of the task as more important than the relationship. However, most of the teams in our study came to work together only after a relationship, often a close friendship, had developed. Most of them seem to value the relationship over the task, seeing their publications as happy by-products of their personal and professional associations.

Furthermore, we were not just interviewing academics who work together: we were interviewing academics who write together, and the creation of common text and voice, a necessarily shared vision, and the expansion of understanding to encompass two or more consciousnesses seemed to deepen the relationship they brought initially to the task. In searching for a way to talk about these relationships, we came upon a model developed by Cynthia Sullivan Dickens and Mary Ann D. Sagaria in their 1997 study of collaboration among women scholars. They interviewed (individually, not as teams) twenty-six women who had co-authored with other women, and they found that four collaborative profiles emerged: (1) "pedagogical collaboration: nurturance" promoted growth and learning through a common intellectual project and often involved a more experienced woman who nurtured a less experienced one; (2) "instrumental collaboration: pragmatism" centered around a need for expertise, a specific task, or a desire to work with a particular person; (3) "professional partnership collaboration: shared agendas" was characterized by common research interests, several projects together, and an extended professional relationship; and (4) "intimate collaboration: intellectual and emotional closeness" involved "an emotional and intellectual closeness, shared understandings, and an ease of communication" (87).

We were especially interested in the "intimate" category because of our study's interviewees' emphasis on the affective and ineffable qualities of their own relationships. Dickens and Sagaria point out that their study "differs from antecedent scholarship on academic teams . . . by identifying intimate collaboration as a fourth relationship pattern, one which has heretofore been invisible and or undocumented in published work" (95). They go on to say that "affective qualities enmeshed in academic research relationships have not been captured by traditional quantitative research methods" (95). Sociologists Dee G. Appley and Alvin E. Winder agree: "Most social scientists are patently unaware of the expression of caring which underlies collaboration. It is therefore necessary to form some awareness that some significant and vital conceptions of human behavior have been omitted" (1977, 283). In addition, most studies of collaboration in academia up to this point have focused on men with "no mention of intimacy as a quality of those relationships" (Dickens and Sagaria, 95). For instance, Smart and Bayer consolidate scholarly collaborations into "master-apprentice," "supplementary," and "complementary" collaborations (Austin and Baldwin 1991, 20), corresponding roughly to Dickens and Sagaria's "pedagogical," "instrumental," and "professional partnership" categories. But Dickens and Sagaria call for more focus on intimate collaborative relationships and for research involving interviews with pairs or teams and "other collaborations that display power and status differences, such as those involving women and men, junior and senior faculty, and African American and white faculty" (97). Our study addresses several of these areas with sometimes surprising results: the ease with which most of the teams, even the male-male teams, fall on some level into the category of intimate collaboration is compatible with one of our key findings, one that has to do with gender and a feminine approach.

A FEMININE APPROACH: DEFINITION OF TERMS

As we said earlier, a central finding of our study is that all of the co-authors approach writing together from a standpoint which involves care, connection, and nurturance, a standpoint which we choose to call feminine, so explaining our conception of that standpoint is important before we continue.[1] We would like to make it clear at this point that we know the terms *feminine* and *masculine* are somewhat controversial, and that some readers will resist them.

In a conversation with Chuck Schuster, who has written about Bakhtin's chain of utterances in relation to collaboration, Michele explained our theory that the co-authors in our study approach co-authoring from a feminine standpoint. He listened, was quiet for a minute, and said, "Isn't it a shame we have to call it a feminine approach because then the only other approach is masculine." Michele agreed with him but defended our choice of terms by saying we knew no better and more succinct way to describe what we were finding, and he concurred that, at present, feminine is the best and most familiar term for a nurturing approach.

Several voices have echoed Schuster's, encouraging us to use the terms; in their imperfection, their incompleteness, they may still contain enough life yet to invigorate themselves, to make themselves useful. We feel that our many exchanges about these terms—between us, and between us and other readers—have dialogically sharpened our views and ensured that the terms remained productive. If a feminine approach involves caring and its cultural work in relationships, ethics, and social discourses, then it deserves to be explored rather than dismissed as baggage.

Part of the resistance to these terms stems from the fact that many people, scholars or not, see the terms *masculine* and *feminine* as naming biological and sometimes essential characteristics, and they also often see those terms as dichotomous and as carrying negative connotations. In deference to those critics, it is possible to use other terminology to describe competitive, individualistic standpoints and nurturing, interdependent standpoints; in their 1977 article, Appley and Winder develop such terminology. They call for a paradigm shift from "a cycle where competition and hierarchy can serve as a value base for survival" to "collaboration as a value system" (280). They

> define collaboration as a relational system in which: 1) Individuals in a group share mutual aspirations and a common conceptual framework; 2) the interactions among individuals are characterized by "justice as fairness"; and 3) these aspirations and conceptualizations are characterized by each individual's *consciousness* of his/her motives toward the other; by *caring* or concern for the other and by *commitment* to work with the other over time provided that this commitment is a matter of *choice*. (281)

According to Eric Trist, this paradigm shift is necessary because "evidence is mounting that the individual by himself, or indeed the organization and even the polity by itself, cannot meet the demands of these more complex environments. A greater pooling of resources is required; more sharing and more trust" (qtd. in Appley and Winder, 280–81). Neither Trist nor Appley and Winder explicitly associate the collaborative value system with a feminine value system, but in their work, Dickens and Sagaria find that Appley and Winder's and Trist's theories "evoke themes of caring, commitment, and consciousness (or reflexivity) that tend to be characteristic of feminist inquiry" (82). And Appley and Winder's paradigm intertwines with other feminine concepts and theories.

Certainly Nel Noddings's ethic of care (1984), which she calls feminine, supports the paradigm Appley and Winder call for. In addition, the feminine valuing of intimacy, and the intimate nature of some of our interviewees' relationships, coincides with Appley and Winder's belief that individuals must be "able to experience psychic intimacy in the work setting . . . which requires the caring and commitment [that is] part of the value base in a collaborative system" (287). Furthermore, this psychic intimacy should "allow the investment of self . . . without the compulsion of necessity," echoing Iris Marion Young's belief that in asymmetrical reciprocity, gifts of understanding must be given with no expectation of receiving a gift in return. According to Appley and Winder, these free gifts of oneself, one's time, and one's talents, can only be given if "work is not related to survival"; they must be given by choice, which "requires a participative mode that we have little experience with. It means investing in the people we work with as much as in the product produced. It means . . . we confirm each other day by day as we move from making a living to making a life" (288).

In 1977, Appley and Winder called for a shift from a competitive and hierarchical paradigm, which they go so far as to characterize as dysfunctional, to a collaborative one, which they see as necessary for human survival. They could have called for a shift from a masculine paradigm to a feminine one, but the terms do not matter; the concept is the same. The world in general, or at least western culture, and certainly academia, is still—over twenty years after Appley and Winder published their research—in need of more nurturing, caring, and interconnectedness, and we believe the co-authors in our study represent a small microcosm of people whose work seems pointed in this direction. We choose to call their approach feminine partly because feminism—in all its manifestations and definitions—is well established in contemporary western scholarship, and partly because we find it interesting that the men in our study approach co-authoring from a feminine standpoint (as we define it) and acknowledge the problems with the masculine approach.

As we worked on this chapter, we began to wonder if we were both equally compelled to continue to call the stance of the co-authors we studied feminine.

Michele: On my worst days I say "feminine shmeminine."

Kami: [irritated] So you 're saying we should just abandon the feminine thing and go with "collaborative value system"? You know Pat (Hartwell) even said we should stick with feminine in spite of the reservations he had.

Michele: Well, some people cringe at feminine . . . you know? . . . and others embrace it. Even though I see strong similarities with the collaborative value system and a feminine approach, no, I'm not saying we should abandon the term *feminine*. Here are my reasons. Despite its being considered loaded, *feminine* is a far more accessible term. Collaborative value system doesn't go as far or include as much as *feminine* in terms of possibilities. *Feminine* is more far-reaching in terms of ethics and attention to difference than it seems on the surface. Collaborative value system comes out of business and sociological models, and even thirty years after Appley and Winder, you don't read about it. It hasn't caught on as a worldview, but *feminine* has. Sociologists recognize caring as central to a collaborative value system, but it has yet to be interrogated in that system.

Kami: Why do you say "on the surface"?

Michele: Because *feminine* suffers from essentializing and stereotyping—cartoons of behavior.

Kami: Do you think that the fact that we're lesbians has anything to do with our choice of the term *feminine*?

Michele: I think it's ironic that we choose that term. I think it's somewhat unexpected of lesbians who would certainly privilege female-identified ethics and actions but reject the social constructs of *feminine*. So sometimes it feels like we're going backwards.

Kami: Are we?

Michele: I think we're trying to revive this term—it's a much richer term than it appears. That doesn't mean it isn't loaded, that it doesn't have critiques and problems. I think it's too bad it's been locked up with women—been limited to women.

Kami: I think it's too bad that because postmodern feminism is so focused on difference—so self-conscious about admitting its ties to white, western, straight, privileged women and problematizing those ties—that the gains made early by second wave feminists in terms of recognizing the strengths of traditionally feminine traits like care, nurturance, and responsibility are now mentioned almost with embarrassment—and sometimes regarded with hostility—by feminists. As we talk, I've realized one reason I might want so much to hang onto the term *feminine*. When I first became aware of feminism in the late '60s, I was threatened by it. It seemed to me all about breaking down the traditional role of women, a role I was convinced at the time was inevitable and necessary for me. I married a man and gave birth to five children and lived out that role, not resentfully but, I admit, somewhat unconsciously. When I started grad school in 1989, after staying home with my children for seventeen years, I started to wake up, but I never felt as if the work I had done in caring for my children and others had been wasted or was less important than some of my friends' "professional" labor (certainly few people thought I had a career) outside their homes, or the work men do. I still feel it's the most challenging and most important work I ever did. When, in the early '90s (yes, I was late), I became aware of Gilligan and Chodorow and others, I felt validated. Here were respected researchers saying the work I had done, the characteristics that defined me, were something to be studied seriously, valued, even emulated. I guess it seems to me that in worrying so much about essentializing, feminists are losing a great deal of what offered—and still offers—so much hope to both men and women.

Michele: Right. Because caring is not easy, or for the faint of heart, and it's not a behavior of passive, dependent sheep. It involves real consciousness and choice.

We would like to make it clear at this point that we know gender is constructed (as well as performed, provisional, and possibly chosen), although not determined. We know that, likewise, the feminine characteristics discussed by theorists such as Nancy Chodorow and Carol Gilligan are, to a significant degree, the result of social construction. We also understand "gender as relation" and the dangers of "too closely focuss[ing] on the details of masculinity and femininity" (Chodorow 1989, 18), and consequently we resist essential and dichotomous descriptions of human behavior. With Barrie Thorne (1999), we believe that

> the contrastive framework has outlived its usefulness. . . . The view of gender as difference and binary opposition has been used to buttress male domination. . . . A sense of the whole, and of the texture and dynamism of interaction, become lost when collapsed into dualisms like . . . hierarchical versus intimate, agency versus communion, and competitive versus cooperative. . . . We need, instead, to develop concepts that will help us grasp the diversity, overlap, contradictions, and ambiguities. (108)

However, evidence of gender differences found and explored by western psy-chologists, philosophers, scientists, sociologists, feminists, and linguists such as Chodorow, Bakan, Guttman, Gilligan, Young, Harding, Lakoff, Coates, Penelope, Romaine, Thorne, and many others cannot be dismissed—even the earliest research which necessarily focused on the differences in biology and the sociocul-tural result of those differences, or gender. This rich mix of disciplines has con-tributed to an "interstanding" (Ballif, Davis, and Mountford 2000, 589), a more comprehensive, productive term for how conceptions of gendered knowledge and action intersect, interact, and can also result in dissonance and discomfort.

These scholars would agree the masculine and feminine stances lie along a continuum, and that certainly a feminine stance is not displayed only by women (any more than a masculine one is displayed only by men). In dis-cussing the gender continuum, Chodorow points out:

> Some women are far more nurturant than others . . . some men are more nurtu-rant than some women. I agree that all claims about gender differences gloss over important differences within gender and similarities between gender. . . . Still, I believe that the intergender differences are socially and politically most significant . . . it is crucial to take full account of structural and statistical truths about male-female differences. What is important is not to confuse these truths with prescrip-tion. (1978, 215)

Yes, "intergender differences are socially and politically most significant," but, as Benhabib notes, gender is infinite in its varieties and yet tedious in its similarities (1992, 229). More recently, Louise Wetherbee Phelps and Janet Emig (1995) remind us that it's possible for both men and women to "embody or enact culturally feminine values" ; Phelps and Emig speak of "feminine attributes" as "principled choices: not so much claimed about women as chosen by women [and, as our study shows, also chosen by men], proposed for women and perhaps men, offered as a basis for constructing new models for writing, learning, teaching, and rhetoric" (409). We under-stand Phelps and Emig as foregrounding the ethical choices inherent in a feminine approach, and the authors of *Feminist Consequences* (Bronfen and Kavka 2001) identify "the issue of ethical relations for feminism as a way of making contact with one another without assuming each other all to be the same" (xxiii).

In choosing the terms *masculine* and *feminine*, we are not looking for easy, discrete, unreflective ways of conveniently characterizing co-authors, the kind of essentializing that was brought to our attention by Bette London (1999) in her critique of Sandra Gilbert and Susan Gubar's well-known description of their work together. London wonders at their inability to articulate not only the deeper reasons for but also actual processes of their co-authoring. She goes so far as to say they

> reproduce tropes employed by their turn-of-the-century predecessors. Indeed Gilbert and Gubar seem at pains to domesticate—even trivialize—their undertaking, relegating it to the conventionally feminized sphere of the "psychologically useful": a support service, a form of nurturing, a kind of cheerleading, an act of comforting. (80)

Our greatest detractors might criticize our claim that care and nurturance are primary to a successful co-authoring relationship. Yet, we are confident that we can meet London's critique head on because we go well beyond simple "domesticating" and feminizing to problematizing and challenging the conditions under which co-authors must write. London claims that Gilbert and Gubar "do not seem to recognize collaboration as a category of *writing*. For when they do not insistently and narrowly personalize their collaboration, they come close to universalizing it out of existence" (81). Our call for reflection, for making co-authoring processes more visible, seems to us to be a clear alternative to what London accuses Gilbert and Gubar of doing.

We find Lyotard's interpretation of feminine and masculine stances particularly useful in helping us see femininity as an alternate space, a place other than the masculine but not necessarily having to do with the sexual differences of men and women. In an interview with Gary Olson, Lyotard insists that "the enormous, extreme, huge importance of the question of gender is precisely that this question has no answer, and that's the only way we can continue to think about it" (qtd. in Olson 1995, 186). He characterizes "real femininity" as the "refusal of the temptation to grasp, to master" (170), which is compatible with Raman Selden and Peter Widdowson's explanation of feminist critical theory as "contradiction, interchange, debate . . . constantly and innovatively in flux— challenging and subverting and expanding not only other (male) theories but its own positions and agenda" (1993, 205). Lyotard posits that "another sexual space could be substituted" in which "differences traverse individual bodies rather than opposing a 'woman's' body to a 'man's.'" For him, what is important is not the differences between men and women but the fact that "a biological or social male" can also be female (qtd. in Olson, 187). Lyotard says that "what is needed is to move away from a discourse of mastery and abstract cognition toward a way of being that recognizes affect, the body, and openness," a posture he defines as "feminine" (170). Specifically about writing, Rebecca Moore Howard (2000) reminds us that collaboration's suspect state hinges partly on the "gendering of authorship": "Collaboration involves one writer being influenced by another, whereas in the male-dominated authorship of the modern

West, authors are supposed to be autonomous. If they must collaborate, they must do so hierarchically not dialogically" (477).

So, when we use the terms *female*, *feminine*, and *feminist*, we are thinking (usually) not of female biology or essential preferences and characteristics, but of

> processes which tend to undermine the authority of "male" discourse. Whatever encourages and initiates a free play of meanings and prevents "closure" is regarded as "female" ... if there is a female principle, it is simply to remain outside the male definition of female. (Selden and Widdowson 1993, 212)

However, it is important to note that our conceptions of feminine and masculine are specific to mainstream American culture and that postmodern feminists resist the notion that all women share the same position (Caughie 1998, 119). Brady (1998) critiques Chodorow's, Gilligan's, and Belenky, Clinchy, Goldberger, and Tarule's use of the narratives of a few western women to represent all women, and Susan Jarratt reminds us that feminism has as much to do with addressing "the specificity and materiality of difference" (1998, 9) as it does with political activism and valuing a nurturing and connected stance.

The characteristics we call *feminine* and *masculine* are historically and culturally derived from observations and experiences of white western men and women, and until recently, differences among women have not been part of the feminist critique. Certainly we, as white western middle-class women, cannot speak for African American or Asian or Hispanic women, nor can they speak for us. As Sandra Harding explains, "people coming from marginalized groups and testifying to their experience is crucial. . . . [I]t creates the kind of subject that can go on to make history and knowledge [while not being] . . . defined by the way the dominant group defines who you are." However, she goes on to say that women's individual stories must be told and valued, but this telling is part of a 'collective process.' It's done in front of other people. It's done together." These narratives report "individual participation in a collective experience. . . . a collective subject of knowledge, not the kind of individualist subject who becomes a genius alone, and not the kind who joins a community and never has a thought outside the community either" (qtd. in Hirsh and Olson 1995, 41–42).

The narratives of individual women have created a kind of meta-narrative from which all people can learn. Recognizing the danger of creating such a meta-narrative, a strategy which has the potential to elide difference, Nancy C. M. Hartsock nevertheless proposes "to lay aside the important difference among women across race and class boundaries and instead search for central commonalities" (1987, 163–64). In their article "Negotiating the Differend: A Feminist Trilogue," Michelle Ballif, D. Diane Davis, and Roxanne Mountford

(2000) explore the differences among feminists. In an attempt to illuminate the tension between valuing difference and finding solidarity, they turn to Lynn Worsham, who believes feminisms can "form an alliance that recognizes that our histories and experiences are not only diverse in all the ways we have learned to name them, they are also intertwined in complex and mutually determining ways. The lesson to be remembered . . . is that there is no need to eradicate difference to find solidarity" (584).[2]

Several contributors to the collection *Feminist Consequences* (Bronfen and Kavka 2001) predict a movement toward "reclaiming universalism" (xx), a universalism which "does not erase otherness. . . . and which will include but extend beyond subjects who happen to be women" (xxii). The meta-narrative we discovered in our study is connective tissue which has the strength to span differences and provide "fundamental supplements to more abstract structural information and analysis as well as sources of theoretical concepts" (Phelps and Emig 1995, 410). In a listserv discussion about the "trilogue," Mountford (2000) closed her posts with a quote by Muso Soseki: "Do not say that your wisdom and my ignorance belong to opposing worlds. Look: China and Japan, but there are not two skies."

Acknowledgment of the risks of choosing the terms *feminine* and *masculine* does not preclude us from using these terms to describe the behaviors of any person from any culture if those persons display feminine or masculine characteristics as we—along with Gilligan, Chodorow, Lyotard, Noddings, and others—have defined them. In choosing these terms, we recognize with Worsham that "there can be no safety in words chosen, no refuge . . . in abstract, dematerialized categories of difference" (1998, 336), but we also believe with Worsham that "a choice of words always remains for each of us to make individually, a choice that will place us alongside one another in a side-by-side relation of association and alliance" (330). Although the terms *masculine* and *feminine* can be problematic, they seem to us to convey best what we want to say about the co-authors we studied; these terms evince the nature of these successful co-authoring relationships. Our choice is supported by Worsham. For her, concepts like "the one most troubling to feminists, 'woman,'" are only inadequate if we expect them "to provide the precise summing up, the final word. An alternative view and a more modest expectation is to see that a given concept places in our hands particular possibilities and thereby suggests a direction for thought and action" (332).

For us, the concepts or terms *masculine* and *feminine* provide a way to talk about our findings and "suggest a direction for thought and action," both in analyzing our findings and in articulating the implications of our study. We choose to name successful co-authoring as feminine because "naming, like rhetoric, is neither good nor evil; rather, it is the condition we are thrown into by language" (Ballif, Davis, and Mountford 2000, 597).

We believe we can say that the co-authors we interviewed are feminine in that their nurturing, heterarchical, noncompetitive, caring, connected, contextual, affective approach—not to mention the possible risks of challenging and subverting academia's sacred cow of single authorship—most often locates them in a space that is not limited to competition, autonomy, hierarchy, and rationality. Of course, we are not saying that these co-authors are never competitive or self-promoting (or that autonomy and competition are never appropriate). For example, many of the co-authors in our study saw the value of autonomy in some circumstances; indeed, several of the interviewees maintained that autonomy is a prerequisite for successful collaboration. However, for the most part, we heard little evidence of that more masculine standpoint as the co-authors discussed their collaborative work, and no one seemed to feel the necessity to establish autonomy as a member of a writing team. As a result of listening to and analyzing what the co-authors said, we believe much of their success is a product of the choices they make—in approaches, epistemologies, and methods—and the actions they take from a nonmasculine standpoint.

From our standpoint, too, we recognize that not all the interviewees consciously *choose* a feminine approach. The word *feminist* involves conscious choice and connotes political action involving women's struggles in a patriarchal system, and the word *feminine*, as we said before, connotes a space "outside" or other than masculine, a space where caring, cooperation, and context are the standard. According to Stephen Heath in "Male Feminism," "Feminism is a social-political awareness of the oppression of women and a movement to end it" (1987, 27), and while we suspect the interviewees sympathize with that movement, we cannot say all the co-authors, either male or female, identify themselves as feminists. When we asked the teams about what seemed to us to be a feminist stance, most said they had not previously thought of what they did in that way. Three teams connected feminism with their co-authoring— Elizabeth Kent and Matthew Oldman, Gilbert Adams and Julie Knight, and Lisa Ede and Andrea A. Lunsford—but two of those made the connection as a sort of afterthought. Kent, in analyzing the valuing of collaboration in their department, mused, "I always felt comfortable . . . in fact I think it's feminist"; and Oldman realized that their assigning of first author to a department member who needed it professionally could be characterized as "female negotiation." When we asked Adams and Knight if they had ever thought the reason they work well together involves a feminine approach, Adams said they had "never had that feedback," and Knight looked at him and exclaimed, "Well I'm

glad you finally got some outside feedback on this . . . that's absolutely the reason we get along." So, in most cases, the perception of their feminine stance is
our perception, although most of the teams saw the validity of that perception
when we questioned them about it, and we think the data supports that perception as well.

Only two of the co-authors, Ede and Lunsford, identified their approach as
consciously feminist; their connection with feminism is more explicit, inten-
tional, and political. According to Ede,

> Our commitment to feminism is an important part of our collaboration and lends a
> kind of multiple significance to the work we do collaboratively. When a lot of people
> work collaboratively, they have personal reasons for wanting to collaborate, and they
> find that to be a positive, productive process so they keep doing it . . . but I think there
> is a kind of overt termination of significance. It feels like it's a feminine statement to
> work collaboratively . . . so that in addition to whether we think "Representing
> Audience" is a better article because we've done it together, there is sort of always
> already some kind of "and we've done it collaboratively" that adds to it.

We found her phrase "overt termination of significance" a provocative way
to describe the value of co-authoring beyond the creation of better products.
She and Lunsford consciously choose co-authoring as a feminist practice,
while the other co-authors in our study exhibit a feminine approach but have
not consciously chosen a feminist stance or have not explicitly named their
approach as feminist.

Since a number of the co-authors in our study mentioned the terms *ego* and
egolessness, distinguishing between the feminine and masculine ego is necessary here. Feminist theorists have not overlooked the feminine tendency to
focus more on the "other" rather than the self (but not always at the expense of
the self), and Chodorow (1989) turns to psychologists David Bakan and David
Gutmann in her 1989 discussion of ego. As we established earlier, Chodorow
sees "gender as relation" (18) but finds analyses of traditional female and male
characteristics useful in illuminating the terms *feminine* and *masculine*. Bakan
focuses on the distinction between male and female egos; for him the male ego
"manifests itself in self-protection, self-assertion, and self-expansion; . . . the
urge to master" while the female ego "manifests itself in the sense of being one
with other organisms . . . [and] in noncontractual cooperation." Gutmann
supports Bakan; he characterizes female personalities (and for him this characterization applies to all sexes) as "part of a larger social organization and system of social bonds" and the male personality as making "himself or herself . . .
the focus of events and ties." Consequently, female egos are likely to be more
flexible, or less "insistent on self-other distinctions," more oriented to the pre-

sent, and more subjective (qtd. in Chodorow, 56). We would characterize the egos of the interviewees as feminine in their cooperative, contextual, flexible approach.

Just as we've asked that definitions of authorship be expanded, we are asking that definitions of feminine be revisited and revived in light of our findings. We're not just calling for a "different space" or a "space outside" or for walls to come down inside the house to open up the rooms, or even for an addition built on to accommodate us. We want, if not a tearing down of the old structure and new plans drawn, at least a full, thoughtful renovation that reflects new and old understandings of how people may be writing together and why. Whatever their preconception of feminine may be, we hope readers will with us see "feminine in the deep classical sense—rooted in receptivity, relatedness, and responsiveness" (Noddings 1984, 2).

NOTES

1.   Our use of *standpoint* is not to be confused with *standpoint theory*. Laura Brady (1998) critiques Sarah Ruddick's appropriation of "standpoint theory" as one "based on the idea that women, as an oppressed group, must know their oppressor—men—in a way that the oppressor does not need to know the oppressed." Like Brady, we are mindful of taking any path that can "imply the moral superiority of women [and] and easily become essentialist" (38). Our intention is to use standpoint in a more prosaic, traditional way.

2.   We understand that the word *difference* can imply a foundational concept, like a "'proper' feminist against which to judge difference." Ballif, Davis, and Mountford find Derrida's term *differance* more appropriate and useful in that it "embrace[s] an unending play of differences and attend[s] to the exclusions that are created in the name of feminist solidarity" (2000, 585).

3.   It was serendipitous that as we were searching for support for our choice of terms, we subscribed to a *PRE/Text* listserv discussion around Ballif, Davis, and Mountford's article (2000). From the article and the stimulating listserv discussion, we gained a better understanding of what others in the field of composition and rhetoric are thinking about in terms of contemporary feminism, especially the struggle to turn toward difference without abandoning the possibilities of common ground. Our work attempts to suspend naming in some ways and invigorate it in other ways. Like these writers, our biggest challenge, and simultaneously our greatest pleasure, has been playing with this language.

4 COMPLETION OF CARING
Successful Co-authoring as Relationship

The test of my caring is not wholly in how things turn out; the primary test lies in an examination of what I considered, how fully I received the other, and whether the free pursuit of his projects is partly a result of the completion of my caring in him.

Nel Noddings

THE FRAMEWORK FOR OUR FINDINGS

Having clarified the central terms we will use in presenting the data from our study, we would like to explain how we used Dickens and Sagaria's study to give structure to what we learned from the interviewees. We find it useful to think about the co-authoring teams in terms of Dickens and Sagaria's categories as we take both a phenomenological and hermeneutical approach. Consequently, we will narrate the interviewees' own perceptions of their lived experience and use the categories developed by Dickens and Sagaria to sort those perceptions, keeping in mind that we are studying what the co-authors in our study said about their co-authoring, not the co-authoring act or co-authored text itself. However, like Dickens and Sagaria, we found that the participants described collaborative relationships that we could not necessarily assign to discrete categories. Furthermore, the categories overlapped, the relationships changed, and no relationship fit only one category. Unavoidably interwoven with the phenomenological approach will be the hermeneutical one which postulates reasons for the teams' successes.

Discussion of how the teams in our study fit into Dickens and Sagaria's "pedagogical collaboration: nurturance" category is prominent in this chapter because most of the elements of successful co-authoring the team members emphasized have to do with nurturance. Combining "nurturance" with "pedagogical collaboration" *only* may be a weakness of Dickens and Sagaria's study, or at least a mislabeling, since the definition of "nurturance" includes "warm and affectionate . . . emotional support and care" (Steinmetz et al. 1996). This nurturant attitude spills over into at least two other categories— "professional partnerships" and "intimate collaboration"—as is evident in the observations the co-authors make and the stories they tell. Dickens and

Sagaria acknowledge this overflow but do not refer to nurturance as they discuss the other categories. For us, "pedagogical collaboration: nurturance" is the primary category and the other three are subsumed by it. Therefore, as we said, the lion's share of this chapter will be devoted to the "pedagogical" category, and we will conflate the last three categories—"instrumental," "professional partnership," and "intimate"—in the final section, not because they do not merit as much attention but because we find it impossible to extricate them from each other and because they are implicit in the "nurturance" category (or that category is implicit in them). For instance, several collaborations which began as instrumental grew into professional and, finally, intimate friendships, and it is not possible to discuss those categories discretely.

MENTORING LESS-EXPERIENCED COLLEAGUES

Basically my job was to nurture graduate students.

Duane Roen

The "pedagogical collaboration: nurturance" category refers to interest in and concern about the development of others, and involves teaching and mentoring: "A majority of the participants [in Dickens and Sagaria's study] agreed that working closely with another scholar on a shared intellectual project was an important way to foster growth and learning" (1997, 87). In Dickens and Sagaria's study, this category usually depicts a more experienced faculty member collaborating with students or less experienced colleagues, and such relationships do exist in our study, some within the teams and some with authors outside the teams. Dickens and Sagaria do not cite Vygotsky, but they are clearly describing an example of his "zone of proximal development," which Vygotsky (1978) defines as "the distance between the actual developmental level as determined by independent problem solving and the level of potential development as determined through problem solving under adult guidance or in collaboration with more capable peers" (86). Vygotsky's studies involved children, but his definition includes "collaboration with more capable peers" and therefore applies to adults as well. We would certainly maintain that the adults in our study were continuing to develop intellectually and personally and were part of zones of proximal development that they created with each other as "capable peers."

When we think about the more experienced faculty in our study talking about nurturing students or junior faculty, Duane Roen and Stuart Brown come immediately to mind. The topic of nurturing was important enough to Roen that he returned to it several times after the conversation in our interview had left it behind.

Roen: If I could go back to something we talked about earlier . . . about the nurturing thing . . . nurturing makes me feel good. When I was at the University of Arizona . . . basically my job was to nurture graduate students.

Brown: I really valued the opportunities I had to collaborate with Duane and Theresa [Enos] when I was in graduate school.

Roen often co-authors with graduate students, and, in fact, Roen and Brown began co-authoring when Brown was Roen's graduate student. They both spoke of a later collaborative project, a collection of essays, in which they involved every graduate student in a course they had designed together. Brown remarked that they decided to "turn graduate students into real researchers," and Roen added that "everyone learned something . . . about collaborating and about doing that kind of research . . . writing for publication." Lunsford also told us about writing with graduate students, and even about a project in which a whole class was involved. However, even though one of the teams we interviewed included a graduate student, Roen and Brown, and Ede and Lunsford, were the only two pairs who mentioned nurturing students either inside or outside their co-authoring pair.

The one team we interviewed which involved a graduate student was the three-member team which included Ben Ellison; Cybil Pike, who is a full professor, had enjoyed a positive working experience with Ellison in the past, so she and Alexander Davis, also a professor, "brought Ben on board." Initially Ellison was a research assistant, but "he had ideas of his own" and Pike and Davis began to realize that they "were all sort of thinking along the same lines and that Ben's contribution was growing . . . far beyond what [they] had imagined, and it began to be appropriate to suggest that he might like to become a co-author." Davis also told a story of Ellison's organizing students to speak to the dean in his [Davis's] behalf when he was up for tenure, but Davis emphasized that asking Ellison to work with him and Pike had nothing to do with "a system of rewards . . . it was simply based on the fact that he knows [community issues, ecology metaphors, et cetera]." Pike stressed that Ellison "holds his own . . . is a substantial writer on his own." Bringing him on as a co-author seemed to be more about what he could contribute than about furthering his academic career; all three co-authors insisted they were peers. This team had also involved another junior-senior configuration early on: Davis felt that Pike "took it upon herself to have a type of mentoring role for me as a new professor in the department," and Pike agreed that she thought of herself as mentor "kind of" because she recruited Davis and felt responsible. However, both she and Davis agreed that they had decided to co-author because of shared interests and that they interact less as mentor-mentee than as friends.

The team of Oldman and Kent is an example of an experienced faculty member more overtly expressing concern about the professional development of a less experienced one: Oldman was tenured and Kent had been on the faculty for about a year. Kent often brought up the fact that she was not yet tenured, and Oldman spoke several times of her having "to be concerned about getting some publications." However, they did not mention concerns about Kent's promotion as a reason for co-authoring; their collaboration had more to do with shared interests and proximity. In another pair, Karen O'Quin was a relatively new faculty member and Susan Besemer a graduate student (but not O'Quin's graduate student) when they began working together. However, O'Quin did not speak of wanting to help Besemer professionally. They met when Besemer asked O'Quin, who was working in computing services as a faculty intern, for assistance in analyzing some quantitative data, and their first article grew from that experience. They came together because they had complementary areas of expertise and continued to work together when combining those areas proved successful and enjoyable.

I have considered Michele my mentor since the beginning of our relationship. When we met, I had been teaching college part time for about five years, and Michele had been working with college students full time for about six years. Her experience with academic culture and conventions was vast compared to mine, and I looked to her to help me learn that culture and those conventions. She was (and is) a fluent writer of academic discourse, while I tend to write in an informal narrative style. She taught me how to compose memos, curriculum vitae, grant proposals, and other tasks requiring a more formal style. A skilled researcher, she showed me that searching the library and online sources could be exciting rather than daunting. She helped me prepare for interviews, coached me about social expectations, filled me in on protocol, and generally made me more aware of what's appropriate and what's not in academia.

As we looked at how the participants in our study came together, we realized they differ from those in Dickens and Sagaria's study. In that study, even though "pedagogical collaboration" is defined as "nurturing the development of others" and working closely with another scholar on a shared intellectual project," this type of nurturing pedagogical relationship is characterized by Dickens and Sagaria as involving senior faculty and "junior and usually less-experienced colleagues." These more experienced women faculty felt that joint authorship was a fairer way to involve graduate students than just paying them to gather data, and also a means of helping women and minority students who might not have been prepared well enough for the rigors of academic life.

In our study, on the other hand, even though most of the teams began on unequal professional ground, the senior member did not invite the junior or less-experienced one explicitly into a mentor-mentee relationship. They came together because of shared ideologies and interests, friendships, complementary areas of expertise, and a common vision. Another difference between Dickens and Sagaria's study and ours is that we also define as nurturing the collaboration occurring between co-authors of equal status professionally. Like the more experienced–less experienced collaborations, these heterarchical relationships are examples of "zones of proximal development," "collaboration with more capable peers" (Vygotsky 1978, 86), peers who each bring different expertise or experience in some areas—more knowledge—than their partners do. For example, concerning the writing process, one author might have a gift for metaphorical language, and the other might be more adept at visualizing a clear organization of ideas. The team members in our study felt these complementary collaborations resulted in significant personal and intellectual development.

As the interviewees discussed their co-authoring, revealing ways they nurtured and complemented each other, they focused on appreciation of cognitive gains, feelings of trust and respect, and friendship; but one of the best examples of their nurturing, feminine stance is their approach to decisions about first author position on publications.

FIRST AUTHOR POSITION

Who needs it?

Mark Hurlbert

In their study of faculty collaboration, Austin and Baldwin, as part of their discussion of critical issues surrounding collaboration, point out that "conflict concerning the order of authorship can erupt" because "in a meritocracy like higher education, it is not sufficient to recognize all contributors to a joint publication. The system demands to know who contributed more and who contributed less to the collaborative endeavor" (1991, 67), and even assigns first author position to an "honorary author . . . an individual who has not been directly involved with the research reported in published papers" (Ede and Lunsford 1990, 98).[1] It's clear that with the competition for positions in academia and the pressure to publish, disputes might arise as to whose name will be in the first position since usually publications are listed by first author; subsequent authors are not always recognized because database retrieval systems are not usually programmed to find authors other than those listed first.

We saw this elision of authors beyond the first one when we attempted to learn the number of collaborative dissertations included in the UMI database; we were told the system had never been set up to search for two authors. Also, several teams explained that in their departments points are awarded depending on author position: for example, O'Quin wasn't exactly sure what the formula in her department was, but she thought maybe she got 100 points for single authorship of an article, 40 points if she was one of two authors, and maybe 5 points if she was one of five authors. It's not a stretch to suggest that if a faculty member needed points in order to earn tenure, he or she might insist on first author position.

To be honest, we had not thought of the issue of first author until the first interview of our study when Roja Grant and Emily Hui spontaneously brought up the topic. Austin and Baldwin include some of the solutions to the "problem"—listing names in alphabetical order, attention to significance of the contribution, heed to seniority (1991, 68–69)—and indeed, Hui and Grant decide first author on the basis of who does the most work on the publication (and for them, the initiator of the project does the most work). They agreed that "whoever physically wrote most of the article at the beginning should be first author." Hui's name appears first on their article, and Grant pointed out that the order of their names is clearly not alphabetical and therefore the one who did the most work is obvious, "which is good." Grant added that she would rather not have to think about who is first author, but "you have to think about those things or you're going to get burned . . . for something as silly as where your name is in the list. If I had tenure, I really wouldn't care . . . that would be one of the first things I would get rid of." Neither Grant nor Hui was tenured, but before they co-authored, Hui had published several articles already on which she appeared as first author. Still, Grant is second author on the article they wrote together although she is not first author on any of her other publications and could have benefited from the first author position. Hui initiated the project, and she is the first author based on their own rule; they were one of the few teams who, in deciding first author, took an approach based more on fairness and justice than on context.

Another team, Knight and Adams, talked for quite a while around the issue of "rank" and their decision about who would be first author. According to Adams (who had been the junior faculty member at the time of their first collaboration), "The only way for me to get in the proceedings [a collection of conference papers] was to team with Julie," and Knight remembered she invited him to "write the chapter" with her. So, Knight and Adams decided who would be first author based on experience and who conceived of the project. Adams explained:

The decision of order of authorship was in my mind. It may not have been in your mind [Knight's]. Not so much rank but experience. You were established here in the program . . . it was my first semester as a faculty member here, so it wasn't a question about who ought to be first author. You were also the co-host of the conference and co-editor of the book, so it just seemed like the natural course in terms of the writing process.

Adams added that "it was about who goes first . . . like who starts." This pair and the pair of Hui and Grant were the only ones who talked of solving the first author "problem" by listing the principal contributor first or by considering the professional reputation and experience of the authors. The other teams took a more nurturing stance—one that asks, "Who needs to be first author?"

This concern for the professional needs of each other is not even mentioned by Austin and Baldwin, but it showed up in the second interview with Oldman and Kent and was part of most of the subsequent interviews with the other co-authors. Oldman and Kent talked about a proceedings chapter they had both been involved in writing, and Oldman commented that in an ideal world,

We would give it [first author] to the person who is generally thought to be either the conceptualizer and, therefore, the lead thinker *or* the person who most politically needs it . . . that's why I want to believe that if I go pull that document, you're [Kent] lead. I want to think, "Jeeze, we would have done that for you."

Kent, as it turned out, had not been listed as lead author—she hadn't even begun to teach in the department with Oldman at that time—but Oldman still felt she should have been first author because she needed the publication professionally.

For the other teams, including the team with a graduate student, first author status did not seem to matter. Kathleen and James Strickland talked about books they felt they actually co-authored but on which only one of their names appears "a teeny bit for political reasons." In response to our questions concerning the issues of first and single authorship as they impact tenure and promotion, they answered, "We can honestly say it doesn't affect us." Their co-authored book won an award at their university (they both teach there but in different departments), and they agreed no one "has ever mentioned anything about the work being co-authored."

When we asked them how they decided Kathleen would be first author on their book, Kathleen turned to Jim and laughed, "Ask him," to which Jim replied, "'Cause I put her first." They had discussed alternating names on their co-authored publications, but Jim thought that would be confusing, and they both insisted several times that "they couldn't care less whose name goes first."

They had decided Kathleen's name would always be lead "for ease of readers and for people using our work."

Katherine Johnson acknowledged that Mark Bonacci was responsible for her name's being listed first on their co-authored textbook. We asked who had conceived of the book and she said Bonacci had. He immediately added that "it evolved," and she went on to explain that he had been thinking of writing such a book, that she was going to write a chapter, and that it became a mutual effort. The following exchange is a good example of a pedagogical, nurturing relationship:

> *Johnson:* And see, he put my name first . . . I give him credit for that. It's like "Katherine, I'll put your name first," and I said, "Don't do that."
> *Bonacci:* Oh, no no no . . .
> *Johnson:* He was really responsible for that.
> *Bonacci:* No, to tell you the truth I felt that Katherine organized the whole book, and then the other thing was that I didn't give up anything because I had published, I think, four books prior, so it's not like I gave up the first author. I *mean* that.

Bonacci exhibited a concern for her professional welfare, and their trust in and respect for each other was evident as they tried to make each other's contributions clear to us.

When we asked Pike, Davis, and Ellison who would be first author on their book, there was a moment of silence as they all looked at each other, and Pike said, "His name [Davis's] starts with D [laughter]." Ellison added that he didn't know who would be first, and even when we redirected the question to Pike in terms of whether their names would appear alphabetically, none of them could give us a definite answer. They seemed to have not thought of it until that moment, an omission which seemed, on the surface (and that's all we were privileged to see), to be an indication of its lack of importance to them. Our sense during the interview and as we read the transcripts was that they had indeed not considered whose name would appear first, and that deciding would be difficult (or as easy as flipping a coin) since they considered each other's contributions to be equally valuable. On the other hand, perhaps they avoided discussing first author position because they anticipated a thorny issue that would be difficult to resolve; or perhaps they were naïve about the issues of rank and position that might come up in a discussion of first author position.

In a conversation with Ellison after our study was completed, we asked him whether he and Davis and Pike had decided whose name would appear first on their book. He said they had not addressed that issue yet, but he went on to tell us that for their conference presentations, they usually list their names in alphabetical order (in the interview, we had not addressed this issue pertaining to presentations). However, sometimes Pike insists that Ellison's name be listed first since he needs the first authorship position professionally, and sometimes they list Davis or Pike first if they feel the first author needs the authority the Ph.D. conveys.

Upon first consideration of this topic, O'Quin said that whoever "puts it together is typically the person . . . [who] is going to be first author" and that she and Besemer "usually agree fairly early on who's going to take responsibility." However, Besemer saw it differently—"Well, it's also who needs it"—and O'Quin agreed. They consider each other's career needs and went as far as to say that "it's not a matter of either of us has such a big ego . . . 'Nope, gotta be first author here,'" and Besemer added that she "really appreciated that with Karen."

At one point, Ede and Lunsford tried to persuade the publisher to put one of their names on the title page and one on the spine of a book, but they were not successful: "It screws up the librarian." However, they have continued to list their names in one order for one publication and the other order for the next. Their conviction that their work is really "fifty-fifty" is illustrated in their story about Ede's tenure review process. The dean's committee solicited Lunsford for "unsolicited letters speaking to the nature of [their] collaboration," and the committee also asked her for a "line count . . . of how many lines [Lunsford] wrote and how many lines Lisa wrote." Lunsford, in "calm and logical argument," explained that they could not do a line count. Ede was eventually tenured because her department was supportive of her and Lunsford's work, but other stories abound of requests by promotion and tenure committees that scholars highlight the sentences they have ostensibly written *on their own*. These stories illustrate the still widely held belief that first author position on a publication always represents the amount of work done.

Brown felt that one of his biggest struggles in his co-authorship with Roen is that he can't get Roen (and another co-author, Theresa Enos) to take the credit they deserve. When we asked them how they decide author order, they joked that they "have a big fight about it" and then added, "Usually we end up drawing straws or flipping coins or something . . . 'you go first' . . . 'no you go first' . . . it's not what you think it is." Roen went on to say that of his over seventy-five co-authored publications, "most often first person has been the person who most immediately needs to have this publication . . . someone who's finishing a degree and is going on the market. In my career I've never really needed that . . . so I've always felt pretty comfortable." He did admit that he would be listed as first author on their next publication, and Brown made sure we knew it was "very deserved . . . it was Duane's idea . . . from inception . . . in fact Theresa and I were talking the other day . . . how guilty we feel about how much more work Duane did on the project." But they both insisted they would not necessarily assign first author to the person who had the original idea. Roen has written first drafts, invited a graduate student to co-author the revision with him, and then listed the graduate student as first author. "That person needs it . . . I don't need it . . . especially now in my career I don't need that."

Mark Hurlbert and Michael Blitz echoed these teams in terms of the arbitrariness of name order. They simply take turns now, but Hurlbert conceded that when he became a full professor before Blitz, they purposefully considered name order: "We agreed . . . well we didn't have to agree . . . it just happened . . . that his name went first on everything . . . you know . . . who needs it."

How did we determine whose name would appear first on this book? Neither of us needs first author position: Kami is on the faculty of a community college and is not expected to publish in order to be tenured; and Michele's staff position as writing center director is not tenure track and does not carry the expectation of extensive publication. If either of us needed to publish in order to advance professionally, we would decide author order based on need. That would be easy. But, the decision to put Kami's name first caused her some angst. Why didn't we just flip a coin? What does it say about our view of co-authoring? If we believe that author order does not matter, that contributions cannot be teased out and ranked, why didn't we choose randomly whose name would appear first? Well, Michele understood implicitly from the moment we broke the dissertation in two that although we were going to work with each other on two dissertations, this study was Kami's "baby." Also, we decided when we began to think about publishing that we would alternate names, and the book we plan to write next about student co-authoring will have Michele's name first. Essentially, we're responding to the institutional constraints that created two different studies, and we cannot help but recognize our individual imprints on those studies despite the amount of work we did with each other on them. So we made the decision with no conflict except Kami's inner ones. And, if one of us "needed it," her name would certainly appear first.

The issue of first author, rather than being the thorny problem described by Austin and Baldwin, seems to be either a nonissue or an easily resolved one among the teams we interviewed. For a few of them, consideration of who did the lion's share of the work or who conceived of the project played a part, but for those teams the first author was obvious and there was no conflict (some had even played with creating hybridized or team names).² The rest of them took a more nurturing stance: it usually doesn't matter who is in that position, but if it does matter, first author position goes to the one who needs it professionally.

This approach is in stark contrast to accounts involving exploitation and masculine ego. O'Quin told a story about a graduate student who did all the research and wrote the notes into a book for a famous scholar in her field but was not even recognized in the acknowledgments. Roen recounted working as a graduate student with a faculty member for a year and then one day seeing the article in a journal with no mention of his name anywhere. One of the interviewees in our study had to insist on first authorship of an article derived from her master's thesis; the chair of the department had assumed he would be listed first because of his prestige in her field.

Author order seems to depend, in part, on the discipline: Engers, Gans, Grant, and King (1999) found that most co-authored papers in economics journals—and many in chemistry, physics, and biology—are "ordered lexicographically" (1), while author order in psychology has more to do with the significance of the contribution.[3] In the field of health, Nicholas K. Iammarino, Thomas W. O'Rourke, R. Morgan Pigg Jr., and Armin D. Weinberg (1989) created a useful question for determining co-authorship status based on contribution:

> Would completion of the project, or the paper, have been possible without this individual's contribution? A no response would indicate the individual deserves authorship credit. If the answer is yes, the assistance probably was the type of advice or critique rendered routinely as a professional courtesy. (103)

Other attempts to provide guidelines on assigning credit for authorship (Fine and Kurdek 1993; Lukovits and Vinkler 1995; Spiegel and Keith-Spiegel 1970) have found their way to academic journals. Karen Morris (1998) and Susan Boykoff (1989) recommend that co-authors sign an agreement—a kind of co-authoring prenuptial—specifying author order and such things as deadlines, royalty splits, veto power, how credit will be assigned, how labor will be divided. Roger B. Winston has even developed a weighting schema procedure to help determine order of authoring by assigning points to various co-authoring tasks (1985). A contributor must accrue a certain number of points to be recognized as an author, and of course the author with the greatest number of points is privileged to be listed first. We were impressed that the teams we interviewed did not need such quantitative measures to ensure fairness; in fact, they were not at all worried about fairness. They trusted each other to take equal responsibility so first author was not about getting credit. Or, if they believed a larger share of the work should be recognized, they knew taking more responsibility would not go unrewarded.

Assigning first author position to the writer who did most of the work or conceived of the project is compatible with the masculine concept of a morality of rights, justice, and fairness, and impartiality, but giving the first author position to the "one who needs it" is harmonious with the feminine attention to context and caring. Roen might have written the first draft of an article, but he had no trouble listing the graduate student who co-authored the revision as first author because the graduate student needed the publication professionally. If first author had been decided impartially or according to who had the right to be listed first based on who initiated the project, Roen's name would have appeared before the student's. Of course, the simple fact that these co-authors care about each other's professional development is congruous with feminine morality, a morality that centers around responsibility, care, and nurturance.

The notion of ego is central to decisions about first author. As we said earlier, in western culture, we tend to assign to the general term *ego* the definition given to "masculine ego" by Bakan and Gutmann (qtd. in Chodorow 1989, 56): self-focused, self-protective, self-assertive, displaying the urge to master and control, a definition compatible with Lyotard's notion of a masculine stance. However, even though the co-authors in our study did not define the term *ego* when they used it, they seemed to be referring to a more feminine ego with the term *egolessness* and a more masculine ego when they used the term *ego*. Furthermore, they saw ego as potentially problematic and egolessness as an admirable trait. In some cases, co-authors described as egoless by their partners were less interested in getting the recognition they undeniably deserved than in making sure a co-author received the recognition they needed. In other cases, what the interviewees called egolessness made author position a nonissue. In a telling statement, Roen declared emphatically:

> Especially in the academic world, especially in the humanities where it's sort of the individual being smart . . . do it on your own and impress the world with what you know . . . when you share there's less opportunity to impress the world with what I know. If there's an idea that would be of interest to people, get that idea out there . . . I don't care if a hundred people co-author with me to get it out there.

Roen's statement is refreshing in view of the competitive, masculine ego-saturated atmosphere in much of academia, where "departmental rhetoric refers to evaluation 'on the basis of individual merit'" (Verrier 1994, 121) and usually values singly published work over co-authored projects. Besemer and O'Quin remarked that neither of them had "such a big ego" that they had to be first author, Kathleen Strickland commented that Jim does not "have an ego problem," Blitz described his co-authoring with Hurlbert as "almost egoless," and lack of ego (as defined by the co-authors) is implicit throughout the interviews. With Bakan's and Guttman's definitions in mind, it is more appropriate to say the co-authors display feminine egos rather than lack of ego. In addition, their ability to give up recognition for individual contributions, and their flexibility concerning first author position, indicate their lack of insistence on "self-other distinctions."

ISSUES OF HIERARCHY

Real awareness of seniority, whose domain you're starting to enter.

Julie Knight

Feminine egos are reflected not only in how decisions are made about first author position but also in the nonhierarchical relationships between the team members, even when more experienced-less experienced configurations are involved. In discussing their work on their first project, Knight and Adams both insisted that their senior-junior ranking in the department was not a factor in their co-authoring. Knight said, "It had nothing to do with it . . . everything kind of dropped away for me . . . the whole social context and all that stuff was really kind of annoying, but we took it into account and just wrote." Adams agreed; for him, "All those things in terms of rank and those kinds of issues kind of melted away." Pike, Davis, and Ellison insisted they were peers, but their team was the only one in which we sensed some residual hierarchy; Ellison, the graduate student, did not use Pike's and Davis's first names. He called them Dr. Pike and Dr. Davis even though they called him by his first name, and he spoke very little. We did not notice the name inconsistency until we transcribed the interview, but we did ask during the interview if he felt their relationship was at all hierarchical. His answer supported Pike's and Davis's assessment of their team:

> That's what I think is so interesting; if there is a hierarchy it's because I've placed it there. I came into this and they've always made me feel very included, and I guess that kind of struck me because I'm so used to . . . as a student . . . the hierarchy, so trying to even break free of that mold . . . I mean they've always gone out of their way to make me feel like it was more a true relationship, so I gotta break out!

It may be that they had asked him to use their first names, but he was not comfortable with that familiarity, or perhaps he felt a more formal approach was appropriate for an interview. And, of course, he might have responded differently to our question if Pike and Davis had not been present.

The issue of hierarchy came up with other teams, not in terms of their own relationships but in stories of negative and even unpleasant other co-authoring experiences. We want to make it clear that all participants were careful and sometimes reluctant to discuss negative cases, which is another indication of the kind of people they are; they never named names, and their stories, for the most part, did not contain specific examples (many of the participants asked us to delete from the transcripts references to negative experiences they had).

Some may have feared repercussions, but we sensed that most respected even colleagues with whom they did not enjoy co-authoring. Even if trust and respect had not been part of the unproductive collaboration, the authors in our study seemed to feel that keeping the details to themselves was a more professional and ethical route to follow.

The interviewees reported that some unsuccessful or unsatisfying co-authoring experiences were a result of too much attention to, or even abuses of, power and position. Knight was part of one project in which she felt "facilitated" by a senior colleague who thought she needed some help professionally. What she didn't like about the collaboration had to do with rank, and she found the whole experience "noncreative, nonproductive," and a "crash all the way around for the other person" and for her. She acknowledged that such "facilitating" gets a project done, but she found the motivation to be only extrinsic, and to her the final product "ha[d] no life in it . . . no part of [her]." Adams called his other co-authoring experiences "different" rather than negative, but he felt they were "much more formal . . . you're real aware of who's got seniority . . . real aware of whose domain and whose area of expertise you're starting to enter."

Just as a feminine ego seems to be important to successful co-authoring, masculine ego can be a player in unsatisfying ones even where hierarchy is not involved. James Strickland compared his writing relationship with Kathleen to others he's found more frustrating, all of which were with men:

> Those are the ones that have broken down because of control issues. When I was a graduate student I did a co-authored thing with a guy who's now a good friend of mine, but in that case he was the senior graduate and took more control, so I just gave in and said, "Fine, I can live with that." After we graduated I tried to co-author with him and it didn't work because I wasn't as willing to give him that control.

Jim had thought that because they were friends they would be able to co-author, but his friend could not give up control even though mutual respect and a shared philosophy were in place and hierarchy was gone. Kathleen pointed out that she didn't think Jim's friend's need to dominate was necessarily a "gender thing," but conceded that "there's tons of research that would support that in our culture women are taught to negotiate" and men are not. We agree that the need to control is not exclusive to males; however, it is a characteristic of the masculine approach whether that approach is taken by men or women.

Both Brown and Roen, as we talked about their other co-authoring experiences, realized most of their successful co-authoring had been with women; they each named two other men—the same men—they enjoyed co-authoring with but agreed that their attempts with other male writers had been less than pleasant. Brown confessed there are people he would not work with again, and we asked, "Is it because they weren't good at listening?" He laughed and said, "Yeah—actually that's a politer way of putting it." Brown characterized unsuccessful writing relationships in which he was "beat up pretty badly" and "pushed around" as "intellectual bullying," and Roen elaborated with, "Sometimes you work with people who say, 'It's got to be done this way.'" Brown continues to work with Roen because egos do not get in the way, and he trusts Roen not to "bully him around." The feminine egos of both the men and women in these writing teams contribute to the success of their co-authoring.

CO-AUTHORING AS EPISTEMIC

> *Doesn't your brain just think more?*
>
> Roja Grant

Even more evident in the interviews than the issues of first author and hierarchy was the enthusiasm with which one co-author characterized the contributions of the other(s)—another example of feminine ego, but also having to do with the "pedagogical collaboration" category in that these co-authors valued "working closely with another scholar on a shared intellectual project [as] an important way to foster growth and learning" (Dickens and Sagaria 1997, 87). Adams expressed a collective conviction when he said, "If I had written it on my own it wouldn't have been nearly as good as it was," as did Grant with her exclamation, "Doesn't your brain just think more?!" For all the co-authors, the cognitive advantages of their collaboration went beyond what they believed to be excellent products.

Lunsford told a story of being asked to come up with four words that could guide the creator of a PBS series about writing. After thinking about this request for awhile, Lunsford came up with *epistemic, social, metaphoric,* and *violent,* and she went on to focus on *epistemic* for our interview. She and Ede had described earlier an essay that gave them difficulty, and she went back to it as a "good example of how we just wrote ourselves in and out and back in and back out and couldn't have ever imagined where we were going to get before we started." She felt that in fields other than writing, authors often see writing as "simply a transcription tool," but she and Ede see it as a way of making meaning. Furthermore, they characterize all writing as collaborative, as do Reither and Vipond (1989) and other teams in our study from the field of composition—Hurlbert and Blitz, Strickland and Strickland, Roen and Brown. It follows then that one of the reasons writing is epistemic might be that it is always collaborative, even if one of the collaborators is alive only in his or her work.

In another story, Ede told us of their dilemma about what to do with all the information she and Lunsford had for *Singular Texts/Plural Authors.*

And somebody said, "Well, we'll just stuff it in there . . . we'll just put them in there," and then one of us said, "Well, what will we call them?" "Well, we'll call them inter-texts" . . . and that was an example of doing something together that I certainly wouldn't have had the courage or probably the insight to do alone, and the head-notes from Burke came the same way.

They went on to say that they

don't really challenge each other, but we have a good way of raising questions to each other. That's the chief cognitive gain . . . that multiple . . . having a kind of safe but still challenging environment where you can try out ideas and try them out with someone other than yourself.

Additionally, Lunsford pointed out that Ede knows "a lot more about feminist theory" while Ede added that "Andrea knows a lot more about other things" and has a remarkable memory.

Oldman acknowledged Kent's contribution to his recent publication, even though Kent had only been in the department for six months when Oldman sent his book to the publisher. Oldman felt the ideas "flowing in and out of our offices are absolutely cutting edge" and remembered sticking his head in Kent's office the first week she was there to ask her questions about learning in order to enrich his knowledge about teaching. Their relationship is characterized by a great deal of talk, especially on their trips to conferences and schools to do research and consulting, and they told a story of a four-hour trip during which they both "moved positions" on theories of constructivism and behaviorism. Oldman is passionate about "those of us who have all the answers need[ing] to be ready to be confronted with people who don't think we have all the answers," and Kent thrives on "changing my ideas because of what someone else has said."

We explained earlier that Knight was first author on the publication with Adams partly because of her more extensive experience, but they also recognized how each other's experiences contributed to the project: Knight brought to their co-authoring the knowledge she'd gained from organizing an academic conference, and Adams had recently finished his dissertation in a compatible area. In addition, Adams spoke enthusiastically about Knight's feedback on another project: "Just recently I wrote a chapter and . . . I had a couple of people read it, and she just gave me outstanding feedback that really had a very positive impact and really lifted the level of the quality of that piece . . . if I worked alone it would suffer tremendously."

Kathleen and James Strickland's first co-authored book, *Un-covering the Curriculum*, came about because Kathleen could not find a text she wanted to use for her courses in education. Peter Stillman, the editor at Boynton/Cook at the time, told Jim he'd prefer an authored book (rather than an edited one), so Jim agreed to do it if he could co-author with Kathleen, "the expert on whole language." They too talked with us about combining their different experiences, and Kathleen insisted that Jim has taught her a lot about writing since he was a writing teacher before she was. She confessed to feeling "humble" when they began writing together, but she added, "We have both gotten better at what we do, and I'm just tickled pink that I have somebody to work with that complements what I do."

Jim, a great storyteller, shared a story he heard David Sanborn, the jazz musician, tell which characterizes Jim's attitude toward co-authoring. Sanborn said, "Whatever I play I always try to play with musicians who are better than I am," and Jim thought, "Boy, that's really perceptive . . . when you're playing together it's like writing together . . . the piece emerges as you each make contributions, but if you're going to get better, you want to play with someone who's better, and that's how you grow."

As we mentioned earlier, Davis and Pike brought Ellison into their project originally as a research assistant and then, as his expertise became evident, they began to think of him as a co-author. He also proved to be helpful in setting up a web page for Davis and Pike's co-taught class. This team grappled, though, with describing the cognitive gains of their co-authoring apart from the affective and ineffable elements. One way they think of their relationship is in terms of the "affecting presence," a concept developed by Robert Armstrong (1981) and involving the influence humans have on each other (and inanimate objects have on humans). Pike described their work, which she finds "enormously clarifying," this way: "I'm constantly experiencing the presence of these two . . . constantly this feeling that goes like, 'Bingo!'. . . I mean it's learning . . . but the thing is they just articulated what I've been thinking . . . and I go, 'yes . . . yes . . . yes.'" Davis attempted to explain this phenomenon as "the sensitivity of the poet" (both Pike and Davis are poets), and Pike tried "supernatural," but finally they resisted what they saw as possibly artificial categories to describe what they do. They seemed almost afraid to dissect their process for fear of disturbing the magic.

Besemer and O'Quin came together because Besemer needed O'Quin's expertise in analyzing quantitative data and then found that their skills complemented each other. They both agreed they produce "more and better" than either of them could alone, and O'Quin credited Besemer with being the "brains of the gang . . . because it's her theory initially . . . it's sort of like the kernel . . . Sue is the germinal one." Roen also subscribes to the "more and better" theory; he is so confident that "co-authoring always leads to a better product" that his seventy-five-plus publications are mostly co-authored. For him, "The important thing is that more than one mind is coming together," even if some of them have "been dead for two thousand years." Brown enjoys the fact that another mind provides "a different critical perspective that gets you kick-started."

Hurlbert and Blitz's long-term collaboration has resulted in an almost spiritual connection between them, and for them, as with Pike, Davis, and Ellison, separating out the cognitive and affective gains is difficult. Early in their co-authoring, according to Blitz, Hurlbert was "up to the minute" on issues in composition and rhetoric because he was teaching classes in those areas, so he was more adept at drawing on those sources. Now, though, chances are they independently buy the "same book in the same week" or they find they have read different sources relevant to the same topic. In the beginning, Hurlbert thought of himself as the rhetorician and Blitz as the poet (although both of them write poetry):

> Michael was the one that had brilliant flashes of insight that would just blow up what we were doing . . . spark it . . . start a fire . . . push it in a new direction . . . and I would be the one who would sit there with a text and tease it out into an argument . . . work out abstractions and applications. But I think over the years I've become more of a poet and Michael's become more of a rhetorician so that we're somehow both all four at once.

Blitz added that his writing with Hurlbert is the "best learning curve"; his knowledge is enriched about the topic of their writing but also about himself. Not only do they learn from each other and produce a better product together—they have changed each other in significant ways. Hurlbert and Blitz even agreed that "in some really meaningful ways you become each other."

One of the reasons Bonacci and Johnson chose to co-author was that they wanted to write an interdisciplinary text, combining their individual expertises in sociology and social psychology. Bonacci remarked that "there's so much sociology in here [referring to their book], and people would have said to me, 'What do you know about sociology?'" He admitted that, for instance, before he worked on the book with Johnson, he didn't have a solid understanding of the term *ethnocentrism*, and Johnson agreed that they learned from each other—both about content and about writing.

For some team members, enthusiasm about what they learn from each other involves their appreciation for the professional "savvy" of their partners. Grant sees Hui as a mentor in this way, although Hui did not invite Grant to work with her with that relationship in mind: "She [Hui] understands the field . . . it was having a mentor and authority . . . it's like I got indoctrinated and acculturated into writing papers and everything in the world of math education without being openly directed. No one said, 'You're writing your first article.'" Besemer, in addition to crediting O'Quin with "inspiring" her to write a paper on her own, felt her own writing had been "all over the place," and said she likes "to get credibility by working with somebody who knows something about the field . . . it could be published because they have some sort of credentials where I never have any credentials except as a librarian." Besemer also feels that "Karen writes the right way for a psychological journal . . . and that's a certain standard style that I can move toward." Obviously, they feel that to be taken seriously as scholars, and to get their work published, they must adhere to certain conventions, and they rely on O'Quin's knowledge of those conventions rather than resisting them. On the other hand, O'Quin draws on Besemer's experiences writing "all kinds of articles," some in a more informal style, when they need to write for the layperson, since O'Quin is used to writing for academics only.

> I think one real benefit of our working together is that we started looking at collaboration and writing collaboratively at the same time. Over these years then we've both grown together—we share a common vision and passion and knowledge base. Kami has such commitment and such a strong work ethic that I am motivated to keep learning, to keep pushing. She has taught me to pay attention to details, to follow through, to focus my dispersed thinking. And, for example, Kami has a better background in classical rhetoric, but I read more widely and bring to our work models of collaboration in other fields. She is such a great learner too: that gives me the opportunity to always bring new things to the conversation. I am continually motivated to stretch, to find more, to deal with tough things because I know she is willing to.

RESPECT AND TRUST

> *Neither of us is possessive about our language.*
>
> Susan Besemer and Karen O'Quin

The interviewees often described their collective writing processes in a way that revealed their feminine egos and their appreciation of each other's strengths. They respect each other's suggestions, revisions, voices, and styles, and they trust each other to do what is best for their co-authoring process and product. We see this trust as a necessary element for or even product of interdependence, connectedness, and relatedness, and therefore integral to a feminine approach.

Almost without exception, the words *respect* and *trust* were used explicitly in the interviews with no prompting from us, and in the interviews where the

terms were not explicit, they were certainly implicit. Knight, in trying to articulate the vision she and Adams had beyond the product, said

> Fundamental to the whole thing is it's about respect. When you deal with different
> styles, you deal with all the complexities that go into what co-authoring actually
> requires. It's about respect because I respect Gilbert as a person and I respect his
> abilities and I respect his background . . . and oftentimes I've worked with people
> and I have not felt that there was real respect for the ability that I did have. Respect is
> absolutely essential.

All the team members respect each other's strengths and styles and trust
each other to make good suggestions and revisions. Grant acknowledged that
she's "not good at getting it started . . . not good at taking a whole thing and
organizing it . . . so she [Hui] does the organizing at the beginning." Hui sees
Grant's strengths as being "very good at details" (to which Grant replied,
"That's true") and "the tone of voice . . . like sometimes I could write a sentence and the tone of voice may not be appropriate . . . and she [Grant] could
just smooth it down." Grant also values Hui's role as taskmaster:

> Emily's good at giving directions like, "No, we're going to stay up and finish it . . .
> work another hour" [they both laugh]. And she prioritizes . . . she tells me, "You
> should go take a shower while I work on this part." Or she'll say, "I'll put Maya
> [Hui's daughter] to bed . . . read over this section."

Grant often pushes for perfection too early, while Hui is aware of deadlines
and what a first draft really means. They admit they both like to "get our own
way," but sometimes one of them just says, "OK, fine, it's a stupid quote but you
can have it." When we asked why they would "give in," Grant answered, "Because
I trust her judgment . . . she thinks it's good . . . she knows what she's doing."

We have no trouble agreeing on what to take out. As we were
reading through chapter two *again*, we came to a paragraph that had
given us trouble. Kami read it, was silent for a minute, and said, "I don't
think we need this now." Michele said, "I was thinking the same thing—
take it out." It's been a little eery sometimes to be in such complete
agreement. On the other hand, deciding what to put in is a different
story, and sometimes we agonize over a single word. In chapter one, we
had a long discussion about the word *yet*. We had written: "Our
language moves through our individual bodies, and feminist theory has
enabled and encouraged any and all to acknowledge, embrace, and
honor this physicality. Even when Hélène Cixous (1992) calls for women
to 'write through their bodies,' she ultimately invites them to join with
others to 'articulate the profusion of meanings that run through it . . .'"

Michele wanted to add "Yet" before "Even," and Kami didn't want to.
Michele: We need to hit it harder. It doesn't mean contrary, it's extend-
ing it. We need to puncture assumptions. You hear all this "writing
through the body." We need to try to capture the point Cixous made
that some people might have missed.
Kami: But *yet* signals a change in gears.
Michele: OK, leave the *yet* out. I guess it's a little over the top [pauses
and watches Kami write down what they have said as they've been
talking]. I think I write with you because I can escape the self-
consciousness of writing alone. And now you force it on me with this
meta shit! :-) [These inserted reflection pieces were actually Michele's
idea.]

A week later, Kami reread the section and realized the *yet* was
necessary. She asked Michele why she hadn't insisted they include the
requisite transition. Michele answered that our conceptions of our
readers are so similar that when Kami insisted the *yet* was not
necessary, she trusted Kami's judgment. (We guess this could be an
illustration of the dangers of trusting a co-author, but it also shows a
good relationship can let some things go for a while, and also that we
trust our editor!) We see that writing together sharpens the decision-
making process; for one thing, we have an immediate audience in each
other. Also, our conceptions of readers differ just enough that we not
only consider a wider audience but we are constantly providing checks
in that we each answer to a portion of the audience that the other does
not share.

In another exchange, Kami had written that before this study, we had
a "narrow definition of co-authoring." Michele didn't like *narrow*; for her,
the connotation was negative. She preferred *precise*, but Kami thought
narrow conveyed what we meant better—that our early definition had
fewer features and pertained to fewer authors. But Kami typed "narrow
and precise"—there seemed to be no reason why both words could not
be used. In the end, Michele said *narrow* worked better and we left it.

Roen and Brown had a little trouble talking about their process—"We need
to do a better job of documenting how we work." But what they could talk
about certainly indicated a lack of possessiveness about their individual contributions. In describing their co-authoring with Enos, Roen said they each read
different thirds of the draft and exchanged them until they had all read all
parts. But what is interesting is that Brown "wrote over the top of it [a draft] . . .
then it went to Theresa . . . she wrote over the top of it." This process is much

like the one Belenky describes in discussing her collaboration with Clinchy, Goldberger, and Tarule (Ashton-Jones and Thomas, 1995). This group of women authors sent a hard copy draft from person to person so that even if one wrote a suggestion for revision over another's words, the words of the original author would still be there. This process ensured that their individual voices would be heard at least until the final draft, just as Roen, Brown, and Enos are able to hear each other's voices during the revision process. In a story about another collaboration, Roen told of asking Andrea Lunsford to make some changes in a draft of a chapter she had written, and her response was, "OK." Not, "Well, I'm an expert in my field and I know what I'm talking about," but just, "OK." We remember hearing a well-known author speak, and we were surprised to hear her say she is scornful of editors because she feels they have no right to tell her what to do with her own language; but Roen, Brown, Enos, Lunsford, and all the other experts we interviewed are receptive to other insights and perspectives because they are teachable and because of their respect for and trust in their co-authors.

Besemer remarked that "neither of us is possessive about our language . . . if she [O'Quin] reads something that I write and she rewords that I'm just so grateful . . . and when I've made a change it's generally received well . . . it's not received with any question or hostility." As we mentioned earlier, they value each other's individual writing styles (which we would call voice)—Besemer's conversational one and O'Quin's academic one—and expect one or the other to take the lead depending on the appropriate style for the piece they are writing. They talked about O'Quin's ability to bring Besemer's personal or journalistic style "down to a much more concise, less wordy, less fiddling around" style and the possibility that O'Quin will "move more toward a sort of conversational style." The issue of voice (what many of the interviewees called style) also involves trust and respect because a collective voice does not necessarily obliterate individual voices, but certainly individual voices are not as distinct in a co-authored piece, especially if sections are not written individually and pasted together.⁵ Individual writers must be willing to give up outside recognition of their unique contributions, respect the voices of their co-authors, relinquish possession of their own language, and trust that the collective voice will represent them well.

We came up with the concept of (first person)² early in our co-authoring relationship to describe (1) our melded (Ede and Lunsford's term) voice, and (2) our sense that knowledge, insight, productivity, rhetorical sensitivity, creativity, the ability to find common ground through negotiation, appreciation of the strengths of others, etc. have the potential to grow exponentially when people write together. As we were writing note three, Michele asked, "When you read what we've written, do you still hear *you* there? When you read a sentence you know we created together word for word, do you get a sense that you're not there?" Kami had no trouble denying such a sense, and Michele agreed: sometimes we can identify a word or sentence one of us wrote (Kami has a tendency to string together clauses with conjunctions, and Michele likes complex, embedded sentences—so we've married boring with tortured), but mostly we hear *us*.

In the CCCC workshop, Blitz described the "welcome danger" of co-authoring—the exhilarating risk of having your words challenged, judged, and possibility erased. From the beginning of their co-authorship, Hurlbert and Blitz agreed that what they wrote individually would not be held sacred. Blitz explained:

We've had this unwritten rule that either one of us could change the other person's words completely. We could chuck it and the other person wasn't going to go, "Hey, what are you doing?" It was clear early on that the common goal was that we wanted to say things that mattered in the best possible way we could say them.

One of them might have an idea and email a draft to the other, in a process much different from that of Belenky, Clinchy, Goldberger, and Tarule, who write over each other's suggestions so the original is still visible. Blitz explained that "the other person can get rid of it down to a single syllable and send it back . . . and there's never ever been a moment when the other person has acted offended or defensive." There is an

egolessness, and the writing process is simply an extension of a kind of appreciation of the hard work of the other person, so even though when we reject things out of hand . . . except playfully . . . we would never put the other person on the defensive because it's not in our natures to do that.

In the workshop, Yancey described the downward spiral once the collaborators begin to make claims on "their own" words:

"How many words do I have?" You can say you wrote every word. "But I thought of it first." You can parse this down to the lowest level of unit analysis though I don't know why you would want to. The minute somebody wants to start moving in that direction, I know we're in trouble. That's one of the signs for me. It should never be about how much of *you* is there . . . it's all about the needs of the text.

We thought perhaps Kathleen and James Strickland might report instances of hurt feelings or conflicts resulting from disagreements since often married couples are less guarded about their language than others who choose to work together. Dickens and Sagaria (1997) found that "collaboration with a close relative . . . meant that they [the women in their study] have to deal with feelings of jealousy, competition, and resentment" (93). However, the Stricklands were insistent about the level of respect and trust they maintain.

> *Jim:* When you're writing together you need to feel comfortable with changing somebody else's words.
> *Kathleen:* And that person needs to be comfortable with your changing them . . . that's grown . . . I think in the beginning that was hard for us probably because I was much more insecure than I am now. But Jim is so careful . . . we don't think about those things anymore. Anything that Jim would change would be a welcome change to me because there's such respect back and forth for the process and what we can each bring to it.

Jim told the story of taking sixty-four pages of freewriting to Kathleen when she was away at graduate school. He was struggling with it, and he knew she could help him get control of the material. On the other hand, Kathleen looks to Jim to enrich their written language. During the interview, when Kami described her own style as unmetaphorical, full of air, and unoriginal in terms of vocabulary, Kathleen exclaimed, "That sounds like me . . . that's why I said Jim is the eloquent one!" She said it was her job to say, "It's time to go write now," and Jim's job to "come up with all the wonderful language." Jim conceded that sometimes she uses the same word three times in a sentence, or the verb *to be* too much, so Kathleen looks to him to "fix that" because he "has a real grasp of good words." (Kathleen's observation, not Jim's). They agreed that they model their collaboration after Ken and Yetta Goodman's, who "maintain their own personalities but they write together and they do so in a respectful way."

Johnson and Bonacci also have complementary roles. Johnson admitted to "lagg[ing] a lot" and Bonacci is the "time oriented" partner. In talking about what we think of as voice, Johnson said she writes in what they define as a more "masculine style" (which they described as linear, scientific, organized, formal), and Bonacci's style is more "feminine" (which they described as expressive, creative, fragmented, emotional), but neither of them feels they have to "defer" to the other; their collective voice blends their styles in a way that works, an example of Lyotard's definition of feminine—outside the masculine. Bonacci appreciates Johnson's ability to write in a more academic, less "over the top" style: "I liked the feedback because ever since I've been writing people have argued that I'm not subtle and I go a bit beyond the pale, so when Kate said, 'Look, Mark, try to make this a little more balanced,' it was fine." Johnson gave a humorous example of suggesting that Bonacci delete the word

"APPALLINGLY" (we capitalized the word to show her verbal emphasis on it) from a sentence so readers would not be put off by overly "hard hitting" language. And Johnson, who admitted to not trusting her "feminine voice," feels Bonacci helps her move toward a less formal style.

Their recognition of the part trust plays in their relationship was especially explicit: "The big thing is that we respect each other and trust each other and know that what we're getting from the other person is real quality." Such trust was evident as they tried to describe their actual writing process: they exchanged drafts, "messed up the other person's draft," and then discussed revisions as they worked on the textbook. Bonacci told a story (one he'd never told Johnson) of being away at a conference and deciding to look at Johnson's latest changes, which he had brought with him. He opened the folder and thought, "Oh my God . . . back to the drawing board . . . but five or six hours later after I was flipping everything around and cutting and pasting I could see that it was much better." He credited her with being able to see how the book should be organized because his style is to "put in all my thoughts and then I try to juggle things around . . . whereas Kate has an outline which is much more organized."

Bonacci also acknowledged that when he suggested a change, "Kate is so good-natured, she's always like, 'Whatever,'" a word which we interpreted, from his tone of voice and inflection, as having to do with her trusting his suggestions rather than being sarcastic about them. When we asked if they had ever created any ground rules about being honest or not getting angry, Bonacci replied that they "didn't have any kind of pact . . . it was more implicit because we know each other so well." In speaking of a co-authoring project they were involved in with another colleague, Bonacci acknowledged the trust and respect in that relationship as well—they trusted the third author's expertise in library science and never felt they had to check up on her contributions. They even spoke of their "implicit trust" in Johnson's mother, whom they described as a "silent writing partner" and free "professional editor."

Knight and Adams characterized their respective individual writing styles as "global" and "sequential" (what we would call linear). Adams remembered that when they were working on their proceedings chapter, "Knight just started kind of writing in the middle of it . . . and I couldn't understand how she could write without knowing what came before that." He also sees Knight as "very good at conceptual kinds of things" and himself as focused on "discrete units of information"; Knight as going "with the flow" and "waiting for things to emerge," and himself as perhaps moving "too quickly toward closure." When we asked how they resolved their different styles, Adams remarked, "We never actually talked about this, so I'll just have to say and realize this probably shows nonawareness on my part," but Knight said she "didn't think it was a problem . . . it was just something we adjusted to. I didn't feel so much tension that it got in my way . . . it was nice." In describing what they saw as the advantages in bringing their styles together, both writers observed that they balance each other, and Adams described a zone of proximal development: "In fact it's a real strength . . . there were times where it felt uncomfortable because it stretched me, but it wasn't a problem." Their trust made pushing beyond their comfort zones into unfamiliar territory possible and even desirable.

As we mentioned earlier, Pike, Davis, and Ellison had difficulty articulating their process, giving the impression that they trust each other completely and almost blindly. They describe their process as "organic" and even "supernatural" and resist analyzing what they do for fear of disturbing a process and relationship they feel works so well. Davis and Pike had been writing together for some time when they realized that "without being explicit about it . . . we [had] sort of grown . . . we'd just go off and write stuff and bring it together and start pasting it together." At some point, remembered Pike, "Alexander started saying, 'This really dovetails here,' so that we were getting to the point that we didn't have really say anymore." We did not mean to write "have *to* really say." By "we didn't have really say anymore" they meant that there seemed to be some higher (or at least other) benevolent power controlling their co-authoring. They even told a story of a colleague commenting that she wasn't sure they knew what they were doing since they couldn't make it explicit.

Most interesting to us as an illustration of complete, essential trust and respect is the way they talked about how their individual writings are combined into one piece. Each writes sections singly, which are then cut and pasted, "integrated," but when we asked them how they put the sections together and how they make suggestions about each other's contributions, Pike provided this revealing explanation (concerning all three of them and their work on conference presentations and early drafts of the book they were working on):

> The amazing thing to me is just that . . . I had thought initially that when we would go off and write things, we would bring them back and go back and forth and mark up each other's work . . . and we never have. The only time any one of us ever made a step in that direction was me, and it was a mistake because Alexander had mentioned . . . was it Mao? . . . talking about race as a construct, and I said, "Oh, well you know Engels did that about sex and you can find that dadadada" . . . and I just experienced that so strongly as an intrusion on what Alexander was doing. It just became clear to me that this is not the way we write . . . I just knew it. There's just a level of trust that I experience from my guys here that doesn't make it necessary really for us to mark up each other's work . . . and then besides the fact that it seems to fit.

When we expressed mild skepticism about the efficacy of such a process and asked for clarification about how they bring a piece together and finish it by cutting and pasting, Pike answered, "We don't even do that . . . we just write it and come back and say, 'Well, that'll be good,' and go on to the next thing." At this point Davis offered the metaphor we mentioned in the first chapter, the one of sewing the pieces of a garment together to make a whole. We think the exchange about this metaphor is worth including:

Day: So you really have pieces that just kind of fall into place . . . is that what you're saying?

Davis: Yeah . . . I may have sleeves and Cybil the body and Ben the lapels . . . essentially when we tailor it, it comes together into a uniform piece.

Eodice: And you think it comes together so well because you conceptualize it together from the start?

Davis: The frightening part is that . . . just as Dr. Pike laughed in her lecture last week in class . . . [laugher from all of them] . . . telling her students, "Now don't try to understand this [we're not sure what *this* is] . . . [laugher all around, especially from Pike] . . . don't go home . . . don't go home and put it into any type cognitive . . ."

Pike: So literally we don't mark or change sentences or anything. We just look at it and say, "OK, that's done" . . . like Alexander says, "There's a sleeve done."

Day: So it just fits together . . . you don't even have to . . .

Pike: And we just go right on.

Day: You [Davis] wouldn't take something of hers [Pike's] and put it in the middle of one of your paragraphs?

Davis: It's possible but it would go there unchanged . . . and it would fit . . . the transition would be quite smooth.

Day: So you're not into rewriting sentences.

Ellison, Pike, and Davis: No . . . uh uh.

They admitted that a few small changes might be made with editing, which is a group effort, but such changes would involve "about one mark for every thousand words."

We think they enjoyed our incredulousness, and of course as composition specialists we were fascinated with the claim that even transitions get minimal attention as sections authored by different writers are being sewn together. We wish we could see the suggestions that are bound to be made by the editor of their current project (or maybe we're making huge assumptions about the field of history here). On one hand, we admire these three co-authors' trust in one another and are moved by the unconditional respect they have for each other's contributions. On the other hand, we wonder if this might not be a case of valuing trust and respect over a potentially better product. We cannot speak to this issue because our study is based on what the participants say about their co-authoring, not on an analysis of products. But we think we *can* say that their co-authoring might be an example that trust and respect, and the way the process is carried out, could be much more important than any products that might result.

RESPECT, TRUST, AND THE CREATION OF A COLLECTIVE VOICE

We have written ourselves into a voice.

Lisa Ede

Voice is more than just writing style; compositionist John Schultz (1978) defines it as "gesture . . . culture . . . contain[ing] the powers of the unconscious and the conscious and the possibility of style" (151). As we mentioned earlier, and keeping in mind that the concept of voice is complicated by our belief that all writing is collaborative, co-authors must be willing to have their individual voices—their styles, writing gestures, cultures—subsumed by the larger voice which is created when two or more voices are consciously combined. Ede and Lunsford are able to set aside the pleasure many writers find in the distinct sound of their own voices because of their faith that the "third" voice is stronger and richer than either of theirs alone.[4] Ede and Lunsford have been co-authoring for years, and the duration of their writing together plus the number of pieces they have co-authored are testimony to the trust and respect in their relationship. Their talk about their collective writing voice versus their individual ones illustrates not only their feminine egos but also their trust: in Lunsford's words, "Without theorizing . . . we have written ourselves into a voice." When we asked how they would characterize their mutual voice, Lunsford replied, "I'm not a very visual person . . . when I read novels I can't see the scenes . . . I think that really shows up in my writing . . . my writing is not very richly textured." She even told us that one reviewer characterized her writing as "simpleminded," but Ede reacted to Lunsford by saying, "I think you have a tighter and clearer sense of . . . and I can get more elaborate sometimes." Lunsford added, "When we started writing I used dashes a lot and you hated dashes . . . and now we have very strong stylistic tics [in the joint style they have developed]." Now, they agreed, no reader would be able to dissect their co-authored pieces to tell whose voice is speaking where.

Hurlbert and Blitz also contend that "there's no way to know who's saying what."[5] Hurlbert told a remarkable story to illustrate how they worked "very hard early to make this voice":

Early in the process of becoming us we had to do something for *Composition and Resistance* pretty quickly. I was at [Blitz's] house, and we were sketching lots of ideas . . . I took the disk home back to Pittsburgh, and I started to work on it. Of course

Michael couldn't be with me, but over about a year we taped our phone calls, so I had these tapes. So what I did was . . . I had a little Walkman. I put the headphones on . . . the tape of us talking to each other . . . and I played it very low just so I could hear Michael's voice and the rhythm of his voice so that as I was finishing and working it would be very present . . . of course now I can't turn it off [laughter].

Besides hearing Blitz's voice, Hurlbert can adopt Blitz's stance as an aid to creating their collective ethos:

I'll be working, and I'll get stuck, and I'll sort of sit back . . . there's a way Michael has of sitting at the computer when he wants to make something happen. I will take that body pose . . . I can see myself doing it . . . and I will even start hitting the keyboard the way he does . . . and then once he's helped me get started I let him go, and I go on.

In addition to Ede and Lunsford and Blitz and Hurlbert, most of the other teams asserted that distinguishing the individual voices of their team members in their collaborative work would be next to impossible, and having read their co-authored pieces, we agree. Hui and Grant described their voices as "intertwined"—they, like Hurlbert and Blitz, sometimes work with two keyboards hooked up to one computer. Davis, Ellison, and Pike described theirs as "unity in diversity or diversity in unity"—sort of "neat scary!" No one seemed concerned about having a certain idea or style credited to them. They all appeared to be confident that the collective voice of their shared project would represent them honestly and well, and that the published product would be one on which they would be proud to see their names.

When we asked Brown and Roen to characterize their individual voices, neither one of them could. Brown admitted, "I haven't thought about why . . . I mean I just know they're different," but of their collective voice, he said, "We seem to be able to smooth it out." This positive depiction of co-authoring evidences his trust in his co-authors since he also characterized collaboration as "intrusive . . . you're getting into that other person's head at least on the text . . . and manipulating or changing what's going on in this person's head." The thought of such manipulation would certainly be frightening if he could not trust the judgment and character of the "manipulator."

Brown also described their collective voice as "a different ethos" which is compatible with the ancient Greek meaning of ethos, "a habitual gathering place," and LeFevre's extended definition, a "socially created space . . . the point of intersection between speaker or writer and listener and reader" (1987, 45–46). Ethos has to do with how credible and trustworthy the audience finds the speaker (or the reader finds the author), so ethos is necessarily about more than one person: at least one speaker or author and one audience member or reader must be present. It follows that the voice, or ethos, might be different in co-authoring since a reader might find two or three or more authors—a number of experts in agreement on, or equally passionate about, a topic—more credible and trustworthy than one author. In our case, we find ourselves more and more likely to respect the work of scholars who co-author; the fact that they work successfully together might indicate that they incorporate feminine values in their scholarship, in their interaction with colleagues, and in their pedagogy.

COOPERATIVE DISCOURSE

> *Adams was so much there—really a presence—that I felt as if they were talking equally.*
>
> Kami Day

The dynamics between the co-authors in the interviews illustrated their nurturing and respectful feminine approach. Jennifer Coates, a researcher in the field of sociolinguistics, reports that in a number of studies "men dominate conversations by interrupting women, controlling topics of conversation and also by becoming silent" (1993, 139). We have, on occasion, observed such attempts to control, so even though we did not expect men to dominate completely in mixed gender teams, we would not have been surprised if they had controlled the conversation to some degree. However, our study seems to refute the claims of Coates and others; we did not witness even one such attempt to control. In fact, in most of the male-female teams, the women did more talking, and the quietness of the part of the men was not a case of "becoming silent" to control a conversation passively. The men in these teams were contributing in ways that Coates usually sees women contributing, using "minimal responses to signal their active listenership and support of each other" (138). Kami wrote this note after she transcribed the interview with Adams and Knight:

> As I look at the transcript, I realize that Julie did most of the talking, but I did not realize that at the time. Gilbert was so much there—really a presence—that I felt as if they spoke equally. I didn't include all the approval words, but I can always hear him saying "Yeah" or "Right" or "Uh huh."

After the interview with Pike, Davis, and Ellison, Kami wrote, "Cybil did more talking than the other two, but I didn't get the impression that Alexander and Ben felt left out. Alexander was quieter than Cybil, but he had no trouble speaking up when he had an insight or even a question" and was also supportive with minimal responses. These men, along with the women, "developed topics . . . accretively . . . building on each other's contributions and arriving at a consensus" as well (Coates 1993, 138) rather than jumping "from one topic to another, vying to tell anecdotes" as participants in all-male groups often do (188). Transcribing Hurlbert and Blitz's interview left Kami with this impression:

> As I looked back over the transcription of Mark and Michael's interview, I realized it seemed that Michael did a lot more talking, but I didn't feel that he was during the interview. I think I had a sense they were both completely engaged because Mark always nodded his head and quietly supported Michael (and me) with expressions of "Yeah" and "Mmmmm" and "Right." It was almost as if they were both talking, but the words were just being articulated physically by Michael, and of course Michael offered the same kind of support when Mark was talking. It might look as if Michael dominated, but they were equally involved.

Hurlbert and Blitz also built on each other's utterances, and they exhibited another characteristic of feminine discourse: a willingness to talk about relationships and feelings (Coates; Romaine 1994). The only other team as open about their feelings was a female-female one, Lunsford and Ede. Perhaps another indicator of the feminine standpoint of the team members is their direct talk about their relationships—and their talk, sometimes indirect, about their feelings for each other. "Talk is central to women's friendships" (Coates, 138), and it is certainly central to the work and the relationships of these co-authors.

The only team in which we saw any competition for "the floor" was with Oldman and Kent, and we all found this "jockeying" humorous at various points in the conversation because Oldman was consciously trying not to dominate the conversation, and sometimes Kent had to raise her voice a little in order to finish her thought. Oldman saw himself in some ways as a typical male, the "old guy, a card carrying member of the men's club" who could fall into masculine patterns of interruption, domination, and control if he were not constantly vigilant. He wanted us to know that he and Kent "try to do that empathy thing . . . what would Kent think about this? . . . if I guess wrong I've got to listen . . . and embedded in all that stuff is the gender thing." He even acknowledged beginning our interview with the "gender thing" in mind. He had launched immediately into a long speech about his co-authoring and the department, but realizing he was doing all the talking, he turned to Kent and invited her to talk about their other projects. "That's my lead-in?" she laughed, to which Oldman replied, "I'm going to pass the buck here because I'm not going to figure out how to turn it over otherwise."

We found ourselves appreciating Oldman for what appeared to be his genuine reflexivity concerning what he perceives as his "masculine" approach. He is an extroverted, enthusiastic, kinetic man with a deep, strong voice and imposing presence. He could have easily taken over, and we think that would have been his natural inclination, but he was constantly checking himself (and so was Kent!) to make sure he didn't. Kent acknowledged that they've often "switched gender in terms of conversation . . . in our partnership I think you [Oldman] take the one down," meaning he tries to take the role of learner rather than expert. We think his practice of scribbling some of his thoughts during a discussion is his way of saying all he wants to say without taking control of the conversation. Oldman seems able to convert his considerable energy from expert to novice, and that ability convinces us even more of the power of collaboration to effect not only cognitive but personal growth. Collaboration has helped him create a new dimension of himself—or discover a latent one—which makes possible his valuing the strengths of his students and colleagues (and perhaps friends and family members), and his ability to see that giving up control makes him more teachable.

We want very much to hear what each other has to say, but our thinking and working styles are different enough that we do find ourselves competing for the floor fairly often. Michele talks and thinks at the same time—to her, talking is thinking. She also is prone to take long pauses in the middle of a thought as she formulates her next words. Kami, on the other hand, sits quietly for long periods, staring off into space getting a thought together, and then starts to talk so she will not, in a Senior Moment, forget what she wants to say. Often the thought she has begun urgently articulating lands in the middle of one of Michele's pauses, which is very frustrating to Michele because she then loses the train of what she was saying. Or Michele begins to think Kami is not listening because she is silent for so long. As we wrote this book, Kami learned to write down a thought so she could save it until Michele was finished, and Michele learned that even if Kami was quiet, her silence did not mean she wasn't listening. And we both also worked at supporting each other with minimal responses to keep the talk going.

ASYMMETRY AND RECIPROCITY

Maybe our skills complement each other well.

Karen O'Quin

Kent and Oldman and all of the interviewees see their differences in gender, expertise, and styles as stimulating and necessary. They used words like "challenge," "stretch," "push," "question," "stimulate," "inspire," and "discomfort" to describe what happens when they work together. Although their individual contributions create a balanced whole, their relationships are not symmetrical. Rather than valuing a "correspondence in size, form, and arrangement" (Steinmetz et al. 1996) to each other, they take a more feminine approach in valuing their asymmetry, their differences—creating a complementarity in which mutual and individual growth take place. Like the co-authors in Knott and Valek's study (1999), the co-authors in ours seldom used the word "conflict"; they spoke more in terms of appreciating differences. Anthropologist Mary Catherine Bateson's insights into symmetry and complementarity are useful in characterizing the co-authors' relationships (1990). Bateson describes a successful collaborative experience in terms that apply to the teams we studied: the co-authors enjoy a complementarity based on their valuing of "genuine differences that allow each of [them] to meet the needs in the other, pursuing mysteries that only the other could unravel, with a delight in mutual teaching and learning" (100). The writers we studied seem to recognize that symmetry, which Bateson says can be limiting "since it is difference that makes interdependence possible" (104), is not necessary or even desirable for a productive, satisfying relationship, and that "to be nurturant is not always to concur and comfort, to stroke and flatter and appease; it often requires offering a caring version of the truth, grounded in reality" (155). In the words of one of the co-authors in Allen, Atkinson, Morgan, Moore, and Snow's study, "Too much respect would prevent members from challenging one another and would thereby lessen the group's creativity" (1987, 81). Thus far we have included many examples of how the co-authors do not shrink from pointing out changes that need to be made in a certain piece, even if making that suggestion means writing over (as Roen and Brown do) or even deleting (as Blitz and Hurlbert do) a writing partner's words.

This view of symmetry and complementarity is enriched by Young's theory of "asymmetrical reciprocity," an attitude of "moral respect . . . that depends less on unity . . . and more [on] the specific differences among people" (1997, 41). It might seem that the co-authors in our study are a uniform group, but actually the group is quite diverse. For instance, in the team with three members, there is a difference of about twenty-five years in Ellison's and Pike's ages; Pike is a lesbian and the two men are straight; Ellison and Pike are white, and Davis is African American. Pike spoke of being touched that Davis was reading all he could get his hands on about lesbianism and queer theory, and she pointed out that she "is always trying to undo her whiteness." She looks to him to help her understand "what someone like Richard Wright is experiencing in his own life and in his work" and is proud of how they "deal with the consequences of things that have come to divide us, yet being able to work together irrespective of sexual differences and racial differences in a fairly harmonious project." Like some of the participants in Valek and Knott's study, these co-authors saw sex not as an issue but as a difference, and they affirmed that difference. The variances in age, gender, and race are essential to this group's work.

Our differences have challenged and stimulated our work, and our lives, together. Of course, we are both women academics in the same field, we have compatible worldviews and politics, we are both committed to good teaching, and we tend to like the same kinds of books and movies. Also, we are both oldest children and Leos (in fact our birthdays are on the same day). However, our differences far outnumber (although they don't outweigh) our similarities and certainly influence our work together. Michele comes from a working class background in which education was not as valued as in Kami's middle-class, military background. Michele is a lifelong lesbian who has supported herself since she was seventeen; Kami spent her "middle years" as a wife and stay-at-home mother in a heterosexual relationship. Both were born into homes in which the parents claimed connections to orthodox religions, but Michele rejected that part of her culture at an early age while Kami remained faithful until rather late in her life. Michele is an extrovert, and Kami scores on the extreme introvert end of the Myers-Briggs continuum. Michele struggles with a reluctance to disclose personal information, has trouble practicing what she advocates about reflecting on and telling stories about co-authoring. Many times as we wrote reflections, she resisted what seemed to her to be self-indulgence. Conversely, Kami has been inspired by the words of Elspeth Stuckey: "We've got all these lives and stories that have led to the moment like the one we [are] at, and we act like they weren't the fuel that brought us here . . . we act as though what got us here were simply the books we've read and the classes we've taught and the theories we espouse . . . what about all this life?"[6] We cannot claim to never have conflicts, but we certainly value our differences and view them as enriching and challenging.

Gender differences enrich four of the other groups, and within groups, as we have shown and will show, are displayed differing disciplines and areas of knowledge, writing and working styles, pedagogies, and attitudes toward the value of single authorship; we're sure an exploration of their cultural backgrounds—religion, ethnicity, class, etc.—would reveal even more differences. They do not necessarily take each other's standpoints or always understand each other, but they seem to see the value of "getting out of [them]selves and learning something new" (Young 1997, 53). In describing Barbara McClintock's work with genetics, Evelyn Fox Keller says, "McClintock, in her relation with ears of corn, practiced the highest form of love, which is intimacy that does not annihilate difference" (qtd. in Palmer 1998, 6). The co-authors in our study have learned to perform the intimate act of writing together while still respecting the differences that distinguish them.

In Buber's concept of I-Thou relationships, "relation is reciprocity" (qtd. in Noddings 1984, 73), and Young's use of the term "reciprocity" is also important in understanding the relationships in our study. Young feels reciprocity has to do with gift-giving: "the gift is a unique offering," and "the relation of gift-giving is an asymmetrical reciprocity" in that if we are given a gift, giving back the same gift or one like it is not appropriate, and we should not think of the gift we give in return as a payment of debt. We simply accept, and if we give a gift later, "it is a new offering" given out of generosity and caring (1997, 54). Young turns to Habermas in order to relate this concept to communication; every speech act involves an "offer" and an "acceptance," and Young interprets this exchange as asymmetrical since we "respond . . . not by saying the same thing back . . . but by making another, different move in our language game" (55). Of course, the writers in our study are participating in this reciprocal act in the hours of talk that are necessarily a part of co-authoring. In both their writing and personal relationships, they give each other gifts, and gifts are given freely in return as gifts, not in payment of a debt. Furthermore, according to Noddings, these relationships, for which reciprocity is integral, fit the definition of caring: she proposes that "as we examine what it means to care and be cared for, we shall see that both parties contribute to the relation; my caring must be somehow completed in the other if the relation is to be described as caring" (1984, 4).

COMMITMENT AND RESPONSIBILITY

Sometimes you do it just to not let the other one down.

Kathleen Strickland

Just as "commitment is elusive without trust" (Bateson 1990, 208), mutual commitment is essential to building trust, support, and a sense of responsibility to a co-author and to the shared project. Carol Gilligan and Nona Lyons have shown that "responsibility orientation is more central to those whose conceptions of self are rooted in a sense of connection and relatedness to others" (Belenky, Clinchy, Goldberger, and Tarule 1986), and we have shown that the members of the teams we studied are connected by trust, respect, and care, which leads them to respond with commitment (Noddings 1984).

Blitz and Hurlbert addressed the issue of responsibility when they agreed that "the biggest problem [in co-authoring] is people just not coming through with the work that needs to happen," and Blitz alluded to being "left in the lurch with a committed piece." They conceded that "the same kind of luxurious synergy" they enjoy is not always possible but emphasized that co-authors must have similar work ethics. Blitz pointed out the work load in collaboration is more, not less, and added that

> to follow a project from start to finish . . . the amount of commitment is not common, and it's easy for people to run amuck if it's a project that takes more than a year or two. Suddenly things come crushing in on the commitment, and there's not a lot of people who clear enough space, so gradually it's become Mark and I collaborating with each other mostly; this one works best . . . it's reliable.

Blitz and Hurlbert concurred with our observation that co-authoring means somebody is "there to make you continue"—they would not think of letting each other down, not because of obligation or duty but because of their trust and shared commitment.

The first other co-authoring venture I entered into after starting to write with Kami was with a fellow student in a grad class. By my reckoning, we simply never got off the ground together, never really communicated our plan of action, and to my mind, never really completed the project. I am sorry to say that I never got his take on this; I simply turned in a section of the paper to my professor, not wanting to tattle, and left it at that. To this day I don't know what he did or did not do on this project. I thought at the time I was employing language to facilitate our getting the work done, but I never had the sense we were on the same page, never got any feedback or sense of commitment. Now, I work with graduate students all the time, in very high energy meetings where we develop ideas and map out plans for research and co-writing about writing center work; this has been extremely satisfying for me and for the students. I would hate to think the difference is that I am more clearly a facilitator now than I was then, because it would imply that I couldn't work in the role of peer with someone in my class, and must be playing mentor to get into the project.

At one point in our conversation with Kathleen and James Strickland, they agreed that they complement and compliment each other. Kathleen said

> I think we're each other's cheerleaders . . . because this [writing] is so difficult it is sure less painful to keep going when you have somebody supporting you. Sometimes I say to Jim, "Do you really mean that or are you saying those things so I'll keep writing?"

Because we took a feminist approach to interviewing, most of the co-authors felt comfortable asking us questions, and on this topic Kathleen asked us, "Do you ever find too that sometimes you do it [your share of the writing] just not to let the other one down?" She went on to say that

> there are times when I haven't wanted to do this or I'm burned out and I'll say, "Well he's not here" . . . you [to Jim] would never say anything . . . but it would make him happy if I did this much, so I'll do it basically at that point for him.

Lunsford and Ede echoed Hurlbert and Blitz and Strickland and Strickland, in terms of support and shared commitment. They "have shared work styles and shared ways of negotiating [their] professional lives that make [their] collaboration also possible." Ede said, "We meet deadlines if we possibly can and I think we both respond . . . we trust," and Lunsford emphasized "that level of trust":

> I know that if we say we're going to do something, Lisa will not leave me in the lurch. We've been through some very hard personal times together, and we supported each other through those times and still met our deadlines and whatever it was we had to do. I don't know many people that I could go down that road with . . . have that absolute faith.

Lunsford's statement exemplifies how Dickens and Sagaria's collaborative categories—pedagogical, instrumental, professional partnership, and intimate—conflate and resist discrete classification. It suggests nurturing, pragmatics, shared agendas, and close personal friendship.

The teams of Hui and Grant, and Brown and Roen, referred indirectly to commitment and support. Hui considers one of the advantages of co-authoring to be that "talking back and forth pushes me forward when I know there's another person I need to respond to." Roen admitted his energy is limited and that he needs someone "holding my hand" or "nudging" him sometimes to complete a task. When we asked Besemer and O'Quin about their experiences with other co-authors, Besemer offered a careful answer, obviously reluctant to criticize others she's worked with:

> I think when you're working with somebody on something like this, you decide you're going to do something . . . then those regular old work skills of "you do what you're going to do on time" kick in. If you say you're going to send them a copy of something, do you send it? I think doing what you say you're going to do goes a long way.

She went on to describe how their complementary "biorhythms" and personalities contribute to the support they give each other:

> There's another thing about working together that I've liked, and it's been nicer with Karen than with anybody else. Although Karen is an extremely positive and cheery

person, I have actually spoken to her when she has [O'Quin is laughing] been a little down, and I have had an opportunity to sort of buck her up [O'Quin agrees]. It's usually the other way around . . . I'm usually the one that's throwing up my hands and saying, "Why did I ever get started in this . . . it's irrelevant to everything . . . and I'm not qualified and even when I become qualified they're not going to believe that I'm really qualified and blahblahblah." And that's when she gives me a little pep talk.

We would like to make it clear that we do not equate a feminine ego and responsibility to others with the selflessness or self-sacrifice often associated with traditional women's roles. When asked to describe themselves to themselves, the women in Gilligan's study (1982), even the highly educated, successful, professional women, always spoke in terms of relationships: "The standard of moral judgment that inform[ed] their assessment of self is a standard of relationship, an ethic of nurturance, responsibility, and care" (159), but for some of them, such a nurturant stance meant denying their own needs. Gilligan wrote *In a Different Voice* almost nineteen years ago, but many women continue to cheat themselves by equating morality with selflessness, virtue with self-sacrifice. By focusing on their responsibilities to others, they are not responsible to or for themselves. From this putatively altruistic position, helping themselves might be seen as hurting others; they might think of their own needs as unimportant, or they might believe they have no choices and therefore abdicate responsibility for themselves, resulting in irresponsible behavior, dependence, and self-negation.

We did not see any such irresponsibility to self in the co-authors, male or female. Nine of the men and eight of the women had published on their own (although we hate to cite that fact as evidence since it seems to support the prevalent view that apparently autonomous work is necessary for respect from the academy), so they were not depending on their co-authors to help them with promotion and tenure. One of the women who had not published on her own was already tenured and did not need a publication for professional advancement, one was involved in a major research project on her own, and Ben was writing his master's thesis. None of the co-authors have nurtured their writing partners at the expense of their own careers. In fact, they see their co-authoring as career-enhancing, and more importantly, as personally enhancing in terms of knowledge gained, productivity, and rewarding friendships.

All of the participants spoke at some point of the importance of being able to "stand on your own," or of their own individual accomplishments, strengths, and abilities. They would find support in the writings of Winnie Tomm (1992), who reminds us that a person is a "person-in-relation" and that the "highest degree of interconnectedness" can only be attained if an individual has a strong

awareness of self (108). Bateson (1990) agrees that "the capacity to be self-sup-
porting is a precondition to genuine partnership and responsible participation"
(187), but there must be a balance: an "emphasis on autonomy can hamper intimacy" (104). Knight articulated the need to strike a balance between autonomy
and interdependence:

> You need to be able to maintain your individuality and the strengths that you bring
> to bear with the skill that it takes to work together with other folks . . . so that you
> can learn about yourself and understand that adds back to your individuality. Folks
> will understand that that sort of thing can give them sellable skills, but that it can
> add back to an individual . . . something more about yourself that you learn from
> the interaction that adds to who you are . . . that you then take with you.

None of these co-authors exhibited a dependency on each other in terms of
being able to write well or think creatively. They all felt they could write better
with their co-author(s), but none admitted they were afraid they could not write
and publish alone. In addition, none spoke of the other's success or well-being as
more important than their own. Their success lay in utilizing their own abilities
to the fullest and acknowledging that co-authoring enhanced these abilities.

Would this book have gotten written if one of us had to do it alone?
When we thought of this question, both of us immediately answered
"no." We said that partly to make each other feel good, and partly
because we both believe in our heart of hearts that it's true. Roen said
he does not like to write alone, that he relies on co-authors to give him a
push or hold his hand sometimes, and his words ring true for us.
Actually, Kami does like to write alone, but she does not have the savvy
about publishing or the interpersonal skills and contacts that Michele
has, so if she had written this alone, it would probably have languished
until it was too out-of-date to publish. Michele does not like to write
alone, and her kinetic energy and innate restlessness make tying
herself to a project for very long difficult. She thrives on doing
research—the more information coming at her, the happier she is. She
is a master at juggling several projects at once, and she's a skimmer
and chunker, reading voraciously and retaining large amounts of
information. Kami, on the other hand, has learned that she functions
best when she deals with one or two projects at a time and one or two
information sources at a time (the Internet can make her crazy). She
likes to read the articles and books Michele finds word for word, and she
can patiently work through a knotty problem or analysis, sitting at her
computer or on the couch for hours without moving. Michele's
restlessness leads her sometimes to find lots of things she needs to do

besides work, but Kami is the one who says, "OK, let's get going," and makes sure we meet our deadlines. The combination of Michele's energy and ability to research and read and remember so much, and Kami's willingness to keep working methodically through something until it's done, makes a whole writer who knows the field and does the work necessary to contribute to that field.

O'Quin and Besemer and the other co-authors in our study create a nurturing environment within their teams (and sometimes outside them); they teach each other, provide support, take their responsibilities to a shared project seriously, look out for each other professionally, and honor each other's contributions. They all fit easily into Dickens and Sagaria's "pedagogical collaboration: nurturance" category.

However, while the next category, "instrumental collaboration: pragmatism," is applicable to many of the teams, we find it impossible to talk about the instrumental beginnings of some teams without discussing at the same time how those beginnings led to professional and intimate friendships. For example, Hurlbert and Blitz began working together because of a chance conversation and mutual desire to create a meaningful panel for a conference presentation. They knew each other only casually when their collaboration began; they came together because of a common interest and complementary expertise, and their relationship has grown into first a professional and then an intimate collaboration. It seems unreasonable to mention their instrumental beginnings separately from their professional and intimate collaborations since one grew organically out of the other. Consequently, we will conflate the last three categories—"instrumental collaboration: pragmatism," "professional partnership collaboration: shared agendas," and "intimate collaboration: intellectual and emotional closeness."

INSTRUMENTAL, PROFESSIONAL PARTNERSHIP, AND INTIMATE COLLABORATIONS

Dickens and Sagaria define their second category, "instrumental collaboration," as one that is "formed to accomplish a specific objective or to work on a single project." This kind of collaboration, characterized by efficiency and expediency, happens for "primarily practical reasons, such as needing someone with a particular skill or resource to complement their own research expertise" or for the "experience of working on a particular project . . . or with a particular person" (1997, 89).

In Dickens and Sagaria's study, the third category, the "professional partnership" collaboration, is found less often than the other types, but in our study, it appears to be the most common type. It certainly applies to each team at some point in their collaboration. "Professional partnership collaborations" involve "shared research agendas and long-term relationships" that continue for years and through a number of projects. They are "cordial and friendly, but they lack the intensity that characterized intimate collaborations" (91). One participant in Dickens and Sagaria's study "portrayed her relationships as friendly 'but never to the point that it [being friendly] dominates.'" The families of the co-authors in a professional partnership might even be on friendly terms, but "there is a difference between a collegial friend and a good friend. There is always a little reserve with a collegial friend that you're not going to have with a personal friend" (91).

The fourth category, "intimate collaboration," includes women who "shared their ideas and their scholarly lives with very close friends, life partners, and other family members," and "collaborating with a loved one added another dimension to an already complex and emotionally intimate relationship" (93). As we mentioned earlier, studies prior to Dickens and Sagaria's had not identified an "intimate collaboration" category, therefore essentially omitting any consideration of the affective characteristics of collaboration. This oversight is significant, especially in light of what we heard the co-authors in our study saying; with Deborah Tannen, we see that "*intimacy* is key in a world of connection where individuals negotiate complex networks of friendship, minimize differences, try to reach consensus, and avoid the appearance of superiority, which would highlight differences" (1990, 26).

This category became the one most interesting to us; over the years, as we have watched our students co-author, we have observed that the affective aspects of co-authoring are as significant as the cognitive gains, so seeing this observation borne out in our study was affirming, especially since we had not expected it. Moreover, we had anticipated the interviews would focus on what the co-authors *did* when writing together, but they focused more on the relationships, all of which were professional or intimate friendships. Dickens and Sagaria, who also call the relationships in their study pedagogical, professional, instrumental, and intimate *friendships* as well as *collaborations*, report that O'Connor's review of research concerning women's friendships finds that "women's friendships have been overlooked and frequently trivialized as an area of research" (83). We would extend that omission to include men's and mixed gender friendships. Feminist researchers have found that women are more likely to develop intimate friendships because they are more likely to connect with others, but, at least in American men, "close friendship with a man or woman [is] rarely experienced . . . most men do not have an intimate male friend . . . [or] an intimate non-sexual friendship with a woman. . . . We need to understand why friendship is so rare" (Levinson qtd. in Gilligan 1982, 154). Interestingly, in our study, one of the most intimate friendships is between two men, Hurlbert and Blitz. It was our interviewees' talk about this kind of relationship—and the trust, respect, and caring it involves—that revealed the most about their success as co-authors.

INSTRUMENTAL BEGINNINGS: COMMON INTERESTS AND PROXIMITY

Our collaboration is what started our friendship.
Susan Besemer

A few of the collaborative relationships in our study seemed to have started out as "instrumental collaborations" in that they had no previous relationship before their first joint task; they came together because they needed each other's expertise or had a common interest, and their work grew into a friendship. The most striking story of a pragmatic relationship evolving into a friendship is the one told by Hurlbert and Blitz. They had been acquaintances in graduate school and then had gone their separate ways, but at a Conference on College Composition and Communication in 1987, they ran into each other again.

> *Blitz:* When we were getting ready to leave on the last day of the conference in '87, I saw Mark slumped on a bench looking miserable, and that was exactly how I felt then. I felt like I had been through three days of disappointment and confusion about panels and the papers I was hearing. Not just that . . . it was also behavior . . . behavior of people at the conference . . . the star network . . . the struggle that graduate students have getting recognized as full-fledged participants. So when I saw Mark looking that way . . . seeing him look that way . . .
> *Hurlbert:* Triggered something sympathetic [laughter] . . .
> *Blitz:* When we started talking to each other . . . just commiserating . . . we realized, "All right, complaining is one thing but we're not whiners by nature . . . let's be more constructive about this."

So they put together a panel, and while it didn't accomplish what they wanted it to, proposing that panel was the genesis of their co-authoring relationship.

It is difficult to recount their story without talking at the same time about the friendship that developed from a largely pragmatic beginning, so we won't try. When we asked them how they knew they would be able to work together, Hurlbert answered, "That's the weird thing," and Blitz added, "We didn't know . . . we had no idea . . . well, no conscious idea." From this "felt sense" (Hurlbert's words) grew a close friendship, one that fits Dickens and Sagaria's "intimate collaboration" category. References to their friendship are woven throughout their interview—they could not separate their work from it. At one point, when Blitz was talking about his other collaborations, he said,

There may be thousands of people I'd have great collaborations with but life is very limited. It's like when you have a family you want to make sure that family is sustained . . . Mark is my family and I intend to enjoy that as long as it is enjoyable.

A little later, Hurlbert went back to Blitz's words: "Michael used the word family . . . and I was thinking the word family."

Their book *Letters for the Living* (1998) seems to us to be the kind of collaborative project that could only come out of a close friendship. Hurlbert and Blitz told us that the book was born of years of students' stories of pain in their lives or "something about our teaching that is really very painful or in our own lives," so it came "out of commiseration . . . the kind of commiseration you could only have with your best friend." They described the writing as "harrowing," and often one of them, reading over a draft, would say, "Are you sure about this? . . . Do you want to do this?" and the answer from the other would be, "This is what we have to write about." In bold evidence here is the trust, respect, caring, and emotional support that would make such a risky project possible.

In a note Hurlbert attached to the returned transcript of their interview, he referred to the transcripts as "a gift, a record of one of the most important social-personal relations of my entire life" and went on to say, "Certainly I am a fuller human being for my relations to him [Blitz]—so the value is personal—or even spiritual. . . . To put it simply, my life is more meaningful for Michael's presence in it."

Another collaboration that began because of a "shared research agenda" and a need for the expertise of the third co-author is the team of Davis, Ellison, and Pike. Pike and Davis had worked together before, but bringing Ellison in for a particular project because of his specific knowledge partially qualifies this relationship as an "instrumental collaboration" that became a "professional partnership." The three of them came together over a project, but they are certainly cordial, friendly, loyal, and respectful of each other's contributions. In addition, they clearly have shared agendas; according to Pike, "The joy of this relationship is that we're in the same place . . . all three of us care pretty passionately about what we're talking about." For their co-authoring sessions, they meet in an informal setting, on Pike's back porch, to talk over ideas and share what they have individually written. When they are invited to conferences to give papers that all three have had a hand in writing, they insist that all three go. Also, Davis spoke warmly of Ellison's efforts on his behalf when he came up for tenure: "Something I constantly think about in terms of Ben and our voice . . . and our work to continue the political struggle . . . he and some other students headed up a movement and spoke to the dean about my situation." As we mentioned earlier, another indication of a "professional partnership" is that, during the interview, Ellison called Davis and Pike "Dr. Davis" and "Dr. Pike," never using their first names (although Pike and Davis called him Ben), and Davis called Pike both "Cybil" and "Dr. Pike." This form of address seems to indicate a some-what formal but cordial and friendly relationship, and beyond their gatherings on Pike's back porch, they did not speak of participating in social activities together.

On the other hand, these distinctions are complicated because the terms "instrumental" and "professional partnership" seem to apply to their collabora-tion among the three of them, but elements of a more "intimate collaboration" are evident in Pike and Davis's relationship and even in Pike, Davis, and Ellison's. Their insistence on the ineffability of their process, and of always being "present" for each other even when they are working alone, indicates a relationship that goes beyond cordiality and shared agendas. And Pike and Davis, who had a friendship before they began to co-author, told stories that pointed to a more intimate relationship between the two of them. For one thing, Davis compared their joint work to hearing "a musician say it was great to be getting paid for something you'd be doing anyway." He insisted that rather than being pragmatic, they just decided to combine their interests and see what happened, that there was no "real teleological expectation." Also, the women in Dickens and Sagaria's study who were part of intimate collaborations "reported the importance of shared understandings"; they spoke of implicit codes: "we can say two or three words and she'll know what I'm talking about" (1997, 92). The notion of the "affecting presence"—which Pike, Davis, and Ellison feel informs their collabo-ration—involves such silent influences, and Pike described the connection between her and Davis in much the same way: "At first when we want to do something we just kind of look at each other and be quiet until one of us thinks of something to say." In addition to this almost preternatural unspoken under-standing, Davis and Pike enjoy a friendship that includes elements of an intimate one. Pike laughed that one of her colleagues tells her she (Pike) feels maternal toward Davis, but she denied it, calling their relationship "a happening thing" and explaining that people have trouble fitting them "into any particular box."

There was evidence of a not only intellectual but emotional closeness. We wrote in our notes after the interview, "When Cybil looked at and talked about Alexander, she regarded him with great affection, even fighting tears when she talked about what good care Alexander took of his mother when she was dying." And Davis conceded that Pike had mentored him concerning what he needed to do to get tenure, but insisted that "it was more than that . . . it was also a type of friendship that developed as well in regards to visiting her home and becoming friends with her family . . . just things like that." The relationship these three co-authors share is even more complex and difficult to take apart and analyze than other teams', and insisting on such analysis is not necessarily consistent with a feminist stance anyway. So as we stand back and look at it holistically, we see that even though they maintain a bit of formality and distance, we get a strong sense of the affection and care and deep appreciation they feel for each other, a sense which seems to characterize most of the successful teams in our study.

When we told Besemer and O'Quin that many of the participants in our study had an established relationship before their collaboration, O'Quin said, "I think we're the opposite," and Besemer added, "Our collaboration is what started our friendship." We asked them how they came to co-author, and O'Quin exclaimed, "It was serendipity!" As we related earlier, they met because Besemer needed help with the design of a quantitative research project and O'Quin was working as a faculty intern in computing services. An article grew out of their work on Besemer's study, so their co-authoring began as an instrumental collaboration and has continued for about twelve years. Because they were not explicit about an emotional connection, their collaborative relationship seems to correspond to the "professional partnership" category: their families have gotten to know each other, O'Quin's family visits Besemer's every summer at the lake, and Besemer and O'Quin often tell each other how glad they are that they work together.

Here's where the professional friendship is blurred with an intimate one, though. They are comfortable expressing their gratitude to each other, and there is that ineffable "shared sense" that Hurlbert and Blitz, and Ellison, Davis, and Pike, tried to articulate. In her account of meeting Besemer and beginning to write with her, O'Quin realized they must have felt some connection. Besemer seemed to feel that O'Quin had no choice at first but to work with her because it was O'Quin's job as a computing services intern, but O'Quin contradicted her with, "Yeah, but during that year I would say that at least another ten or twelve people came to me for help of a similar sort and you're the only one I ended up working with . . . so you know . . . I didn't co-author with anyone else." Like Hurlbert and Blitz, their connection was immediate and intuitive and has carried them through a long and productive personal and professional relationship.

While most of the teams looked to us to get them started with a prompt, and most of them began by talking about how they came to co-author, Oldman and Kent jumped right into describing the collaborative ambiance of their department and their own work together, which at that point involved a great deal of talk and co-teaching. They were co-authors on a proceedings chapter with five other authors, but they did not really come together in order to work on that piece—it was just the culmination of the conference, and everyone who attended participated. So their collaboration could be called "instrumental" and "pragmatic" in that it evolved largely because of proximity—both Kent and Oldman attended the conference, and now they are faculty in the same department, often traveling by car on trips that take up to seven hours—seven hours of animated discussion, according to them. Kent kidded that if she'd taped the ideas that come out of those conversations and written about them, she'd be tenured by now!

Our first impression of Oldman and Kent the day we interviewed them, as they entered the building talking and laughing after having eaten lunch together, was that they enjoyed each other's company and were at ease with each other. Nothing in the interview contradicted that initial sense. Oldman feels they have bonded and are "really good friends," and we could see why— even after all those hours together in close quarters, they continue to be friendly and certainly more than cordial, even to the point of telling stories about each other and indulging in a little teasing. Kent, who described their collaboration as a "partnership," enjoyed telling us about their different roles— what Oldman called "good cop, bad cop"—in an ongoing project to help a local high school achieve state standards. Kent said Oldman is the one concerned with people's feelings, with "bonding," and she's the more structured one ("We got ten more seconds to do this and here's our structure"). They find this dynamic to be opposite the stereotypes of gender roles, and Oldman thinks that reversal is "hilarious." Kent also teased Oldman about not being able to think if anyone takes his pen away (he doodled and wrote throughout the interview). That they talked a great deal about future projects also indicates a solid friendship. They agreed that they have several projects 80 percent done in their heads, and now "it's a matter of time . . . in four quiet hours we could bang out a first rate piece . . . if all we had to do was publish." They have been gathering data for several studies they plan to develop into publications.

But, we would say their friendship is professional, not intimate, because we did not hear any talk in the interview to suggest an intimate collaboration— no stories about socializing outside their work, no talk of emotional support or ineffable connections. In addition, they seldom used first names in addressing or referring to each other. However, they used "Oldman" and "Kent" (not "Dr. Oldman" or "Dr. Kent"), which certainly was not formal and seemed in keeping with their playful attitude toward each other. Clearly, they like and respect each other, share agendas, and look forward to a long-term professional relationship.

Another pair who began working together because of proximity and shared interests rather than in order to accomplish a certain task was Adams and Knight. Knight had been in the department for about two semesters, and Adams was making the transition from student to faculty member. Adams was involved in a "major research initiative," and at some point Knight became part of the process. They both remembered the day they "laid papers out on the table" and "talked about [their] interest in meta-cognition"; "over in the student union . . . we had a chat while we were eating . . . just some kind of getting ready to be who we were." No writing, or at least no publication, came of that project, but in the interview they both spoke of returning to it. Adams remembered that time as "almost an eye in the storm"—multiple projects were going on around them and "this was an opportunity to step out of that and kind of pause for a moment to engage in a very introspective and reflective process." He remembered more of the process than the outcomes, but he maintained that he "wouldn't have gotten the same insights" alone.

In trying to explain their relationship, Knight talked a great deal about the "social context"; she felt it was

> powerful and important for folks when they work together to understand not only their styles and common interests . . . but if you don't clear out some of the things about how you wish to behave together in a social sense . . . I've seen that cause a lot of confusion, so I feel that way about working with my colleagues. Folks can get away and not understand that it probably doesn't make any difference, but what makes the difference is not asking.

We struggled to understand her notion of "social context." At one point she said, "The chapter came out of something around the social context . . . and then we decided what to do around it . . . so to me it was not about rank." From this, and from her later characterization of the "social system" as "crap," we interpret "social context" to involve the hierarchy and politics in the department. She was saying the project began as part of the department system—she was senior, she invited Adams to co-author, Adams was "beginning his wheel as assistant"—but they "decided what to do around it." They found a way to circumvent department dynamics and develop a peer relationship, and friendship, that she perceived as "neat and level" and "fun."

She also mentioned a dinner she and Adams shared "afterwards" (it was not clear whether she meant after they decided to co-author, or after the conference, or after some other event): "one of the many tables at which I cried . . . that I have washed with my tears in this town." This kind of unguardedness with respect to emotions certainly indicates a comfort level that points to a friendship, and Adams told another story that illustrates their comfort with each other. They had been writing in Knight's apartment, where they often worked, and they were both tired. Adams remembers thinking,

> "I'm so tired . . . now if I were home I would just lie down and take a nap," and I forget who mentioned what, but somehow we just got on the topic of we were really tired . . . and Julie said, "Well, let's just take a nap." So she gave me a clock and went to her bedroom, and I lay down on the couch, and we set the clock, and a half hour

later we woke up and we started writing again! . . . and I'm thinking, "I've never done that with anyone, but that's what I would do if I were on my own."

After Adams told that story, we said, "So, you're comfortable with each other . . . it sounds like you're friends," to which he replied emphatically, "Oh yeah, definitely . . . so that stands out." As with all the teams we interviewed, the friendship "stands out." We would certainly place their collaboration in the "professional partnership" category; they are cordial and friendly and their plan to write a text that year indicated satisfaction with their work so far and a desire to continue. And, even though they did not bring up socializing outside professional projects, we might even tentatively suggest the emotional closeness of an intimate friendship, based on Knight's story about shedding tears in Adams' presence. In addition, in a telling comment, Adams defined writing as

> an intimate process . . . and I think when you do it well, and you get to that level of intimacy, then you start to cross assumptions and values, and things of those sorts do come out, and you can't help but develop a good relationship.

This statement may sum up the relationships of the members of the teams more accurately and profoundly than any other in these interviews. When co-authoring is successful—when collaborators recognize and value each other's strengths, watch out for each other, and trust each other to nurture their professional and personal relationships—perhaps intimate relationships are a natural and beneficial outcome.

PROFESSIONAL AND INTIMATE FRIENDSHIPS

> *But we got to be really thick and fast friends, and I think we always thought we'd collaborate on something.*
>
> Mark Bonacci

The remaining teams were all established friendships—and one is a marriage that is also a deep friendship—before co-authoring began. Grant and Hui talked a great deal about how they met and how their friendship grew. Their collaboration fits the "instrumental" category in that Hui needed Grant's insights because of a common experience with a class she wanted to write about, but they were friends before that first project. When Grant was a doctoral student, Hui was a visiting scholar who sometimes sat in on courses Grant was taking. They began getting to know each other, Hui gave birth to her daughter and Grant visited her in the hospital, and their friendship developed from there. Grant moved about three hours away but continued to visit Hui and her family periodically, and it was during one of these visits that they began co-authoring.

In many ways their collaboration is a "professional partnership": they are friends, they have co-authored three projects, they spoke of future projects, and they certainly have shared agendas. Also, although Grant visits Hui and her family and stays in their house fairly often, there was no explicit discussion of an emotional connection or support. There was a sense of reserve about showing these emotions overtly; however, several times their actions indicated an intimate friendship (and in our notes, we wrote "Grant and Hui have a more personal, intimate friendship"). For one thing, they admitted to having disagreements "all the time." Grant said, "We just get irritable . . . we both like to get our own way," and when we asked what they do about that, Hui answered, "We probably stop a minute . . ." We think being able to show irritation and frustration with each other indicates a level of comfort, although most other teams did not admit to such feelings or at least to expressing them. (Kami admits her experiences color this interpretation; she only allows frustration and irritation to show if she is very comfortable with someone.) Also, Dickens and Sagaria's participants report an "ease in communication" with intimate collaborations, and Grant and Hui demonstrate such ease in that they often finish each other's sentences (perhaps a concrete demonstration of Bakhtin's "chain of utterances"!). The following exchange, one example of many, made us smile as we transcribed it and realized what was happening:

> *Hui:* You know . . . like we will finish each other's . . .
> *Grant:* Yeah . . .
> *Hui:* Yeah, like I will start a sentence and she will . . .
> *Grant:* Finish it . . .
> *Hui:* Finish it . . . and then maybe also bring up a new point . . . and then we go from there.

Although Roen and Brown did not focus on their personal relationship or finish each other's sentences, Roen's first speech in the interview was, "Actually, as we're starting to talk the first thing that comes to mind is how we collaborated on other things than writing projects." Brown agreed he had been thinking the same thing and told us Roen had helped him install an oak floor in his house. When we asked if that collaboration came before the co-authoring, Roen said, "Before, during, and after." They acknowledged that they had an established friendship first, even though their first co-authoring project happened while Brown was Roen's student. At one point, Brown said about co-authoring, "It just has always seemed more efficient," which might locate their collaboration in the "instrumental" category, but he continued with "I'm not sure expediency is the sole consideration." Of course, they "investigate[d] topics of special interest" (Dickens and Sagaria 1997, 89) but did not speak of consciously choosing each other because of a need for a certain skill or a need to publish. They were friends, they co-authored an article, they enjoyed the experience, and they continued to co-author. Although they are intellectually close, and even though they spoke briefly about socializing outside their work (they helped each other with home improvements, and Brown mentioned being in Roen's house recently), they did not speak overtly of their friendship or of emotional support or closeness, so their relationship seems compatible with the "professional partnership" category. They have co-authored several publications, they plan to co-author in the future, and they are certainly cordial and friendly.

Bonacci and Johnson share an office and were noticeably comfortable with each other, equally free with praise and sarcasm and not reticent about stories of their shared professional and personal lives. Their collaboration could be characterized as "instrumental" in that they draw on each other's expertise in their respective disciplines (social psychology and sociology) for both their teaching and their co-authoring. However, in most aspects, it does not fit the "pragmatic" category. There was not even a need to publish since publication is not an expectation at the community college where they teach. After several years of sharing an office and talking about their teaching, these two friends simply saw the need for an interdisciplinary text, and they wrote it. And while there are elements of a "professional partnership," Johnson and Bonacci's co-authoring is clearly "an intimate collaboration" involving intellectual and emotional closeness.

Like Oldman and Kent, this team saw their traditional gender stances as reversed, and they had some fun with the discussion of what they called their "masculine" and "feminine" styles.

> *Bonacci:* I just realized this . . . if there's any such thing as masculine and feminine writing styles, Kate has the masculine and I have the feminine because Kate is very organized and methodical, and for me it's just off in all different directions.
> *Johnson:* Are you saying that feminine is off in all different directions? [laughter]
> *Bonacci:* But the feminine has a lot more of the creativity and emotion . . .
> *Johnson:* Are you saying that the masculine is not creative? [Bonacci laughs] I'm sorry . . . I'm just kidding.

We think their ease with verbal banter and kidding indicates the comfort level of a close friendship. Also, even though Johnson asked us to call her Katherine, Bonacci usually called her or referred to her as Kate, a more familiar form and one she seems to reserve for close friends.

Several times during the interview, Bonacci described Johnson and himself as "best friends," a topic that came up early in the interview:

Bonacci: We've been friends for probably fifteen years.

Johnson: Ten.

Bonacci: Oh, we are? OK . . . I can't believe it's only ten years.

Johnson: We were neighbors before we were colleagues.

Bonacci: Yeah . . . next door neighbors.

Johnson: And I had just gotten married . . . and have since been divorced and remarried . . . I'd just gotten married about ten years ago.

Bonacci: Oh . . . I didn't know that.

Johnson: I keep track of these things.

Bonacci: But we got to be really thick and fast friends, and I think we always thought we'd collaborate on something.

Later they told us stories of Bonacci buying champagne with Johnson's first husband to celebrate Johnson's defending her dissertation, a story which is made even more interesting because Johnson's first husband left her that same day and Bonacci supported her through that difficult time. Bonacci also told the story of the day he defended his dissertation. After what seemed like a successful defense, Bonacci's advisor informed him he wouldn't sign the dissertation until he (the advisor) got a publication out of it. So, Bonacci went home in tears only to find his partner and Johnson had planned a surprise party. In addition, Bonacci stayed with Johnson's mother, their third co-author, "at one point when [he]was without housing." Clearly, they have been present and emotionally supportive at significant moments in one another's lives.

Kathleen and James Strickland probably fit most exactly the "intimate collaboration" category. They are life partners who were married before they began co-authoring, and while their writing together adds "another dimension to an already complex and emotionally intimate relationship," they denied having to deal with the "feelings of jealousy, competition, and resentment" that Dickens and Sagaria mention as possible drawbacks to collaborating with a close relative (1997, 93).

> *Day:* You're the first people we've interviewed who are married. Do you think the fact that you're married makes any difference about how you negotiate things? . . . Do you ever . . . have . . . ? [Kami must have made a funny face or gesture—everyone laughs a lot.]
>
> *Eodice:* Let me put it a different way. Because you also have a relationship other than writing together, do you kind of separate those things out? Do you say, "OK, this is our writing time and what happens here is different later . . . we're not going to carry it over?"
>
> *Jim:* I don't think so.
>
> *Kathleen:* No.

Jim: In fact I think our writing together sort of infringes on everything else . . . because we don't separate it. If something comes up that's a writing topic . . .
Kathleen: It's so intertwined in our life . . .
Jim: We'll talk at dinner about something we're working on . . .
Kathleen: Yeah . . . it's very much intertwined in our life.
Jim: At the grocery store . . . I mean . . .

Remembering her own experiences with occasionally stomping out of the room during a co-authoring session with her life partner, Michele, Kami plunged on:

Day: Do you think you're less careful about hurting each other's feelings because you're married to each other?
Jim: [softly emphatic] No . . . I think we're just as careful because there's more riding on it.
Kathleen: And I think we're very . . . part of our marriage is mutual respect, so that carries over into our writing.

They also acknowledged the "luxury" of their proximity—since they live together, they can immediately discuss ideas that "pop into [their] heads." It seems that their co-authoring has added a positive dimension to their lives in that now both their personal and professional lives are "intertwined"—perhaps enriched by each other. And perhaps because they write they have learned to treat each other even more respectfully than they would otherwise, a "chicken and egg" question we will consider later in chapter seven.

On the other hand, they also admitted the disadvantages of such an intertwining. Kathleen confessed,

Sometimes I don't even know where the professional me and the personal me begins and stops anymore . . . and Jim just accepts that and I don't because it's not like I can take a vacation from it or on break we can get away from it. It's very much who we are, and that's cumbersome sometimes.

These sentiments may indicate some resentment because of the demands of their shared work ethic and the scarcity of "down time," but certainly no resentment, jealousy, or competition in relation to each other.

Of course, their collaboration has "instrumental" and "professional partnership" elements. Their first project was born because Jim needed Kathleen's expertise; they have co-authored several publications, and they plan to co-author a great deal in the future. Kathleen admitted that she's "spoiled" and that she "can't imagine working with anyone else," and Jim admitted his other attempts at co-authoring "always fell apart." A marriage does not guarantee emotional closeness, but the chief impression we took from this interview was the respect Kathleen and Jim have for each other and the care they take of their relationship when it might be easy to be careless.

> We think being partners in life, as the Stricklands are, has created some interesting moments in our co-authoring. We can honestly say, though, that the rough spots have seldom been about the work. In fact, the work often helps smooth out the rough spots. Recently, we had a disagreement about something personal on the morning of a day we had set aside to work. We *had* to work, so we went downstairs to the office, silently and rather grumpily, and began writing. We *had* to talk to each other if we wanted to write, and we did, but soon we decided we needed to watch the tape of the workshop once more. As we watched it, we became engaged in an animated conversation and before long, the "rough spot" had disappeared. Our work sometimes helps us find common ground when our differences make us want to go to separate corners and sulk.

In the field of composition and rhetoric, the collaborative relationship and friendship of Lunsford and Ede is almost legendary. Even the setting of our interview revealed the intimate nature of their friendship. We all went to Ede's room in the Palmer House Hotel, host of the 1998 Conference on College Composition and Communication; Ede and Lunsford sat on the bed, and Ede declared that they did a lot of their talking and writing on beds anyway! They were obviously completely at ease with each other, and often, to make a point, Lunsford reached over to wiggle Ede's toes in an almost intimate gesture. They were the only team that engaged in any such physical contact. When we asked them how they came to co-author, Ede told the story of the two of them driving along the Oregon coast "having fun" when one of them said, "'You know we should just do something together,' and it was really like that . . . so we had that experience and enjoyed it, and it was a tax deductible way to get together." We suppose their collaboration could be called "instrumental" in that they contribute individual skills and knowledge to common projects, but they did not start to co-author for practical reasons. They were friends—they describe their relationship as a "deep friendship"—who wanted to spend more time together doing what they enjoyed, and when they began, they were living close enough together to make that possible.

Like most of the other teams, Lunsford and Ede's collaboration is also a "professional partnership" in its longevity—about twenty years—and in the fact that they still have projects planned for the future. But their intellectual and emotional closeness is certainly the overriding sense we felt during the interview and as we transcribed the conversation. This intellectual closeness is best illustrated in a story they told of working on their "Representing Audience" article. Lunsford was talking about how their separate voices are not discernible in the final draft, and Ede was smiling during Lunsford's explanation:

Ede: I'm smiling because I'm thinking of the time when I threw the tin [laughter]! We published this "Representing Audience" article that looked back at the earlier audience article, and that was the most difficult thing we've ever written.

Lunsford: The most frustrating . . .

Ede: The most frustrating. The second one we wrote in three radically different forms . . . the first one was a proposal.

Lunsford: The second one . . . wasn't that the one where Russell Durst just lost his grip? We got the worst review following that . . . he really just kind of had a fit!

Ede: That's right . . . yeah . . .

Lunsford: And he actually had some good points. I think he thought we were really being self-indulgent . . . and he had some very harsh things to say.

Ede: So it took a long time because we were making big changes and then we were not able to be together.

Lunsford: No . . . not at all.

Ede: And there was one point when I . . .

Lunsford: I was at Bread Loaf . . .

Ede: That's right . . . and you didn't have your separate phone line installed yet I think . . . and I was trying to work on it alone. I just got so frustrated I picked up this tin and threw it across the room . . . and that was when I knew I was in trouble and that we had to . . .

Lunsford: AND [her emphasis] . . . it was her favorite tin!

Ede: It was my favorite tin . . . that's right . . . so we took a little break there.

Day: It scared you? You thought you were too dependent on the other person?

Ede: Oh, no . . . that was when I knew I had to say, "Andrea, this is not working."

Lunsford: "We have to be *together*."

Ede: "We have to be together for this."

Lunsford: We've written on the telephone quite well, so it's not that we can't, but in this instance this was a really hard essay. You know one of the funniest stories . . . you know that diagram [they are both laughing heartily] . . . talking to you on the phone . . . and I was saying, "Lisa . . . draw a circle . . . now put a line through the circle [more laughter]."

Ede: It just drove us crazy . . . we worked eighteen months on it.

This story is not about Lunsford and Ede's reliance or dependence on each other; each is a strong and prolific scholar in her own right. Perhaps it does show, though, that they do not usually bring separate pieces to stitch together when they are working on a shared piece: the threads of their contributions are woven together (to return to an earlier metaphor) throughout the process. In fact, they insist that they "start with a kernel together," so (we know we're mixing metaphors here), to describe their collaboration, it might be necessary to go back to the shearing of the sheep!

These two have also shared homes and families. Ede's husband, Greg Pfarr, and Lunsford are close, and Ede told us Lunsford, who doesn't like dogs, has even learned to tolerate the dog Ede and her husband had acquired recently. They wanted us to know they "have lots of fun together," sometimes taking a few days and pledging to relax with each other when they have been particularly busy. As we mentioned earlier, they have "supported each other through some very hard personal times," and when we asked if there was anything else they'd like to address before we concluded the interview, Lunsford turned to Ede and said, "I love Lisa."

Our co-authoring relationship is one that is also impossible to sort into categories. We met the first day of graduate school and began developing a personal relationship shortly after that. Because we felt immediate trust in each other, at first we were reading and giving each other feedback on our writing. Our relationship was pedagogical in that we were helping each other learn new material based on the individual knowledge we had each brought with us, and it was somewhat instrumental because we looked to each other's expertise in researching and writing to improve the individual work we were doing. Before the semester was over, though, we had co-authored (word by word) a paper with another student. After that summer, when we began living together, it just seemed natural to write conference proposals and papers together. Our co-authoring skipped the professional partnership category and went right to intimate collaboration. So, our coming to co-author had to do with proximity, and we did know each other briefly before we began to write together, but our personal and co-authoring relationships grew together and had everything to do with a sense that we could trust each other. We came to appreciate and rely on one another's strengths; it was apparent, as it is for the co-authors we studied, that we could produce something better together than we could alone.

THE "F-WORD"

What all these teams had to say about their friendships clearly illustrates that they value the relationship at least as much as the task and perhaps, in some cases, over the task. Individuals are willing to give up first author position, they are willing to give up their own words, they are willing to acknowledge and use the ideas of their co-authors if they are better than their own (or even if they're not), and they behave in these respectful and trustful and caring ways partly out of a desire to continue their friendships. Even if their collaboration began as instrumental, their writing grew into a friendship, and perhaps the friendships have deepened because, as Knight observed, "When it's well done, writing is an intimate process."

Presenting the findings of this study is difficult for several reasons. For one thing, although we divide the study into sections such as "respect and trust" and "commitment and responsibility," these categories are certainly not discrete. Examples of commitment or cooperative discourse could just as well illustrate respect and trust and vice versa, and all of the examples illustrate nurturance and a feminine standpoint. We have attempted to sort out and analyze different aspects of the relationships, but in reality we see them holistically. Also, thinking and writing about the interviewees' words raises several questions, which we will address later: Does co-authoring engender a feminine standpoint of respect, trust, appreciation of difference, responsibility, and care, or must a person adopt or naturally display a feminine standpoint to co-author successfully? Furthermore, friendship and co-authoring certainly seem to enrich each other, but would friendships continue in every case if the co-authoring ceased? Of course the feminine approach of the team members contributes to the success of their friendships for the same reasons it contributes to the success of their co-authoring. Their ability to care for and connect with other human beings, to trust and respect and nurture, makes unkindness almost impossible. Hurlbert and Blitz attribute their close friendship partly to "a level of kindness" between them, and Kathleen Strickland maintains that Jim's kindness is one of the reasons for their successful co-authoring (and marriage!).

Finally, almost every team brought up the dreaded "F word"—fun—an element sorely missing in most conversations about scholarly work (and in the work itself). When we told Roen and Brown that co-authoring was fun for us, Roen said, rather seriously, "Well, life is short . . . you'd better find every opportunity you can to do the fun things." Hurlbert and Blitz admitted that a project sometimes has a "goofy start" and that they often "play around a little bit." In discussing her one singly authored book, Kathleen Strickland lamented, "I didn't have as much fun . . . I didn't *enjoy* it as much . . . I wouldn't look to do that again." When we asked Lunsford and Ede how writing together is different from writing alone, they agreed that alone they "don't have as much fun," and they wanted us to know that although they both have a sometimes punishing work ethic, they like to play too. Knight described their co-authoring as "a hoot," and Adams said, "It was a blast!" Oldman and Kent had a great deal of fun teasing and provoking each other during the interview, and at one point,

Kent said about their co-authoring, "Your time is gone, that's for sure . . . that would be punishment, but the fact is you enjoy what you're doing so much more that it's not the pay . . . it's not any of that." Echoing Kent, Yancey, in our CCCC workshop, asserted about co-authoring, "It's fun. It has to be fun because it's too much work!"

Intrinsic rewards such as these are possible because, in addition to a feminine standpoint, the co-authors share ideologies and visions. Furthermore, they are able not only to choose to tackle a challenging project but also to choose with whom they will work; they have had time to develop a relationship; their shared writing process is unproblematic and productive; and they are willing to challenge academic conventions and traditional views concerning single authorship. We will explore these aspects of their co-authoring in the next chapter as we look at what they had to say about their material practices.

NOTES

1.   We were impressed with the depth of examination of the issues surrounding co-authorship in the 2000 book *Ethical Issues in Biomedical Publication*. One contributor, Anne Hudson Jones, writing about unethical authorship practices in the biomedical sciences, defines "guest, gift, or honorary authorship" as "authorship that is conferred on someone who clearly does not qualify for authorship" (15). Horton claims that "although editors become agitated about gift authorship (an endemic disease, polyauthoritis giftosa, according to Kapoor [1995]), scientists seem to regard it as acceptable (Sharp 1998)" (Horton 2000, 37). Abuses arise mainly from the listing of authors who are respected or influential in their fields but who had nothing or little to do with producing a paper. In some cases, names of scientists carrying a particular authority in a field have even been attached to a byline unbeknownst to them; in several of these cases, lack of real involvement in the project—or lack of knowledge of the project—allowed fraudulent research to be disseminated widely because these well-known names were attached to it. In the case of John R. Darsee, who was accused of falsifying data,

> [t]hat the co-authors did not recognize flaws in the papers is explained in some cases because the co-authors did not know [he] had listed them as authors until after the papers had been published. In other cases, however, co-authors made statements testifying to their lack of direct involvement in the work reported in papers that bore their names. (Jones 2000, 9)

Surprisingly, prolific publication did not immediately raise concerns in these cases (in one case the output was one paper every ten days!), and when fraud was finally uncovered, the element of gift authorship was seen as "'a disguise for an impossible amount of work by one person' (Engler et al. 1987, 1387)" (Jones, 11). Author order can also reflect honorary authorship: traditionally, the position of last author gave appropriate credit to the mentor of the developing researcher, but that practice has been corrupted in some departments by the convention that the chair or lab supervisor's name is listed last even if he or she has not contributed to the project.

2.   Most of us in composition are familiar with Ede and Lunsford's toying with the idea to combine their names into one: Annalisa Edesford. Thinking in terms of introducing a new scholar into the field, Spooner and Yancey published several pieces as Myka Vielstimmig, "a writing persona, an abstraction" who represents their collaborative partnership. According to Spooner, "Myka is a sort of Russian-sounding jumble of a few letters from our two names. Vielstimmig is a legit word in German for 'multivocal'" (email, August 2, 2000). To read Vielstimmig's work, go to http://english.ttu.edu/kairos/3.2/features/myka/bio.htm. Michael Field (a male poet), was created in the nineteenth century by Katherine Bradley and Edith Cooper and described by Cooper as representing "this happy union of two in work and aspiration . . . sheltered and expressed by 'Michael Field'" (London 1999, 67).

A group of multimedia artists call themselves "ad319," their original room number at the University of Illinois at Urban-Champaign. They prefer this name because it foregrounds and represents the location and proximity that fostered their collaboration. Five writers known as the "U. S. Five" have published a novel, *The Devil's Rood*, which involved doling out forty-four characters to the collaborators by way of a lottery. They revived a true hundred-year-old murder mystery, and the collaboration allowed each writer to contribute about ten characters' perspectives on the murder (Word 2000, 10D).

Ede and Lunsford (1990) quote Ralph E. Weston's 1962 proposal for scientific scholarship urging scientists to "'apply the concept of "team research" logically, consistently, and enthusiastically . . . . [and to] forego the pleasure of seeing their names emblazoned in 8-point Baskerville and accept authorship designated by a group name' (78), such as the Harvard-MIT 'Yankees'" (100). Perhaps Ede and Lunsford's concept of the "constructed nature of authorship" (101) could be better represented in the construction of team names.

3.   Attempts to codify the levels of contribution within the author order structure remain inconsistent and confusing across disciplines. It appears to us that in some fields, last author signifies the largest contribution, and in some fields the opposite is true. Or, last author might signal respect to a senior researcher or mentor, not to mention the gift author complication. Engers, Gans, Grant, and King (1999) found that co-authors in the field of economics appear to collectively decide not to use the criterion of relative contribu-

tion in deciding name order on an article, even though employers want to know about individual productivity. The collaborators seem to be in some way subverting the system by choosing to list their names in alphabetical order, thereby creating an equilibrium that distributes credit equally among the authors. Also, "one explanation for the use of the lexicographic order arises when co-authors have an ongoing collaborative relationship with multiple outputs that involve varying relative contributions" (15). Of the many discussions we've read about author order, this piece was most interesting because it used a complex formula from economics to analyze first author conditions in economics scholarship.

4.   For many of us who have co-authored, it seems easy to admit to what has been variously called a third voice, a new voice, (first person)[2]. For co-authors, this is our most local voice. Spooner describes one aspect of voice as it relates to the Spooner-Yancey "Myka pieces." Spooner maintains that the multiple voices in the Myka writing cannot be parsed, assigning one voice to one writer and another to the other writer. He recognizes that readers have attempted to do such parsing (we think studying what makes people want to do that would be interesting), and related that "we [he and Yancey] added a third and fourth voice, just to make it harder. The principle is that in our kind of collaboration, we both write and rewrite all the voices; we don't divvy things up the way some co-authors do. So the co-pseudonym addresses that principle" (email, August 2, 2000).

Wouldn't it be fun to call on Don Foster, who is most well known for exposing the author of *Primary Colors*, Anonymous, as Joe Klein, to analyze our collective voice, (first person)[2]. As a graduate student, "he identified Shakespeare as the author of a dull little poem called 'A Funeral Elegy.'" His evidence was almost entirely textual, exhaustive, balanced, and plausible. He submitted his manuscript, describing his conclusions to Oxford University Press.

> The publisher solicited anonymous experts. . . . Two reviewers concluded that internal textual evidence is by its nature insufficient to establish authorship and recommended that the book be rejected. . . . Foster gleefully recounts how he figured out the identities of his reviewers solely by analyzing their language . . . and his Shakespeare claim eventually became front page news. (Liptak 2000, 34)

5.   Ed Linn's obituary describes him as "an author and magazine writer who collaborated with the maverick baseball owner Bill Veeck on three books." Linn shared many stories of his work as a co-author, especially his work with Veeck on *Veeck—As in Wreck*, and one story illustrates how the lines between voice, and even authors, get blurred.

After going over the manuscript for the presumed final time, the pair had "the only real argument we were ever going to have."

As Mr. Linn remembered it: "That late in the game, Veeck had decided that he had given Rogers Hornsby a worse pummeling than an old guy, long out of baseball, was worth. I accused Bill—if you can believe this—of running scared, and he informed me that it didn't matter what I thought. "It's my book, and those two pages are out."

He was right of course, right on both counts. In order to explain away my temper tantrum before I left the next day, I said, "You have to understand, Bill, that by this time I think I made you up."

"Don't worry about it," Bill said. "You have to understand that by this time I think I wrote the book." (Goldstein 2000, 16C)

6. Blitz and Hurlbert heard J. Elspeth Stuckey make this statement at a conference, and in our interview they cited it as one of the impetuses for their co-authored book *Letters for the Living* (1998).

5 WHAT THEY DO
How the Co-authors View Their Collaborative Writing Process

People who like this sort of thing will find this the sort of thing they like.
Abraham Lincoln

In this chapter we will concentrate on how the co-authors describe what they actually do together to produce a piece of writing. Four of the teams are made up of composition specialists, and we assumed they would be more articulate than the others about their writing processes, but we found that the ability to discuss their processes was spread evenly over the teams. In fact, Knight and Adams, who are in another discipline, were the most articulate and reflective about both their individual and joint processes, and Roen and Brown, who are well known in composition, had some difficulty characterizing their individual processes and shared voice. However, we learned from the interviewees that process is not an issue and that they had not previously discussed it very much—if ever. In each case, their feminine approach led to a productive, relatively smooth-running procedure that made possible a focus on content. When prompted, though, they were able to discuss their processes, and most of that discussion involved drafting and revision. In addition, in all the interviews, the topics of choice and time popped up as important issues in relation to the writing process itself.

CHOICE AND TIME

Folks do that because they want to.
Julie Knight

Of course, no one forced the interviewees to work together; either one invited the other to co-author or the decision was a mutual one, so choice is understood in all the teams. Almost all the co-authors stressed that collaboration should be voluntary—that writers need to be able to choose their projects, partners, and perhaps even *whether* they will co-author. This conviction about choice, which is tied up with time, seems to be an important ingredient in the formula for their practices. In this section, we are going to use Strickland and Strickland's term "co-writing" to designate face-to-face, word-by-word text production as distinct from co-authoring (working together—

topic and idea generation, research, talk, possible co-writing, decisions about how the final product will look, etc., on a writing project). We were actually surprised to learn that these successful co-authors have so many reservations about student co-authoring, and specifically co-writing, based primarily on the issue of choice.

We know teachers who require collaboration but do not allow students to choose their own collaborative partners, instead grouping them based on such criteria as the Myers-Briggs Type Indicator, birth order, perceived writing ability, gender, the alphabet, work schedules, or any number of other factors. Karen Spear (1988), Rebecca Rule (1993), and Anne Ruggles Gere (1987) (and we include ourselves in this group) require student collaboration but have found there are no guaranteed formulas for creating successful group configurations. We have tried random grouping, grouping based on writing ability or writing apprehension levels, matching cards, and other gimmicks, and none of these methods seem to contribute significantly one way or the other to the productivity of the group. We have also allowed students to build their own groups after a period of time (with about the same results as with teacher-built groups); Julia M. Gergits and James J. Schramer (1994); Romana P. Hillebrand (1994); Gere (1987); Collette Daiute and Brigette Dalton (1988); Donna J. Qualley and Elizabeth Chiseri-Strater (1994) and others recommend allowing students to self-select groups because this choice seems to facilitate group autonomy (having to do with bonding and group identity), productivity, and satisfaction with the collaboration process in general.

On the other hand, Elizabeth G. Cohen (1994) and Paul J. Vermette (1998) maintain that given the opportunity to choose their partners, students of any age will not build the most effective teams: groups will be stratified by gender, race, class, and ethnicity; "friends will build play groups, not work groups"; loners will be left out or group themselves as "losers"; high achievers will seek their own kind; "appreciation for diversity of talents and skills will not be a common event"; and "stereotypes will be enforced" (Vermette, 69). Vermette's students do a great deal of their learning in groups, but he always builds the groups himself. Most of the interviewees in our study require students to work together, but, except for the members of one team, the interviewees who use collaboration agreed that students should be allowed to choose their partners. We think they base this conviction on their own experience with choosing each other and with the challenges of co-authoring, and especially co-writing, even with a partner they have elected to work with.

In thinking about this issue, Susan Besemer views choosing a certain project and choosing a partner to share in that project as inextricable:

Writing . . . especially scholarly writing . . . it's not something everybody does, and it's certainly not something everybody looks forward to . . . and even less is it something that people voluntarily do . . . so for me it's like a hobby in a sense. If you're going to do it, and you don't have to do it, you're a little bit eccentric right to start with . . . so in order to kind of keep yourself going when you don't have to for promotion . . . having someone that you share that with who also believes in the value of doing this . . . at least you have company in it.

She sees herself and Karen O'Quin as "a little bit eccentric" in that they choose to continue to publish together, or even publish at all, when they are not expected to, and she feels choosing the right person with whom to pursue a generally dreaded activity is essential to the success of that activity. As a librarian, Besemer does not teach classes, but O'Quin has written about small group projects, so we asked her if she requires students to co-author. She said that sometimes she mandates a group project and sometimes it's optional: students' projects involve choosing a topic as a group but then usually researching separately and making decisions about how to combine their separate sections. She has tried asking students to actually co-write papers in the past, but the limited success of such endeavors has, at least in part, to do with time. Many students at her institution are commuters who are overburdened with school, full time jobs, and families and simply have no time to meet outside class. More time set aside in class to work on group projects would be a partial solution, but O'Quin labors under the pressures of both covering the material (psychology) and including the writing component. Students do not really have time to become acquainted in order to form cohorts with whom they are comfortable.

Lisa Ede and Andrea Lunsford also incorporate collaboration into their pedagogy, but not necessarily co-writing. All of Ede's students in one class "have to write an essay responding to the same essay"; she tells them they can collaborate, "but in general they do single-authored essays and then do a collaborative discussion on that . . . on the process of working together." So, they can choose to co-author or write responses individually, and those pieces lead to some kind of collaborative project, but it does not involve co-writing, and she did not say whether they choose with whom to collaborate. Ede shares O'Quin's concerns about the complicated lives of her students and the difficulty they have finding time to get together outside class.

Jim and Kathleen Strickland have obviously chosen to work with each other, and so important to them is the freedom to choose their co-authors that they both have some real concerns about student co-authoring, especially college students. Much of Kathleen's work is in elementary education, and she pointed out that "children can choose people they feel comfortable with . . .

you have 180 days all day long. . . you have time to build those relationships," but in college "I have 15 weeks . . . 50 minutes a shot to do something." She and Jim agreed they would not force students to co-write. Kathleen even worried that "it could actually hurt a novice writer . . . I mean if you didn't choose that [co-writing] yourself and choose the person you wanted to write with . . . if that wasn't an outgrowth of something then it could actually hold writers back . . . I think it could sour their taste for writing." Her experiences with the challenges of co-authoring are obvious here. She gives her students opportunities to respond to each other's writing and to learn from and support each other, but "this idea of co-writing needs all the right ingredients and they can't be forced, so I think we could do more harm than good."

Both Jim and Kathleen ask students to work on projects together, but the students are allowed to work out how much writing they do together and how much of the work they want to do individually. As we mentioned in chapter three, Jim and Kathleen do not compose face-to-face, word-for-word—co-write—and they seem to want their students to have at least the same freedom to choose how to co-author—and with whom—as they do. They do not feel that in a semester students have the time to build the respect and trust necessary for successful co-writing.

Duane Roen was adamant in his conviction that "collaboration [joint text production] is only going to flourish in a voluntary community." Both he and Stuart Brown encourage students to collaborate and help them do it if they choose to, and they both allow students to form their own groups. However, neither requires that students "collaborate as co-authors [co-write]." Students do not produce a piece of writing together, but they respond daily to each other's work. When we queried Roen about his reservations, he referred to the freedom he has to choose *his* co-authors:

> Because I know the range of personalities in the world . . . we've both [he and Brown] already said there are some personalities we don't care to work with . . . we choose . . . and I give students the opportunity to choose . . . and the students are in a sort of enforced arbitrary community whereas collaboration is only going to flourish in a voluntary community.

We knew that Roen believes the value of collaboration goes beyond cognitive gains, so we wanted to know what he would say to someone who maintains that the risks of collaboration are worth the benefits. He replied:

> Absolutely . . . we have to agree that we want to do something better for someone . . . for ourselves or some third party or for the world . . . and that's one of the problems with collaboration in the classroom. There are some students who don't want to be in your classroom, and there are some students who take the easiest route to getting

through the course . . . well if someone's forced to work with that person whose only goal is to get a C, you've got problems that are almost insurmountable.

We brought up the conflicting research on choice: as we said earlier, some studies find that students must be allowed to choose their partners, and some find that the teacher, after he or she has taken time to get to know the students, must put them into groups based on their diverse strengths and styles. We admitted we did not know the best strategy, and Brown told us another story to illustrate his commitment to choice:

> I was teaching a technical writing class seven or eight years ago, and I had a couple of young Navajo women in that class, and there was no way I could break them up . . . and they did a wonderful collaboration. They proposed and implemented an adoptive grandparent program on the Navajo reservation . . . but culturally . . . fortunately I had worked with Navajo when I was at Arizona, so I knew . . . especially women in the Navajo culture . . . if they don't know your clan name, you're going to have a hard time establishing a relationship. If I had broken them up . . . assigned them . . . it would have been destroyed. I wonder if diversity is not going to be better met by keeping collaboration . . . let the black students hang out together . . . and come up with projects as opposed to . . .

We have to admit that these statements were somewhat unsettling to us. These interviewees' beliefs about choice called into question our own commitment to co-authoring and co-writing in our classes and made us rethink assigning our students to groups, no matter how well we think we know them. Certainly giving students choices about how they learn is compatible with a caring, student-centered, feminine approach, but what about creating a space where students can begin to appreciate "asymmetrical reciprocity," value and negotiate difference, and find common ground? We will address the questions raised by these views, and the implications for pedagogy, in chapter seven.

Other co-authors in our study also support choice in their pedagogy. Describing themselves as constructivist teachers, Roja Grant requires her students to collaborate and Emily Hui encourages them to. Both allow students to choose with whom they will work—"I just tell them to get in groups" (Grant)—and do not really know how students settle disagreements or make decisions about their collaborative processes. Neither seemed to have thought a great deal about why they allow students to choose their partners rather than assigning them to groups except that they were following the example of a mentor they both respected.

While both Mark Hurlbert's and Michael Blitz's students collaborate, it was not clear in the interview whether they let their students choose that activity, but Hurlbert told us later that he does not require his students to collaborate, even going so far as to say that forcing students to work together is questionable ethically. However, if the students do work together, the students decide whether they will sew individual pieces together, co-write, or a combination of both. When we related a story to illustrate the stress (ours and the students') that often accompanies co-authoring in the classroom, Blitz admitted that "there's been mutinies . . . things can fall apart so easily." On occasion a student even opts to drop his class rather than deal with the challenges of collaboration. They did not speak explicitly about whether they allow students to choose with whom they will work, but they both share Roen and Brown's concerns about the possible imbalance of commitment in a student collaboration, and, with us, they wish students had more time to develop trusting and respectful relationships. Finally, we agreed that students need to be given choice in how to define co-authoring for themselves.

Gilbert Adams's pedagogy incorporates collaboration, including collaborative writing, but his students choose with whom they will work. Julie Knight also values student collaboration, but she acknowledges that the experience may not always be a positive for students because they do not necessarily get to choose whether they will collaborate or with whom. Students in Alexander Davis's and Cybil Pike's classes do not co-author, but they learn interactively and sometimes participate in group projects. Neither said whether their students are allowed to choose collaboration or to choose their partners. However, Davis did acknowledge that problems with student co-authoring might arise because "it seems like a very random type thing whereas I don't see this [his co-authoring with Pike and Ellison] as random." He worries that grouping students randomly, or even allowing them to group themselves without the benefit of knowing each other, can result in unproductive, unsatisfying collaboration. In the Katherine Johnson–Mark Bonacci team, Johnson does not ask students to collaborate at all and Bonacci occasionally asks students to participate in group projects, but Johnson and Bonacci's concerns have more to do with their own lack of skill in organizing collaborative activities and with problems arising from uneven commitment in the groups.

Taking a view that values teacher choice over student choice, Matthew Oldman, who also identifies himself as a constructivist teacher, feels teachers are better equipped to designate who will work with whom. Oldman has written extensively about cooperative learning (Ann D. Chapman, Judith J. Leonard, and John C. Thomas [1992] cite co-authoring as an example of cooperative learning) and insists that teachers must assign their students to groups. Speaking from years of experience teaching secondary school and college undergraduate and teacher education courses, he stresses that a teacher needs to know students' strengths, weaknesses, and even personality styles ("We want to heterogeneously mix them . . . you can't put all your introverts in one group . . . they just sit there and look at each other") so that a group consists of students of differing abilities, making zones of proximal development possible. He does not, however, give his students choice about whether they will collaborate; he wanted us to know his students "don't pass [his] course until they prove they can collaborate," and Kent's students are also required to work together.

Whether they expressed it overtly or not, all the co-authors in our study seem to be aware of the role of choice in developing satisfying, productive writing relationships and in the role time plays in choice. Some feel the benefits of co-authoring are worth the occasional bad match in style or clash in personalities. Others worry that students do not have the luxury of getting to know each other well and therefore do not have the basis for intelligent choices about co-authoring partners. For many of them, students are at risk for having to endure forced collaboration with partners whose styles, abilities, or even cultures are markedly different from their own. Admittedly, institutional time constraints—fifteen-week semesters usually divided into fifty-minute instruction segments—do not allow the "talk time" necessary for students to become acquainted with each other so they can work through these differences or choose partners with whom they are more compatible. Nor do traditionally configured classes, pressed to "cover the content," provide time in class for students to participate in the talk necessary for successful co-authoring.

TALK, INVENTION, DECISION-MAKING

We love exciting dialogue and conversation.

Michael Blitz

When we asked the co-authors how writing together differs from writing alone, they supported what we have observed as our students co-author: more planning goes into a co-authored piece. Roen and Brown agreed that there's "more up front design that goes into a collaboration," whereas when they write independently they "sort of dive in." And most agreed that planning consists of a great deal of talk, which involves negotiation and invention that leads to decision-making, and which we think distinguishes co-authoring from collaboration and cooperation. The co-authors in Allen, Atkinson, Morgan, Moore, and Snow's study "reported that the major and most satisfying collaborative effort usually took place at the beginning of a project when group members met together to talk about and plan the project" (1987, 77). Kent and Oldman spoke about often sitting down in the same room and putting their ideas together in a written piece, but so far, in the year Kent had been with the department, most of what they had done could be called planning. They had several articles in progress, and to begin, they each bring a "skeleton" and create a kind of "synergy." Oldman writes as they talk, one takes the notes and writes a draft, and they continue from there. They feel that 80 percent of a written piece is verbally constructed. Janice Doane and Devon Hodges (1995) would agree; their "talk-work" is essential because they "have come to rely predominantly on the oral—conversation, composing aloud" (56). Ede and Lunsford characterize their talk-work as a "large looping spiral" which "emphasizes the frequency and proportion of talk in [their] process . . . . talk . . . write . . . talk . . . read . . . talk . . . write . . . talk . . ." (1983, 152).

If all writing is collaborative, even solitary writers carry on inner dialogues among their many selves and with other writers, dead and alive. But the importance of talk is even clearer when writers collaborate; their thinking is audible and several pools of knowledge combine in a virtual space to create a deep lake of possibilities from which choices of what is to be written down are made. Spear (1988) contends that the significance of talk in collaborative writing cannot be overlooked: "The act of talking is a process of discovering, articulating, and clarifying meaning based on the flow of verbal and non-verbal cues the interaction generates," and it involves "the more evolutionary, interpersonal processes of composing, reinventing, and revising" (6, 7). In describing Hunt and Reither's co-authoring, Reither and Vipond (1989) assert that "Hunt and Reither tossed their thinking into a pool of knowledge" but they also exchanged drafts for months and then eventually "met in final editing sessions in which they huddled over the same keyboard, reading (often aloud), *discussing* [our emphasis] options" (860).

In all of our conversations with the co-authors in our study, talk came up as part of their planning, composing, and revision. Because the role of talk in collaborative activity is obvious, we do not see the need to show numerous examples of what the interviewees said about talk in their co-authoring, but the interview transcripts were full of snippets like "we usually converse and we plan" (Adams and Knight), or "we love exciting dialogue and conversation" (Hurlbert and Blitz), or "when we write together we talk a lot" (Ede and Lunsford), and we *can* include an example of a peek we got at one team's co-authoring process.

We were able to observe Besemer and O'Quin as they talked through a complex question concerning a draft of a piece they had brought with them; they thought we might want to see them in action. The encyclopedia article they were preparing for publication had begun as Besemer's, but by the day of our interview, the only thing left of that original piece was "the kernel underneath." The article's topic was creative products, and the reviewer had asked, "To whom is it [the product] creative?" We listened as they struggled (O'Quin actually punctuated their conversation with the words "struggle struggle") over issues of subjectivity, social approval, comparison of products, value to the world versus value to the individual, and qualifications of the judges. They arrived at the consensus, without writing a word, that a product is creative to any relevant person, but put off discussion of criteria and of who is relevant until another time. Interestingly, they characterize this talk as co-authoring, but they are a team who never sits down together to co-write. We include this brief synopsis of their discussion because we're sure we would hear similar stimulating exchanges if we could watch all of the teams work. The talk in collaborative writing is the zone of proximal development made visible.

Actually, we *were* privileged to witness such stimulating exchanges in each interview even if the teams were not actually discussing a piece of writing; team members made discoveries during the interviews as they talked about their own co-authoring processes. Roen has written about co-authoring with Robert Mitten, and Ede and Lunsford have written about their own co-authoring, but the other teams admitted to never really thinking about it (Knight called it "a nonawareness" on their part). Besemer admitted that "one of the benefits of this [our interview] session is . . . I hadn't thought about how much my life is formed by things where I purposely chose to work with somebody," and she and O'Quin agreed they had not thought much about their working together. Roen and Brown recognized they needed to document better how they work, and when we tried at one point to wrap up the interview because we were cognizant of their other obligations, they indicated a desire to continue because "it's not stuff [we've] thought about before." They were considering for the first time, especially, characteristics of their individual and joint voices.

As our interview with Kathleen and Jim Strickland began, Kathleen mused, "This is the first time really we've actually . . . we'll probably be discovering this with you . . . we've thought a little about it but truthfully it's happened so naturally." As we talked, Kathleen came to some conclusions about the value of co-authoring beyond learning to write better, and Jim revealed to Kathleen that the co-authoring model he keeps in mind is Ken and Yetta Goodman.

Ellison, Pike, and Davis had not talked about their co-authoring before, and in an effort to be sensitive to their reluctance about artificially analyzing their process (Pike saw as "necessary" the difficulty in "separating it out"), we asked if it was "intrusive for us to ask [them] to talk about this." Davis reassured us with "It just gives me another opportunity to try to understand better what it is that we do . . . the more we talk about it the more we can comprehend it." About what she was discovering as we talked, Knight declared, "It's neat to have the opportunity to talk about this. I think, 'Yeah . . . you've hit on that one, and that clarifies for me the how and why.'" She felt she had realized for the first time her and Adams' shared "vision of the thing they wanted to write about . . . something bigger than both of us." Finally, during the course of our dialogue with Johnson and Bonacci, Johnson realized they enjoyed few extrinsic benefits from their co-authoring because of problems with the administration (tangentially related to their co-authoring); the rewards were mostly intrinsic—she and Bonacci became closer friends, and she "felt good." They confessed they felt so good they would go through all the headaches again for the intrinsic rewards.

When we initially proposed the co-authored dissertation, we believed our study would benefit the students we would study, but we did not necessarily think about whether the experienced co-authoring teams would benefit. As we transcribed the interviews and listened carefully to the co-authors' talk, we became aware that their talk, as usual, had brought them rewards. Their talk was epistemic in that they learned more about each other and about what they do, and what's more, they had fun. In answer to our question, "What's it been like to reflect on your co-authoring?" Kathleen Strickland answered, "Fun . . . no one's ever cared before!" As we said in chapter four, Hurlbert wrote, in a note attached to the returned transcript, that he saw the transcript as "a gift, a record of one of the most important social-personal relations of my entire life—so thank you." And Oldman (who claims he talks a lot because he discovers as he talks), with characteristic enthusiasm, proclaimed, "It's fun. It's its own reward!"

In their co-authored meta-narrative about writing together, Darlene Dralus and Jen Shelton admit: "odd that writing about our collaboration is scarier than the collaboration itself" (1995, 26). I agree . . . never as comfortable telling stories or examining myself . . . wondering why, ironically, I am the one who comes up with this idea to talk about it but won't . . . who tries to articulate why it is great to write with Kami but gets easily frustrated—ready to shut down—at the first interruption or if Kami doesn't appear to be listening . . . "I don't want to be a brat (or a baby, or a didactic who-ha) . . . but . . ." I say . . . "Really, I don't want to <u>appear</u> to be a brat" . . . but know damn well I am sometimes.

On the other hand, give Kami a keyboard and off she goes . . . perfectly comfortable (so it seems) disclosing all her weaknesses, apologizing, telling all the tales of our good times and bad. I sometimes squirm at the honesty and clarity of her stories . . . they seem jarring or too familiar . . . scary . . . and I think: who wants to know this? To read this? I am ambivalent, not supportive enough of this kind of writing—and it ends up being what readers think is the best part.

DRAFTING AND REVISION

If the process is running OK, you can devote more energy to the content.

Julie Knight

Kami has co-authored with five people, and three of those collaborations have been face-to-face, word-by-word text production—co-writing. Michele has co-authored with sixty-two people: one co-authoring team involved Michele, a graduate teaching assistant, and the assistant's forty-three students, but she has co-written (word-by-word) with six other authors. This kind of co-authoring—face-to-face, word-by-word—comes close to Austin and Baldwin's (1991) "full collaboration," which they call "probably the purest and least common form of co-authorship. No clear division or authority exists . . . it requires a great deal of discussion and negotiation to ensure its success . . . relies heavily on consensus . . . [and carries] heavy interpersonal and time demands" (24). However, as we conceded in our discussion of definitions in chapter two, most of the co-authors in our study do not do much composing word-by-word, or co-writing, and many do none. For some teams, co-authorship resembles Austin and Baldwin's "partial collaboration"—the work is divided, and "each takes responsibility for a specific section . . . negotiation is less important" (24). Most of the teams in our study, though, engage in a type of co-authoring not considered by Austin and Baldwin: a combination of face-to-face composing ("full collaboration") and writing sections individually, which are then blended ("partial collaboration"). This combination— and its many subcombinations—illustrate the difficulty of defining collaborative writing; however, negotiation, talk, and consensus are important elements of all their work, whatever approach they take, and the co-authoring teams feel their processes are effective and have developed organically as the team members worked together.

In Hui and Grant's co-authoring, Hui writes the first draft, Grant makes changes, and then they arrange to be together for a few days to work on revisions. At that time, they sit down in front of the computer screen and co-write, which they acknowledge "takes a long time." Grant admitted she would not like to compose the whole piece word by word: "Sometimes it just doesn't make sense . . . I can see how it's going to be good . . . 'Let me just do it and show it to you [Hui]' . . . and then ten minutes later or a half hour the other person shows the other person." For later revisions, they might send drafts back and forth by regular mail or email. Grant's reservations about word-by-word co-authoring echo those of the writers in Allen, Atkinson, Morgan, Moore, and Snow's study (1987): The co-authors who tried to co-write but abandoned the attempt found they were unproductive because they "haggled over words and sentences" or "their styles were so different" (78), and one group which co-wrote successfully decided against it for future projects because it took too much time.

Brown and Roen's process varies depending on the project, but as a rule they also exchange drafts of some sections and co-write some sections (although they do that rarely, being at separate institutions). They sometimes "rough out a plan of action" and then "all go off and deliver," later exchanging drafts by email and regular mail. In editing a book involving multiple contributors with Theresa Enos, they divided the contributions into three stacks. They each read one stack first, passing it on to the next person, who passed it on to the next so each of them read all three stacks. According to Roen, "That really made the editing process a lot easier for the third person." Roen drafted part of the introduction, after which Enos and then Brown wrote all over it until they had a final draft they were satisfied with. We asked Roen about the article on collaborative research he co-authored with Mitten, and Roen admitted that he and Mitten had co-written part of that piece.

Hurlbert and Blitz's co-authoring often begins with "joking" or "playful bickering" about the way things are, or a story one of them tells the other about his teaching. They live in different states, so one might write part of a draft and "ship it" to the other, but they do co-write; in fact, as we mentioned earlier, they sometimes hook two keyboards up to one computer—"when one backs off, the other can go."

We did most of our writing for this book sitting together in front of a computer screen. Kami sits at the keyboard and types as we talk about ideas and negotiate the text. She is also the designated oral reader; Michele likes to hear the text and process it that way, so she listens as Kami reads—usually too fast—sections of the text. In thinking about this arrangement—which is somewhat different than for past projects—we decided that Kami gets to control the keyboard because she's more familiar with this particular text and can find sections more easily. She can scroll quickly and land on what we are looking for, while Michele looks away so she won't get seasick. Occasionally, Michele takes control of the mouse as Kami types. Also, Michele needs, periodically, to get up and pace or putt golf balls, and Kami is content to be more stationary, sometimes typing (as we talk) while Michele paces. On occasion, if one of us is busy doing something else, the other sits and "fiddles" with the text.

In thinking about "the early years" of their co-authoring, Ede and Lunsford remembered "talking it out together," taking notes, doing some writing, and dividing it up when they "reached a certain point of understanding" and could work separately on part of a draft. For their first project, Ede had most of an article written when Lunsford became involved, but with subsequent projects, they started together with a "kernel" and "trad[ed] things back and forth," "heavily rewrit[ing]" each other's contributions. She feels word processors have made a significant difference in their co-authoring; "working in our old IBM correctable typewriters was more isolating." Before word processing, revision meant retyping. They told a story of working on an essay on classical rhetoric:

> *Ede:* I kept moving things around . . . and we had one typewriter . . . Andrea hates to revise, and I'm messier than that. So here's poor Andrea . . . it's her birthday. . . we're in the University Motel . . . we're working on this essay with like five thousand footnotes . . . and I keep coming in from the other room and saying, "Andrea . . ."
> *Lunsford:* "That passage has to go back to the beginning . . ."
> *Ede:* And it means retyping . . . and rethinking . . .
> *Lunsford:* And all the transitions have to be changed . . .
> *Ede:* There was nothing like "save as" and let's just move this around and see how it is . . . it was just unbelievable . . .
> *Lunsford:* I was ready to kill you . . .
> *Ede:* You were . . .

They have never co-authored a piece without being together "physically at least part of the time." For their book *Singular Texts/Plural Authors,* they each took the lead for different chapters, "revised things back and forth," and co-wrote the last chapter. But according to Ede, "I think there's a progression which might be perverse . . . toward writing everything together at the screen . . . the most recent things we have done when we have been physically together we have written together with one of us sitting at the computer." When we sent Ede and Lunsford copies of the transcript to review, we underlined "perverse" and put several question marks in the margin, thinking perhaps we had misunderstood. In the margin of the returned transcript, Ede wrote, "Yes, that can be right. It's crazy in a sense to write this way—crazy and wonderful!" But they do it. In fact, on the day of our interview, we first found them huddled over a laptop computer, working on their latest undertaking.

Knight and Adams "usually start with a conversation and then go off and have some time to incubate and then bring that back together . . . sometimes it's big sections or small sections." In the proceedings chapter they co-authored, these separately incubated pieces were the "chunks between the beginning and the end," but they co-wrote "right there together" the "set up" and the conclusion. Bonacci and Johnson co-wrote part of a chapter together, but most of the co-authoring for their text involved writing first drafts of separate chapters, exchanging them, "messing them up," and coming together to suggest revisions. However, they attributed not doing more co-writing to their hectic schedules: "students running in and out . . . it's not like we really got to put our heads together all that much." They both teach five classes each, so their lack of time is an important player in their collaboration.

The teams we have just discussed do at least some word-by-word composing, but several of the teams do not co-write at all. Oldman and Kent get together after one of them has written the first draft, discuss it, and one of them revises the draft based on their discussion. This meeting, discussion, and revision process continues until they each have a copy of the final draft which they polish individually and then polish together, but they do not compose face-to-face. According to Kathleen Strickland, her and Jim's co-authoring often begins with "sort of epiphanies . . . all of a sudden something happens and I'll say, 'Why don't we write about that?' or he'll say, 'Why don't you write that down?'" Of course, they talk a great deal. One of them freewrites, puts ideas down on paper, the other asks questions, one takes the draft and works on it, and so forth. Kathleen explained further, "At certain points in the manuscript we sit and actually do a lot of talking and work with the manuscript . . . but I think authoring . . . we can co-author . . . but I don't think we co-write . . . we're very different people."

When Besemer and O'Quin began co-authoring, Besemer wrote most of the review of literature for their articles, and O'Quin crunched the numbers from the data and interpreted the statistics. Now, though, they have developed more flexibility and their roles are not so fixed, partly because Besemer took it upon herself to learn how to design and analyze quantitative research. "Talk gets things rolling," and they usually start writing from the data they have gathered, write different sections, "put it together" so the different sections don't sound as if two different people wrote them, and then read the whole thing separately and suggest changes—but they have never written any part of an article face-to-face. Besemer explained: "I wouldn't want someone over my shoulder at first . . . I need to get into it alone," and O'Quin added that she has "trouble thinking with someone else." From this explanation, we understood them to be saying they see thinking and writing as similar, but talking and writing as two distinctly different processes—they seem to be able to think with someone else if they are talking but not if they are writing.

In a study of co-authoring in academia and business, Allen, Atkinson, Morgan, Moore, and Snow (1987) found that the only group that composed together word-by-word on a regular basis was made up of a pair who had a long-term co-authoring relationship. We would like to be able to conclude that the longer the co-authoring relationship, the more likely that co-authors will come to write word-by-word, but Strickland and Strickland and Besemer and O'Quin—long-standing teams who do not co-write—and Knight and Adams, who do co-write but are just now working on their second project, refute that claim (as does our own experience). We can't even posit that the more intimate the relationship, the more likely co-writing will take place since Kathleen and Jim Strickland fit the "intimate" category best. Trying many combinations of longevity of relationship, intimacy level of relationship, discipline, degree of feminine approach, introversion and extraversion, and even age and gender, we could not find patterns or any particular criteria in our group of interviewees that point to likely co-writing, except, of course, a shared feminine approach.

However, a few commonalities among the co-authors who do not compose face-to-face—James and Kathleen Strickland; Besemer and O'Quin; Pike, Davis and Ellison; and Kent and Oldman—do suggest themselves. Almost all the members of these four teams feel strongly that writing is at some point completely individual or that a scholar should be able to show they can write on their own. According to Kathleen Strickland, "Writing is still very personal"—she sees her dissertation as hers alone and feels a person writes alone before co-authoring takes place. In fact, she said to us,

> You said you couldn't separate what you [Kami] and Michele have written together . . . because what you write together becomes one . . . and that's what happens when you co-author . . . but think about the process you went through to get to that . . . you didn't have a mind meld or anything.

Besemer forced herself to do the statistical analysis for her dissertation without any help from O'Quin to prove to herself that she could crunch the numbers on her own, and so no one would "think I was just riding the coattails of someone else." O'Quin sees the need to identify individual products at some point; her concern is for "your perception of yourself" and others as needing a "crutch":

> At least once in your life, dammit . . . you need to go out there and stand on your own two feet . . . do it all yourself. That's certainly based on stereotype, but some stereotypes have a kernel of truth. There are times when it is important for an individual person to accomplish a goal alone.

As much as he values collaboration, Oldman felt he had to singly author his text even though he admitted he would have made full professor if he had co-authored it; he needed to prove to himself that he could do it: "My own personality style is somewhat disorganized and sort of random abstract kind of thing . . . and this is sort of a testament to the fact that when push comes to shove I actually could do it." Kent even hinted that "there's an attitude [in their department] that he might not have been able to [write the book on his own]." Kent also wanted us to understand that not "everything [they] do is collaborative all the time"; she said, "There are personal thoughts of mine that I don't want someone else's thoughts on . . . 80 percent of what I do can be totally collaborative but there still needs to be 20 percent of that that's me . . . that everyone will know it's mine."

Pike pointed out that she and Davis have published on their own and Ellison was writing a "thesis that ha[d] nothing to do with us whatsoever." She went on to say, "In terms of our collaboration the reason it's possible is because each of us stands on our own two feet in the relationship, and so nobody gets swept under the rug." Also, Davis admitted (at the end of the interview after having discussed his growing appreciation of collaboration), "I've always respected putting out a massive volume of one's own . . . having your name solely on the book."

Unlike Ede and Lunsford, and Roen and Brown, who consider all writing to be collaborative, these co-authors believe that some writing is done, and even should be done, on one's own. We might tentatively suggest that writers who hold this view certainly value the epistemic and nurturing rewards of co-authoring but perhaps are less likely to co-write. More research is needed in this area. This view also supports the belief that accomplishing a difficult task on our own gives us the confidence we need to tackle other solitary and collaborative tasks. We know we have felt this way, but we don't know why. We need to resist western culture's irrational insistence that realizing a goal "all by myself" is somehow more challenging and valuable than realizing it collaboratively.

Whatever their views on the value of individual work, we can say that process did not seem to be of major concern to any of the teams; they did not talk of consciously deciding they would exchange drafts, co-write or not co-write. Perhaps their compatibility had to do simply with matching preferences for co-authoring processes; co-authoring would break down if one partner could not write with another person in the room and the other did not feel they could create a complete product unless they composed text jointly. We think, though, that all of them would agree with Knight and Adams, who came to the realization during the interview that "if the process is running OK you can devote more energy to the content . . . it gives [us] a lot more content clarity."

THE PRICE OF PRACTICE

> *[Consensus] can be cumbersome.*
> Elizabeth Kent

Fox and Faver (1984), who interviewed social scientists about collaboration but feel their study "reflects a range of methodologies and types of scholarly projects" (349), mention excessive time, financial expenses, the "personal, socioemotional cost of developing and maintaining a good working relationship," and lack of commitment as "process costs" of collaboration (352–53); "outcome costs" are delays because of a "sluggish collaborator," deciding who gets credit, and possible loss of quality (353–54). In a study of educators who collaborate, Joan P. Isenberg, Mary Renck Jalongo, and Karen D'Angelo Bromley (1987) report similar findings: fully 50 percent of the educators studied related negative experiences with collaboration. In addition, Isenberg, Jalongo, and Bromley found these drawbacks: inability to achieve consensus, the inability to resolve differences in writing styles, and "clash of philosophies and interests," which includes decisions about "purpose, focus, audience, and outlet for the publication." But for the respondents to their questionnaire, the most "pervasive and difficult" problem was "failure to share a vision" (14) (we told a story earlier of Jim Strickland's problems with a co-author who "wanted things to go in different directions").

As we considered the co-authors in our study in light of the above reports, we found that none of the teams brought up money, and while some wished they had more time, and all but one team admitted that co-authoring took more time than singly authoring, they did not see the extra time as a "cost." In fact, Besemer and O'Quin agreed with Isenberg, Jalongo, and Bromley's findings that collaboration saves time because the workload can be shared. In addition, all the interviewees saw the quality of their products as enhanced by collaboration. None of these successful co-authors saw maintenance of a good relationship, allocation of credit, or reaching a consensus as difficult or costly. They saw the differences in their writing styles as complementary and reported no serious difficulty in resolving differences in writing and working styles. Perhaps most importantly, the members of each team shared ideologies, philosophies, and a vision with each other.

However, almost all of the teams talked about unsuccessful collaborations that involved hierarchy and control—problems which created obstacles and incurred costs in terms of working to maintain a productive relationship and assigning credit. And of course, many of the co-authors told stories of unsatisfying co-authoring involving a writing partner's lack of commitment to the project, which sometimes resulted in delays. Two of the teams, though, brought up a disadvantage not addressed by Fox and Faver, or Isenberg, Jalongo, and Bromley, although this drawback could involve time and quality of product. These two teams, Adams and Knight, and Oldman and Kent, whose departments enjoy collaborative ambiances, told stories of collaboration run rampant. Interestingly, the co-authors in these teams all chose pseudonyms!

Kent and Oldman opened our interview by enthusiastically describing the collaboration that goes on constantly in their department. Oldman told us that the eight people in their department "collaborate formally and informally all the time," and Kent added, "Nothing we do individually is individual . . . everything I've written they've all read before it goes in [to the publisher]." They both feel all members of the department are "tolerant of each other's styles" and that divergent thinking is valued, but the fact that "everyone has to come [to the meetings] and say their feelings about something or their ideas before we can vote" can be cumbersome. Kent confessed, "I think our department values it too much . . . we don't get things done," and Oldman agreed.

Their leadership insists on consensus, but as a group, they have difficulty reaching consensus, so both Kent and Oldman favor delegating a decision about a particular issue to a committee, and then supporting the recommendation of the committee. Kent said in the year she's been in the department, only two issues have finally come to a vote; the department knew beforehand that the vote on one of them would be unanimous, and they put off the vote on the second issue because a potential dissenter wasn't present. Oldman and Kent are concerned that when the department hires more people, there will be even more dissenters and even fewer decisions made. Oldman and Kent told a humorous story that illustrates the situation:

> *Oldman:* We actually debated this month in the department to put time frames [on decisions] . . . we'll have an hour to digress and bond but then we'll vote . . . and we voted against it.
> *Kent:* We never got it to a vote!
> *Oldman:* We never got it to a vote . . . I'm sorry . . . exactly right.

They grapple with wanting a voice in departmental decision-making but also wanting the department to run more efficiently. As Kent said, "We're having a huge accreditation review, and we're trying to demonstrate a lot of decisions we've made, but we as a large group can't make any decisions." They have too much of a good thing.

Their struggle spotlights one of the possible drawbacks to collaboration: the need for consensus. The ethical concern is that voices will be silenced in the interest of coming to agreement, but in response to our question about Trimbur's reservations concerning consensus, Roen said, "If I don't collaborate, it's not a matter of silencing . . . there's no opportunity for the other person to say *anything*." All of the teams in our study had difficulty articulating their ability to reach consensus; they spoke of "just adjusting" or "somehow working it out." They all denied having to give up anything dear to them in order to reach consensus. Brown suggested perhaps a facility for consensus has more to do with "accommodation" than "appropriation"—perhaps finding a way to include all views, or at least respectfully hear all views, before deciding which to include. In their co-authored article, Hui and Grant characterize such accommodation as "finding a common ground with multiple alternatives," and Pike described it as "not so much a matter of any of us changing course in any regard as just beginning to see the connections that exist between our ideas and our working styles."

Jim and Kathleen Strickland feel that collaboration has heightened their awareness of audience, and they see a connection between that awareness and consensus: "It makes sense that *we* have consensus if we're taking our readers into consideration." Standing by her conviction that some writing is individual, Kathleen said that consensus is not necessary when students are giving each other feedback on personal essays (or even when the instructor is providing feedback); "The writing still belongs to the writer," and Kathleen gives students the space to make decisions about their own writing. "But in co-authoring," she added, "you lose the right to say, 'This is mine . . . I'm not going to change it.'" She and Jim agreed that writing together means "negotiating meaning," which they do "a lot and easily."

The aptitude for reaching consensus seems to be both necessary for and an outcome of a relationship built on respect, trust, and genuine friendship; it's possible that people who are comfortable with a feminine approach are more willing to "accommodate" views other than their own. Shared vision is also key. Kathleen Strickland admitted that such accommodation "would be different if it's a philosophical issue that would change meaning," but she and Jim "are going the same direction" philosophically. Likewise, all of the co-authors' ideologies, interests, styles, and work ethics are compatible enough with their partners' that consensus is not even an issue. According to Hui, "The common things were just so strong . . . we didn't feel there was a need to sacrifice our own particular idea," and Pike celebrated seeing eye to eye with Ellison and Davis, being "in the same place." The interviewees seemed to take the ability to reach consensus as a given for successful co-authoring—several claimed they had never thought explicitly about it. And they often appeared surprised at our question about whether they saw consensus as necessary or problematic: how would they accomplish anything otherwise? Still, while consensus was not a stumbling block for the co-authors in our study, we think some of their reservations about requiring students to co-author may have had to do with fears of forced consensus. Perhaps a student assigned to a group of students she does not know well enough to respect or trust does not feel comfortable or safe enough to make her views known. Or the opposite is possible: a student who values the closeness and compatibility of his group may not want to "rock the boat" by disagreeing.

Knight and Adams are both also part of a department that, in the past, overvalued collaboration and insisted on consensus. Choosing his words

carefully, Adams told us (and Knight agreed) that under the department's former leadership,

> There was so much focus on collaboration that it actually became too much of a
> good thing, and too much of a good thing can be a bad thing. The metaphor we
> used was like playing basketball . . . everyone had to touch the ball . . . you had to
> pass the ball so many times before you shot it. We collaborated on everything, and it
> was absolutely wearing . . . team projects . . . team writing . . . team teaching . . . it was
> difficult because it got to the point that you couldn't do anything without checking
> with somebody. That extreme kind of put a choke on things . . . and then there were
> also the power trips and control in terms of how collaboration was defined and
> operationalized.

Members of the department felt forced into consensus. Their department
chair at the time was a well-known and powerful man, a man who was responsible for groundbreaking initiatives in their field and who liked to have his
imprint on every project and article (Knight's negative co-authoring experience was with this man). Knight felt that given more time, she and the chair
could have resolved some of their differences "over a glass of wine," but the
leadership changed, and that conversation never took place. Adams thought
she was overly optimistic; he did not think open discussion "would have made
any difference." Adams and Knight have since defined departmental collaboration for themselves; they feel that formerly, "the individual got lost," but that "a
strong department is based on strong individuals who have areas they are
known for and who are able to collaborate."

Both Oldman and Kent's, and Adams and Knight's, departments have experienced the "downside" of collaboration that occurs with forced consensus.
Kent and Oldman's chair looks for consensus out of a genuine desire to give
everyone a voice, and Adams and Knight's chair used his position to coerce
department members into agreement with his ideas and styles.

THEORY TO PRACTICE

There's really a strong interaction between method and substance.
Cybil Pike

Often teachers and scholars in academia—or at least in the field of composition—talk the talk well about the value of collaboration. They know the work of
such theorists as Vygotsky, Bakhtin, and Rorty and agree that knowledge is
socially constructed; they have read what Bruffee, LeFevre, and Gere and others
have to say about writing as a social act and about collaborative pedagogy. Yet,
they are unable or unwilling to walk the walk: they resist incorporating collaboration into their pedagogy and they continue to write ostensibly alone; or they

themselves co-author but are suspicious of student co-authoring; or they encourage student co-authoring but have no idea what such an activity feels like since they have never co-authored themselves. We can say, though, that the co-authors in our study all walk the walk, at least in the sense that they co-author and plan to continue to work together. And all of the team members but one include some kind of collaboration as part of their pedagogy.

Actually, although all the teams embody the theories of socially constructed knowledge, feminism, and asymmetrical reciprocity, most of them never explicitly mentioned they thought of working together as praxis; their conversations certainly illustrated how and why knowledge is socially constructed, and how nurturance and attention to difference contributed to their success, but they did not say they set out to put theory into practice. Most of them did not even talk about trying to exemplify theories they were writing about. They simply decided to work together because they were friends or partners or (initially) because they had complementary skills; their work came to illustrate these theories. They walk the walk in that they "do it"—they co-author, enacting, consciously or not, the theories that support that enactment. Only two teams spoke specifically of their co-authoring as a manifestation of the theory or philosophy that, in part at least, drives their work.

One team who thinks of their work as praxis is the team of Lunsford and Ede. They discussed how their co-authoring represents their theory on two levels, both of which we discussed earlier, so we will mention them briefly here. Lunsford characterized writing (and therefore co-authoring, since she feels all writing is collaborative) as epistemic, and she and Ede told many stories of how they learned together as they co-authored, sometimes arriving at a very different place than they imagined when they started. They are also committed to feminism and feel "it's a feminine statement to work collaboratively."

The other team is Davis, Pike, and Ellison. Davis feels his co-authoring with Pike and Ellison exemplifies what they are trying to say about politics, race, and sex in their book:

> Realizing that we have to deal with the consequences of things that have come to divide us, yet being able to work together irrespective of sexual differences and racial differences in a fairly harmonious project . . . is exemplary of the things we're trying to write about.

Pike agreed:

> There's a really a strong interaction between method and substance. I don't think they're really quite distinguishable . . . I'm sure we can't do the substance without the method we have . . . .and you can't pull the method out from the substance . . . I think they're just integral to one another.

Davis added, "It seems to me it's just a mutual attempt to further understand and conceptualize and put forth what it is we see in looking at these myths and metaphors and stories." In one of his few speeches, Ellison expressed rather emphatically that their work helped him put the theory he was writing about in his thesis into practice:

> I have to say the experience I've had working with them has actually made my thesis very real because I was writing about a perspective that transcends boundaries, and I was always thinking of that in theoretical form until . . . working with Dr. Pike and Dr. Davis it's living it rather than just this theory. . . . it's made my thesis very real.

Ellison's conviction is supported by Fox and Faver's research (1984). They found that "interaction with, and commitment to, a collaborative partner helps take the project out of the purely cognitive realm and makes it a more 'real' or 'actual' endeavor . . . working with others can create a social context and reality for the research" (351). Davis and Pike also feel that, in addition to representing their theory in their work, their co-authoring exemplifies for students the possibilities for working productively through differences in race and gender. When Michele observed that teachers who work together demonstrate through their actions "the kinds of things that need to happen with our students in their futures," Davis agreed that "it was good for students to see us [Pike and Ellison and him] working together."

The co-authors in our study also walk the walk even into the headwind of academic tradition and convention. Many of the co-authors admitted that while their departments valued their collaborative scholarship, their fields outside their departments, their institutions, and academia at large are suspicious of co-authoring. For other interviewees, co-authoring is not valued even in their departments, and they have encountered difficulty with tenure and promotion; many of the co-authors admitted to the necessity of singly authoring at least a few publications so their departments or prospective employers could see they are capable of working on their own. Still, a few of the interviewees have only co-authored publications and have no plans to singly author, so rewarding do they find the experience and so strongly do they believe their co-authored work is better than anything they could write alone. In the next chapter, we will show how their co-authoring situates them in the academy.

6 CO-AUTHORED SCHOLARSHIP AND ACADEMIA

Frame lock, and its cousin tone jam, are the prevailing stylistic constraints of the sanctioned prose of the profession. . . . The keepers of the scholarly flame, a torch passed hand to hand and fist to mouth by generations of professional standard bearers and girdle makers, search committees and admissions officers, editors and publishers, maintain, against all comers, that the argument for this or that or the other must maintain appropriate scholarly decorum.

Charles Bernstein

This chapter will look at how co-authoring, and what the co-authors believe about it, positions them in the academy. Mark Bonacci was the only author who felt confident that co-authoring is valued in his field. Of the other team members, some are sure co-authored scholarship is valued in their departments, but most of the others perceive that co-authoring can be risky in that it is suspect in their institutions and their disciplines. This chapter will also include the interviewees' opinions of co-authored dissertations, and will explore whether their fields' attitudes toward co-authored scholarship affect their own views on collaborative dissertations.

PUBLISHING, YES . . . DISSERTATING, MAYBE

Ahhh . . . of course!
Lisa Ede

When we asked Susan Besemer and Karen O'Quin whether co-authoring was viewed as problematic in their fields (library science and psychology), they shook their heads "no"; they see a great many co-authored articles in their journals. But when we asked if their departments would look askance at co-authoring in deliberations concerning tenure, O'Quin told the story we related earlier about more points toward promotion being awarded to singly authored publications. Of course, Besemer's conviction that she needed to publish something "purely her own" (a conviction applauded by O'Quin) indicated a concern about how the field of creativity studies, in which Besemer was getting her Ph.D., will view her if she has only published jointly.

Their views on co-authored dissertations reflect these concerns. As we did with all the teams in the study, we presented a hypothetical situation: "What would you do if two students asked you to advise a co-authored dissertation?" O'Quin immediately replied, "I don't think I'd be allowed to . . . in psychology a dissertation is seen as being an individual product . . . I guess in the hypothetical [if the institution allowed it], it depends on how much I buy into the idea . . . I don't know." They both thought it would "be interesting in the future to have such a thing," but O'Quin could not imagine a co-authored dissertation in psychology because of the "emphasis on the person." She went on to say, "A dissertation is presumably the one place in the world where this is your product . . . you're being awarded a degree after your name. What are they going to do? . . . give you half a Ph.D.? You've got the rest of your life to work with somebody." As we mentioned in the previous chapter, her concern is for the students' perceptions of themselves and how the world perceives them. She fears the academy would see them as needing a crutch, and that the students themselves would not feel confident about their abilities, would always wonder if they could have done it on their own.

Besemer took a different stance based on her recent experiences writing the final paper for her doctoral program's final project, a set of publishable or published articles. She doubted that co-authored dissertations would be common any time soon because of the "traditional environment . . . which seems essentially antagonistic the way it sets up the ultimate hurdle," but she saw that co-authored dissertations, even with the challenges that working together present, might dramatically alter the loneliness and solitude that usually attend that final academic gate.

> Taking as a given that it would be legal and acceptable, I can argue both ways. I can say, "Oh, this is too hard . . . don't add agony to it by adding the interpersonal dimension." On the other hand maybe that's just what you need in order to make the whole process more palatable . . . more humane . . . because certainly some of the things that have been the most troublesome to me in my doctoral work have been this tremendous isolation and lack of support . . . and that's just what I've gone back to over and over again in this discussion about the kinds of values that working together gives you.

She even wondered if getting her Ph.D. was going to be worth enduring what she saw as "the loneliest experience" she'd ever had; she felt at times that she "was slipping a gear" and sometimes wished she "had never gotten into it." When she said this, we remembered a student in our graduate program warning a group of us who were about to begin work on our dissertations that we were embarking on "one of the loneliest experiences of our lives."

Besemer's yearning for relief from the isolation she has experienced is an example of the reason many scholars seek co-authors; Fox and Faver (1984), in a study of social scientists who collaborate, partially credit increasing collaboration in academia to "the desire to alleviate professional isolation." They found that developing and maintaining an identity as a researcher "depends partly upon having active researchers in one's reference group. . . . collaboration and colleagues are particularly important for scholars . . . who face conflicting demands for other-than-research performance" (350). Besemer, and most of the co-authors in our study, certainly wear many hats—teacher, administrator, researcher, writer—and might well be isolated as scholars if not for their relationships with each other.

We also told Besemer and O'Quin of our belief that all dissertations are co-authored to a certain extent but that the co-authors are not acknowledged, and Besemer admitted feeling guilty for not acknowledging O'Quin's part in her final project for her Ph.D. She had denied herself help from O'Quin for the last article, but "the whole flow of the research has certainly had her hand on it."

When we shared with Mark Bonacci and Katherine Johnson other co-authors' stories of persecution they suffered because they had published with another scholar, Bonacci said, "Wow . . . how weird," and when we added that some had been asked to highlight their individually written sentences in an article, he exclaimed, "Oh how limited . . . it so goes against the so-called credo of collegiality . . . could you imagine us [him and Johnson] redlining what parts of the book we contributed? Oh, God!" To our question "Do you feel those who are looking at your publications value co-authored pieces as much as they would value individually authored ones?" Bonacci answered, "Oh, yes." Johnson asked, "Do they?" and Bonacci answered, "I'm sure of it." Not having published prior to the text with Bonacci, and being tenured without publication, Johnson had no idea how co-authoring would affect promotion in her field, but she had seen numerous co-authored articles and books in sociology.

To our question about co-authored dissertations, Johnson responded, "Whoa . . . that would be a tough one . . . probably because I never heard of such a thing before." Like Kathleen Strickland, she would want to "find out if it's even possible from the university's standpoint . . . go to the dean of graduate students." Based on seeing only one (himself) out of six graduate students on the same fellowship finish their degrees, Bonacci had concerns about "one person falling by the wayside and the other person being left holding the bag," but he thought it was "an interesting concept." If she advised such a dissertation, Johnson would "ask the graduate students to go into great detail about what they've done and what they want to do," which is the kind of reflection we are advocating, but she "would entertain it if it was a possibility." Like Besemer, she felt "having a partner would make life a lot easier . . . and I don't mean to have less work or anything . . . writing a dissertation is a lonely endeavor." She felt as if her dissertation was somewhat collaborative in that she had guidance from her advisor, but Bonacci, who thought his *would* be collaborative, was told, "Just do it and I want a publication out of this at the end."

"It would depend on where you were," was Cybil Pike, Alexander Davis, and Ben Ellison's response to our question about co-authoring and promotion, but they did not really know the climate in their field concerning co-authorship since Pike had been promoted with both singly and co-authored publications and Davis had gotten tenure with a singly authored article. Davis remembered refusing to acknowledge work with Pike on a grant when he was putting together his materials for tenure. He felt he had to "stress individuality" but, having worked with Pike and Ellison, his feelings have changed somewhat—"that was a growing exercise."

When we broached the subject of a collaborative dissertation, Davis said, "I've never heard of that . . . I guess I would advise against it . . . I would think they [the graduate students] would need to distinguish themselves within the context of the dissertation in terms of entering their particular fields." Pike was "intrigued by the idea" but agreed with Davis: "So critical to our relationship is that each of the three of us can stand on our own feet." They were also concerned about how a scholar who had co-authored a dissertation would fare on the job market.

However, later in the interview, when we told them our original design for a co-authored dissertation, Davis said, "That would be really cool," and Pike felt "the idea of the meta dimension was brilliant," but she pointed out that "what's possible in one context is entirely impossible in another," and that a co-authored dissertation is impossible in an academic context. We explained that we had wanted to set a precedent, but Pike observed what we had come to see—that the institution needs a precedent which precedes us, and Davis made us all laugh with his observation that "in some cases you can set a precedent but be so unprecedented it won't be appreciated until it's posthumously!"

About whether dissertations are inherently co-authored, Davis did not think of the work with his committee as collaborative; in fact, he said his experience with having his first topic rejected, and his committee's aggressive feedback as he wrote the dissertation, "made [him] think twice about collaborating." He had considered his committee members as friends with him and each other, and he saw the friendship "crumbling in the process." Pike told a long story concerning her dissertation; her findings "completely contradicted everything [an important scholar in her field] had done," so she and her advisor "negotiated and negotiated and negotiated" because her mentor was worried about offending that scholar. Pike felt that experience gave her practice in dealing with "difficult people," and it certainly sounds as if she and her advisor worked closely throughout the process.

Matthew Oldman and Elizabeth Kent's stories about their department illustrated that, in spite of overemphasis on consensus, they enjoy a local collaborative ambiance. They admitted, "We're odd .. we're not mainstream . . . it's an enclave" and that the emphasis on working together is not "top down [from the university's administration]." In fact, when Kent was hired, the dean told her, "Don't talk to those people [in her department] . . . they're going to take you in the wrong direction." The following exchange shows how the members of the department view themselves and how they think other departments view them:

Kent: We are supporting our own environment . . . there is no supporting our environment . . . not from the closest above . . .

Oldman: No . . . no . . . our dean . . .

Kent: To the furthest above to parallels in other departments . . .

Eodice: So it's really local . . .

Oldman: Absolutely . . .

Kent: They laugh at us when we go to lunch together . . .

Oldman: Yes. . . that's right . . .

Eodice: Yeah . . . OK . . . joined at the hip . . .

Oldman: Joined at the hip . . . and fighting together most of the time . . .

Kent: Well . . . there's all the department sitting at a table [in the cafeteria] . . .

Oldman: Talking shop . . .

Kent: And they're all laughing [people in other departments] . . . and they're telling us to be quiet . . .

Kent: No other place I applied to or interviewed with had that feeling . . . the excitement . . . it's kind of an interesting philosophy.

As far as the attitude toward co-authored publication in their field, Oldman was sure they would not be hurt by writing "collaborative pieces here [in their department] . . . but I know there might be some places where that might happen." Kent agreed; she was even told when she was hired that "the rule of thumb was that collaboration [in their department] was just as good as individual [publication]." Oldman said, though, that he is and always will be on the promotion and tenure committee because there "are a couple of forces of evil . . . that count [co-authored pieces] as half of a publication," and he wants to be sure he is there to champion co-authored works. According to Kent, "a lot of departments outside [of their department] don't realize the value of collaboration," and since she does not know how long she will be there, she, as we mentioned earlier, feels she needs to publish on her own.

Kent's story about her dissertation seems to support the view that all dissertations are intrinsically collaborative; on one hand, she saw hers as "mine and mine alone," "whatever you [her advisor] say . . . goes in there, and that wasn't collaborative." However, she went on to say, "It was me convincing my advisor . . . in terms of the writing he was handing back and forth, and you could find a paragraph or two he wrote." She was clearly not thinking in terms of the intertextuality of writing and Bakhtin's chain of utterances (Michele wrote in the margin of the transcript, "She [Kent] is working alone but with a full load of heteroglossia—multiple voices/perspectives to hear and mesh"). When we explained that we think of input and guidance as collaboration, she acknowledged that her advisor's input, guidance, and standard and deadline setting would fit that definition of collaboration, but she did not think of it as collaboration. She saw it more as doing what her advisor told her to do so she could successfully jump through hoops, and she added that if her advisor had done what he should have, he would be the second author on the article from her thesis. She did, however, define her defense and revisions as collaboration because of the tone of those activities; she had worked collaboratively on earlier projects with the people involved [people other than her advisor], and she felt they valued her ideas and treated her in a more nurturing way. So Kent narrows the definition of collaboration somewhat: working together is not collaboration unless there is respect and care involved. All the teams in our study would fit her definition, but perhaps that definition explains why so many academicians do not see their dissertations as collaborative.

Kent and Oldman's institution will be starting a doctoral program in the near future, so it was not unreasonable for them to imagine advising a dissertation. Kent's first response to our query about co-authored dissertations was, "I would say 'no' . . . not because I don't agree with it but because no one else is going to agree with it, and you're not going to be able to go through the hoops." She went on to say, "I would like to be in a position at that point to challenge the establishment and let them [the graduate students] do it if it were a sound idea"; but at the time of our interview, she felt she was not in a position to change anything, so she felt the only sound advice would be to discourage co-authoring.

Oldman agreed with her, but he was grinning because he had just realized we were the two students in our scenario who wanted to do a co-authored dissertation. He referred to Vygotsky for support of his position: "What we can do together today we can do by ourselves tomorrow . . . even though there's no meaning outside our interaction we have to go make meaning apart," but he acknowledged the paradox there. For him, students' "stand[ing] by their own work" is important, but he did feel that dissertation advisor should be a collaborative role. He also told us a story of hearing a presentation given by a woman whose dissertation topic was collaboration in reading. She had found that 95 percent of the research published in four reading journals over the last ten years was collaborative, and she asked the question, "What prepared me in my dissertation to join that world?" Her question echoes Judy Entes's, who "investigated scholarly writing by multiple authors" but was told the day after she defended her dissertation that she "should publish only in prestigious refereed journals and *alone*" (1994, 48).

In thinking about their field's attitude toward co-authored scholarship, Roja Grant and Emily Hui told us a story about a listserv involving educators in their field. They had followed "a *big* debate" concerning whether or not people whose publications were all co-authored could compete for a grant, and Hui said that "people have very strong opinions that, no, we cannot [co-author]." Grant added, though, that many on the listserv supported co-authoring and wrote messages like "this is what learning is." Hui did not address her own experience with attitudes in her field toward co-authoring, perhaps because, up to that time, she had always worked as an adjunct, and promotion had not been an issue. She had had difficulty securing a full-time position, but we don't know whether the fact that all her publications were co-authored was a factor. We do know that Grant's re-appointment was conditional (but was later made unconditional), partly because her publications were co-authored.

The evening of our interview with Hui and Grant, we stayed overnight at Hui's, and the next morning over coffee, we asked them how they felt about co-authored dissertations (they knew we had written a proposal for one). Hui's immediate response was, "Why not?" She thinks of her dissertation as collaborative because of all the "back and forth" with her advisors and their help with revision, and she wonders why the process could not be the same with peers. Grant had also worked closely with her dissertation advisor. When we narrowed the question to whether they would advise a co-authored dissertation, both answered that it would depend on the students and the project. The students would have to be strong academically and aware of the problems they could encounter in a job search. Patricia A. Sullivan (1994) doubts that co-authoring will be an option for graduate students working on dissertations in the near future because "a formidable array of Romantic and Enlightenment tenets continue to be ranged against such a possibility . . . in the humanities," but she does call for redefining the dissertation as "intertextual, interdependent, and collaborative" (27). We too expressed our doubts about co-authored dissertations becoming acceptable any time soon, but Grant thought the "day is getting close" and that much unacknowledged collaboration already takes place.

We mentioned earlier the problems Lisa Ede had getting tenure because of her co-authoring with Andrea Lunsford. They also told us the story of Ed Corbett's being "horrified," "almost apoplectic," and "puzzled" about their decision to co-author an essay for Robert Connors's book on classical rhetoric and modern discourse, which was their first co-authored project. They had

thought Corbett would "think it was especially wonderful if [they] collaborated," but he cautioned them against it. Other people cautioned them as well
that they would never get tenure, expressing "shock, consternation, or dismay"
at their co-authoring, but Ede and Lunsford were "naïve" in their belief that
they "were not the odd ones . . . everybody in the world writes collaboratively"
(we had no trouble identifying with their naïveté). They had innocently
thought they "would just go out and get this information and people would go,
'Ahhh . . . of course!'" We wondered what made them feel they could ignore the
warnings. Lunsford answered,

> Well, we were just bullheaded. I think I had been promoted, and I had written quite
> a bit that looked like it was by myself even though I don't think anything is really by
> yourself . . . but then Lisa came up for tenure after me, and that was more of an
> ordeal . . . they solicited unsolicited letters from me . . . at the departmental level
> speaking to the nature of our collaboration. At the dean's level I got another letter
> that said, "We want a line count of how many lines you wrote and how many lines
> Lisa wrote."

Lunsford convinced the committee that a line count was not possible, and
Ede was tenured, although she "remember[s] the dean saying very specifically
that if [she] ever wanted to be promoted to full professor [she] would have to
do more single-authored work." In reference to their already published co-
authored articles and their book *Singular Texts/Plural Authors*, the dean
thought they were "very tricky" to "figure out a way to write about [their] collaborative writing"—as if they felt they had to justify their collaboration or
couldn't think of anything else to write about! Interestingly, Lunsford felt they
were "lucky neither one was at someplace like Princeton . . . or [they] would
never have gotten out of the ballpark." We assume she felt convention is even
more entrenched at "prestigious" institutions.

Their story illustrates not only the attitude in the humanities toward co-
authored scholarship, but also Lunsford and Ede's willingness to take risks.
According to Fox and Faver (1984), "For those who challenge established
methods and views, collaboration may be a source of sustenance and support"
(355), and perhaps Ede and Lunsford, even though they attribute their press-
ing on to naïveté, felt on some level safer to challenge tradition because they
were challenging it together. The other teams did not speak directly of taking
risks, but the risk is understood if the discipline does not value collaborative
work as highly as singly authored work.

Ede and Lunsford knew about our attempt to write a co-authored dissertation because we had been communicating with them by email, and they had
been supportive and sympathetic; they both feel it's time for collaborative

dissertations. As we said in chapter one, Ede reminded us in one email message that "academic bureaucracies are terrifically entrenched." She also wrote that she'd received at least three other emails or letters like ours from graduate students hoping "to do a collaborative thesis or dissertation," but to her knowledge, none had been successful (August 2, 1997). Lunsford wrote in an email message that she worked for "two years to get the grad school to 'allow' collaborative research proposals to compete for funding" (August 2, 1997), and in our interview she expressed doubt that she "could get a collaborative dissertation at Ohio State." She would be "willing to try it if somebody wants to do it" but fears even if the department approved a co-authored dissertation, the graduate school would block it. In addition, as supportive as Lunsford and Ede were, they expressed concern about the "red flags" a co-authored dissertation might raise when we went on the job market. Lunsford and Ede have taken this issue beyond mere conversations within the field of composition; they recently issued a challenge to their colleagues in the humanities with a strong statement in a *PMLA* article.

> What might it mean, for instance, to acknowledge the inherently collaborative nature of single-authored dissertations and the impossibility of making a truly "original" contribution to knowledge. Would the sky fall if, upon occasion, Ph.D. students wrote dissertations collaboratively? . . . . What work of redefinition will make way for understanding the contributions of doctoral dissertations come not from some abstract originality but rather from their participation in complex layers of knowledge production? (2001, 358)

When we asked Mark Hurlbert and Michael Blitz how they see the climate in the humanities for collaborative work, Hurlbert answered, "Lousy . . . it's still lousy," and he admitted his co-authoring had caused him some trouble with promotion and tenure committees. He was reluctant to go into detail, but he did say,

> Generically speaking, it's one of the questions that inevitably comes up in all tenure and promotion decisions . . . the hierarchy and relative weight of the work. Sometimes it's as banal as whose name is first . . . sometimes it's a complex as . . . "There's enough collaborative material here . . . overall who does what part of the work?" . . . and that's the question we can't answer.

Blitz added,

> It's provided for both of us some awkward moments because it's . . . especially in the humanities . . . people don't know what to make of collaborations . . . because interesting research in the humanities takes so many different final forms . . . and it's amazing how uninformed lots of people are about what research can look like . . .

what scholarship can look like . . . and so when you add the complication that you've worked with somebody else to produce a hybrid thing . . . then . . .

When we reminded them of Ede and Lunsford's being asked to do a line count, Blitz said, "I think we're ornery enough . . . if that were to happen we would just simply highlight alternating lines . . . alternating syllables." He feels everyone knows there is nothing new about collaboration: "some of the people that have questioned me about it themselves collaborate . . . they're just nervous about it . . . 'Does it mean the same for you as it does for me?' . . . so it's an educating process." In their co-edited book, *Composition and Resistance*, Hurlbert and Blitz (1991) make their position on co-authored dissertations clear:

> In graduate education, we need to argue for the legitimacy of collaborative writing. We need to claim a place, for instance, for collaborative dissertations in our universities and in our profession. And we can begin this work on department graduate and program committees and at conferences and in professional publications. Until we do, our commitment to collaborative writing is just another fashion, just another hypocrisy. (169)

Over a decade later, their position has not changed. When we asked Blitz (in the interview) what he would do if two graduate students approached him about advising a co-authored dissertation, he said, "I would do everything in my power to help them." Of course the problem is that those with the most power continue to block such a dissertation. In a later email message, Blitz added,

> I am prepared to advocate strongly for those who want to do them [collaborative dissertations]. If enough full profs were to speak up/out there would be more response, I'm sure. But mostly people are fearful of rocking a boat they don't realize has already been sinking for decades. (January 3, 1999)

Hurlbert's agreeing to be part of the committee for the co-authored dissertation we originally proposed is proof that he supports such projects, and in a note attached to the returned transcript, he said,

> Given the growing number of scholars in composition who are collaborating on a regular basis, it is only a matter of time until collaborative dissertations become a regular practice. Indeed, it is strange that there is still such resistance to the idea of collaborative dissertations. One can only wonder what motivates this resistance; in fact, wouldn't it be interesting to research and report the sources of this resistance so the profession could make its own determinations on these people and their motives?

When we asked Duane Roen and Stuart Brown if either of them had run into snags with promotion and tenure because of their co-authoring, Roen said his numerous collaborative projects were partially responsible for his struggle for tenure (locating himself in the field of composition was also a factor). He had good relationships with people in the department, but the college committee "voted unanimously against" him, and then the university committee "voted unanimously for" him because some of its members were "sympathetic to the kinds of work he was doing."

Roen was also aware of our proposed co-authored dissertation since we had been exchanging email messages with him as well. In response to our scenario about two graduate students, he wrote in a message, "If two students came to me with a proposal to collaborate on a dissertation, I would do everything I could to support that proposal. That is, I would make the case with the graduate school" (August 1, 1997). During our interview, Brown and Roen agreed it's time for collaborative dissertations; Brown believes we'll get better dissertations, but he worries about the job market. At the time of the interview, two doctoral students at his institution had approached him about a co-authored dissertation, but he was "reluctant to go along" with the idea. He planned to propose a design whereby they could do collaborative research but produce "two distinct dissertations." We wondered if co-authored dissertations continue to get blocked because committees are made up of people "who've never collaborated possibly or had a bad experience," and Brown finished our thought with "like 90 percent of an English department."

Both Roen and Brown talked at length about the unacknowledged collaboration in the dissertation process. When we proposed that the dissertation is collaborative in nature, Brown's response was,

Totally . . . as a director and even as readers your imprimatur is all over that dissertation no matter how hands-off you try to be. I'm becoming increasingly hesitant about the term *director* because it's not my dissertation . . . so why should I direct this dissertation in a certain way?

He admitted that sometimes he has to step in and say, "No, do it this way" because of his expertise, and Roen added, "You know if it [the dissertation] isn't done a certain way, it's going to hurt the person on the job market." He also pointed out that "collaboration exists sort of separate from the dissertation writer among the committee members, and if one committee member has authority over other committee members, sometimes that ends up hurting the student." This observation seemed to support Kent's assertion that a dissertation may mean people are working together, but the collaboration is not always characterized by respect and trust.

For their co-authored book *Un-covering the Curriculum*, Strickland and Strickland received the "president's award for outstanding publication in 1994"—the first time two people from their university had been honored in that way because, according to Kathleen, "they [the university] don't usually do co-authored . . . but the university was pleased because it was two authors from the same university . . . maybe [the response to our co-authoring] would be different if we were from different universities." They have not felt any fallout because of their co-authoring, yet Creamer (1999) reports those who co-author with a spouse or partner have been "challenged during the process of a merit review to identify what role each had assumed" and have received "unmistakable messages about the importance of developing an independent scholarly record" (11). Perhaps the Stricklands had "not felt any fallout" because Kathleen is in the field of education, and she implied that collaboration is more accepted in that field. Also, Jim had singly authored several pieces before he co-authored with Kathleen. When we asked them how they would feel about advising a co-authored dissertation, Jim said, "It'd be OK with me," and Kathleen added, "Me too . . . I would jump at the chance!" She would, though, tell the graduate students, "Let's go through the system and see if this could happen" because

> change is very difficult, and people don't usually have very good reasons for not changing. Saying, "it's always been done that way" is the poorest reason I could possibly think of . . . it's just a cop-out . . . some of that is probably fear and some of it is ignorance . . . innovation and groundbreaking kinds of things are what make names for universities.

We told them some of the story of the struggle we'd had trying to get permission from the graduate school to at least include a co-authored literature review in both our dissertations, and Kathleen exclaimed, "And they'd be perfectly happy if you each rewrote that in your own words . . . I mean that is so foolish!" Jim even thought we should pass around a petition at the April 1998 Conference on College Composition and Communication asking people to support a collaboratively written review of literature. They were both sympathetic to our frustration, and Kathleen encouraged us to "write about the process." She said, "You may make even a bigger impact on this whole idea going through what you're going through than if it went through smoothly . . . you may not be able to do what you planned but this may help you and other people . . . it's a good story."

Knowing one of the central concerns about a co-authored dissertation, Jim asked, "So . . . is collaboration cheating? . . . I mean that's the issue. Do they think one of you is somehow getting away with something? . . . nobody was getting off easy." Kathleen offered more support with "You're not coming off the street to pull something. You've worked through this whole program . . . you have people who will say you are two good people. It's like everything we say about teaching . . . when you know the students in your class." They both understood that co-authoring is more work, not less, than authoring alone, and none of us could imagine two graduate students choosing to co-author if they were not capable scholars and serious about their work; nor could we imagine a teacher or a committee approving such a project if they were not confident of the students' abilities and integrity.

We suspected that co-authoring would be highly valued in Gilbert Adams and Julie Knight's field since team projects are important, but they said, "Not really." Adams explained, "In our [his field's] definition of scholarship, we have rank ordered from what supposedly carries the greatest weight to the least amount of weight in terms of scholarly products . . . and sole authorship of refereed publications is the number one." However, he and Knight did not feel their department operated that way, and Knight went on to say that their field's "scholarship definition is tied to hierarchy . . . this is the way you get promoted . . . I think it's very detrimental to academe altogether." Like Oldman and Kent's situation, collaboration is valued locally but not necessarily in their field in general or at their institution.

In response to our question about advising a co-authored dissertation, Knight said, "Oh, I think it's good," and Adams said, "I would have no problem with that." For some reason we were surprised—we said, "Really?" Adams explained, "This is the direction that we're moving in because we're talking about team-based projects . . . I think we're in a better position . . . our mind set is a little more open than the students' are." Three of his master's students were working on "essentially the same program of research," and when Adams proposed they work collaboratively, they "stated right out front that they did not want to write together." We asked him if he knew what their reservations were, but unfortunately, he did not explore that with them.

Knight had advised a partially co-authored master's thesis, "the first real collaborative piece that was ever done" at her institution. The students had originally been working on separate projects, but Knight suggested they combine it into one chapter of a conference proceedings. "They both got a very powerful publication out of it," and the chapter became the center piece for both their theses. Knight admitted, though, that "there were tensions up and down in style and who did what, and I've often thought in retrospect that I favored one over the other . . . even in my role as advisor and person working with them and collaborator . . . it was very complex." She felt any collaborative thesis would be "hard to advise because you're going to have to advise on content and process . . . folks would have to want to do that and be process aware."

Many of the teams offered suggestions for a dissertation that would at least be partly co-authored. Pike said, "I think if I was the graduate coordinator and had you two in the department, I would suggest two separate committees . . . do your ethnography [to Michele] . . . do your collaborative thing [to Kami]. . . and then do the meta-analysis and have it published word for word in each dissertation." Oldman "would make the collaborative paper part of the candidacy"; he "would like to see the ability to work effectively collaboratively as a prerequisite to studying alone."

We already discussed in chapter one Ede's suggestions for criteria that might make a co-authored dissertation more palatable to a graduate school: "The safest thing imaginable would be a problem/study that could not easily (if at all) be done by one single scholar" (August 2, 1997). Of course, we felt our proposal to study ourselves met that criterion. Lunsford also offered this tongue-in-cheek suggestion: "Why don't you just write a seven-hundred-page dissertation . . . you [Kami] write one page . . . you [Michele] write the next page. What are they going to do?" Of course, we had no trouble imagining what "they" might do, including rejecting the whole dissertation out of hand and requiring us to start over individually from scratch!

Knight thought the best arrangement for a co-authored dissertation would be for the students to write parts together and separately, as her two master's students did. In that arrangement

> you have an array for evaluation . . . almost like a profile of things. To me it's a much more powerful array because you have an array of process skills that are not taught. That's so sellable in terms of things that folks are looking for and need when they go to show the individual ones, so you have an incredible profile that I think is cutting edge.

She believes employers look for applicants who have experience working successfully with other people, and that collaborative scholarly work provides this experience. Her statement was compatible with Adams's view that "there's so much more that could be gained [in the process of co-authoring a dissertation] . . . so many other important skills that are developed." Those "beyond the cognitive" gains are evident in the co-authors' words about their relationships.

O'Quin, although she values the dissertation as a test of individual ability, could see two graduate students working together on data collection:

> You might work together in planning two pieces of a bigger pie, and each of you takes a piece of it . . . then you would collect the data together . . . perhaps even do

the analyses at least partly together . . . but then the individual writing parts would
have to be individualized.

Besemer agreed that "even that degree of collaboration might help with the
isolation . . . enough so that it makes it a very positive, more enjoyable process
to work on that dissertation than the other way."

David Damrosh, professor of English at Columbia University, sees the ability to collaborate as one of the abilities that could be demonstrated with the
dissertation: "Rather than always having to take the form of an individual
monograph, a dissertation could be thought of as a connected series of essays,
some written by the student alone, others in collaboration" (2000). As we mentioned earlier, Pike, Davis, and Ellison, and Adams and Knight, felt a combination of singly authored sections with co-authored sections would be the best
structure for a collaborative dissertation. Brown planned to advise his graduate students to conduct their research collaboratively but publish two separate
dissertations. (Actually, in our email exchanges with Roen, he had advised us
to do exactly that if we did not get permission to co-author our dissertation.)
Besemer and O'Quin, like Brown, were more comfortable with the notion of
collaborative research but two distinct dissertations, and Kent and Oldman
would support a collaborative paper as part of the requirements for candidacy
as proof of the ability to collaborate.

However, Hurlbert and Blitz, Lunsford and Ede, Strickland and Strickland,
Hui and Grant, Johnson and Bonacci, Roen, and Adams—a little over half of
the co-authors in our study, and representatives of four disciplines (six people
from the humanities)—were all able to imagine a dissertation in which the
voices of the co-authors are woven together from page one to the last page. Hui
and Grant, and Jim and Kathleen Strickland, are optimistic about co-authored
dissertations becoming acceptable and even common in the near future. It's
worth noting that all but one (Brown) of the co-authors in our study who are
in a position to advise a dissertation—Lunsford, Ede, Roen, and Hurlbert—
favor a truly co-authored document, one that has two names on the cover
page. Several of them stressed that we just need a precedent, and that they
would do all they could to support a co-authored dissertation; but all were
pessimistic about their ability to get a proposal for such a dissertation past
their graduate schools. The most they could hope was that attempts like ours
would gradually break down traditional barriers and open the door for co-
authored dissertations, especially in the humanities, in which there is yet to be
a co-authored dissertation.

In summary, over half the co-authors in our study think the time has come
for collaborative dissertations in some form and would be willing to advise

such a project. The interviewees who support collaborative dissertations know such support would require swimming upstream against a strong current of entrenched academic tradition, but we did not hear most of the co-authors speak explicitly of how their own publishing together challenges convention or presents risks. Still, their acts of co-authoring are subversive because they "unfix" patriarchal academic constructs (Doane and Hodges 1995, 52). Every co-authored scholarly work defies academic custom, consciously or not, and perhaps the risks become fewer and fewer as more and more scholarly work boasts two or more names on the title page.

When we were denied the opportunity to co-author a dissertation, one of the only things we could laugh about for a while was that those who had blocked our attempt were afraid, in part, that we would open the floodgates and graduate students would flock to advisors with proposals for collaborative dissertations. But some people who know better—those who co-author themselves—knew we would most likely be producing even more—and certainly working even harder and taking longer—if we co-authored a dissertation. We did in fact co-write the literature review, a chapter on collaborative dissertations that showed up in Kami's dissertation, and a great deal of the rationale for the design and methodology for both dissertations. We didn't plan how much we would do side by side, but intuitively we struck the right balance. It meant everything to us to do it that way—productive but not alone and lonely.

IMPLICATIONS FOR SCHOLARLY WRITING

The co-authors in our study, in their discussions of first author position—and of co-authoring with junior faculty, graduate students, and colleagues of equal rank—display a nurturing attitude toward fellow scholars rather than the competitive one that seems to be the norm in academia. One of the implications of our study is that such nurturing relationships are possible and desirable among academicians, and that co-authoring is one way to foster such relationships.

Most faculty at institutions of higher learning want to publish in order to be respected at those institutions and in their fields, but the pressure they feel to publish comes from the knowledge that their names must appear in the table of contents of a refereed journal if they want to hold on to their hard-earned faculty positions. Jeanne C. Marsh, writing in the field of social work, insists that research and scholarship should be the "preoccupation of faculty members . . . and must be a central criterion for tenure and promotion decisions" (1992,

134). In the same journal, Frederic G. Reamer, who takes a different view from Marsh's, relates that in the interview for his first teaching position, he was asked not about pedagogy or teaching interests but about what books he "planned to write in the next seven years" (1992, 130). In his well-known 1990 study, Boyer found that the pressure to publish had reached peak levels, and numerous articles support his findings. In the years since Boyer's study, the pressure has only increased—almost any tenure-track faculty member would concur that they must publish or perish. Of course, the rewards of tenure are professional and fiscal; a study by Stuart A. Kirk and Kevin J. Corcoran (1989) reveals that "not only does it pay to publish, but it pays quite well. . . . Faculty members who publish one article per year will, on the average, . . . receive one percent higher raises than those who do not publish." If an assistant professor published an article that initially earned a one percent merit raise, eventually that raise would amount to more than $12,800 (379–80).

As Reamer's story illustrates, junior faculty labor most under the pressure to produce scholarly writing—alone. A January 2001 issue of *The Chronicle of Higher Education* reports that expectations since 1990 *have* risen: "The most significant change . . . is the overwhelming pressure on young professors to publish early and publish frequently. At some institutions, that shift has come at the expense of teaching and service" (Wilson 2001, A12). In describing the history of their co-authoring relationship, Doane and Hodges admit they felt pressured, as graduate students entering the job market, to "adhere to certain academic notions of property and propriety in our way of constructing a text." By writing separate sections of their first article and combining the sections with few intrusions on each other's independent work, they "tried to respect autonomous authorship" because "an important condition for legitimizing our collaborative work was that we proved through our dissertations (and the books they became) that we each could successfully produce in the traditional way" (1995, 52). An article entitled "Perceptions of Life on the Tenure Track" by David Verrier (1994) explores "what it takes to become and what it means to be a faculty member," and he asserts that "themes appear to converge around the pressures and isolation facing young academics" (97). Junior faculty are expected to quickly distinguish themselves, yet they must do it alone with little guidance from experienced faculty; "they suppose that what matters is little more than hard work, especially efforts carried out independently and privately" (Boice 1993, 333). A study of female academics by Elizabeth G. Creamer and Catherine McHugh Engstrom (1996) supports Verrier's findings, adding that this isolation inhibits scholarly publication. According to Joanne Gainen (1993) and Robert Boice (1993), the challenges are multiplied for women and minorities; these faculty "too often fail in professorial careers" because they are "made to feel overworked and inefficient, incompetent, invisible, and unwelcome" (Boice, 291).

Verrier (1994) interviewed eighteen junior faculty members, and while one might expect that junior faculty, "in the same boat" as each other so to speak, would form a supportive cohort, they instead viewed each other as being "in competition" for tenure (102). The narratives of the junior faculty revealed "a highly competitive culture, where differences in status and prestige are reinforced and propagated through overt and more subtle departmental practices" (114). In addition to competing with each other, they were suspicious and fearful of senior faculty for a number of reasons: they knew several new hires had been let go the year before, and several times senior faculty had insinuated that one of the new faculty belonged in another department. Also, senior faculty were perceived as reluctant "to get 'too close' to junior faculty" because they didn't want to mislead them or form friendships in case the new faculty were not there very long. Even the way office space was allocated and how "public pronouncements [were] made during faculty meetings" (104) widened the chasm dividing senior and junior faculty and exacerbated the feelings of isolation and confusion experienced by new faculty. Their experience is echoed by Eric J. Follo, one of the co-authors of an article about peer support groups:

> I needed a meaningful, well-paced induction into academe. Yet, there was no induction program at the university because well educated, mature faculty members were expected to function effectively immediately. . . . Where was the assistance that I needed? (Follo, Gibson, Tracy, and Eckart 1995, 15)

His co-author, Sarah. L Gibson, adds, "Most department members secluded themselves behind slightly opened office doors and worked studiously at computers" (16).

In stark contrast to these situations, the women faculty in Dickens and Sagaria's study (1997) nurtured the development of others, including junior faculty and graduate students:

> Collaboration as a form of teaching or mentoring was described often and by a majority of the participants. Faculty who collaborated with students and senior faculty who collaborated with their junior and usually younger, less-experienced colleagues practiced this form of collaboration. (87)

One professor explicitly put "energy into helping minority students . . . and some women" who seemed unprepared for the task (88). However, they kept ethical issues in the foreground, cognizant of the possibilities for exploitation. Like the scholars in Dickens's and Sagaria's study, four of the co-authors in our study also spoke of mentoring and co-authoring with graduate students (Pike and Davis write with Ellison, who is a graduate student; O'Quin worked with Besemer when she was a graduate student; Roen and Lunsford both spoke of co-authoring with students) or junior faculty (Knight was senior when she began writing with Adams; Oldman is senior to Kent; Pike was senior when she began collaborating with Davis; Hurlbert, Lunsford, and Jim Strickland were senior when they began co-authoring, respectively, with Blitz, Ede, and Kathleen Strickland). However, most of them denied consciously choosing to co-author in order to help the junior writing partner; they insisted their relationship was nonhierarchical and certainly nonpatronizing. How fortunate for these graduate students and junior faculty that they had the opportunity to work with a more experienced faculty member who was not bound by issues of status, prestige, and competition—faculty members who display a more feminine approach.

Certainly, we in academia should be adding to the body of knowledge in our fields: we must remain vital in our disciplines by knowing current research that contributes to theory and practice and by conducting and writing about research. However, many of us, especially new scholars, might feel less threatened and isolated if invited to co-author with more experienced scholars. The pressure to publish will not abate any time soon, so senior faculty need to move beyond the carefully drawn boundaries that involve their specialties, their power, and even their eminence; their responsibilities should include mentoring and nurturing junior faculty and graduate students since "new faculty faring may depend more on sociological than on psychological factors" (Boice 1993, 334). What better way to nurture than to invite a less-experienced scholar to co-author, to initiate that scholar concerning the most important requirement for success in academia, and to set an example for that junior scholar to follow when he or she becomes a senior member of the department? The women scholars in Creamer and Engstrom's study (1996) "emphasized the crucial role relationships with colleagues played in developing their skills in writing and publishing" (14). However, at present, most senior faculty are recidivists, contributing to the isolation of young, or new, scholars simply because they were isolated themselves.

Of course, the professional benefits of co-authoring are not limited to less-experienced scholars. Experienced scholars need support in their quest to publish. Many a dissertation or first draft of an article has languished for years in a drawer because the author does not know how to begin to turn it into a publishable piece, and does not have the support to embark on the daunting task. We spoke recently to a friend who confessed she delayed for ten years writing an article from her dissertation because every time she looked at the dissertation, she was reminded of the isolation and fear that accompanied its creation.

But co-authoring can do a great deal to alleviate the drudgery and loneliness of writing, as most of the co-authors in our study confirm. As Besemer said, "In order to keep yourself going . . . having someone you share that with that also believes in the value of doing this . . . at least you have company in it."

In a revealing story, Reamer (1992) shares, "I have lost count of the number of faculty around the nation who have whispered to me that they write because they feel they have to, not because they want to or do it well" (131). None of the co-authors in our study spoke of writing because they have to. They want to write, and they have learned that they write better, enjoy support and guidance, and just generally have more fun when they co-author than when they write alone.

In addition to nurturing and relief of isolation, "there is some evidence that the pressure to publish may be leading to a rise in co-authorship" (Reamer 1992, 130). In our workshop, one participant told the group that she needs to co-author. When we asked her why, she admitted, "Well, I need to author!" Austin and Baldwin (1991) cite studies that indicate

> a positive correlation between the number of authors on a paper and the probability that it will be accepted for publication. . . . collaboration seems to help scholars avoid making mistakes or submitting bad work that the scholarly community will not accept. (31)

Writing support groups have sprung up at many institutions across the United States (and we suspect in other countries) because of the pressure to publish. Group members report development of "their identity as scholarly writers" (Gainen 1993, 98), and the creation of writing partnerships (99). During the year Gainen studied a twelve-member writing group (all women), each of the women presented a paper at a conference, everyone "had at least one manuscript in progress intended for a refereed journal . . . three had articles accepted, and one received a book contract." Most of the women acknowledged that the group played a significant role in their success (98). Gainen concludes that "the simple experience of sharing writing conflicts and celebrating both large and small successes may serve to quell self-doubts and strengthen hard-won but sometimes fragile professional identities" (99). In the faculty writing support group which Michele facilitated with her colleague Sharon Cramer, participants reported that the primary benefits were gaining an understanding of the expectations for academic writing and the realization that they were not alone.

Follo, Gibson, Tracy, and Eckart (1995) report similar successes in a writing group called WRITE at Oakland University. Of interest to our study, a feminine sensibility informs this group:

When all members are . . . leaders and followers, providers and receivers, teachers and learners, the resulting synergy exponentially improves each member's opportunities for success, emotional well-being and professional excellence. This collegiality cannot be replaced. Each member gains strengths and perseverance by being a part of *all* members' accomplishments. (18)

This scenario seems to confirm Noddings's "test of caring," which involves our determining whether someone's success "is partly a result of the completion of [our] caring for him" (1984, 81). The success of the members of these groups, and of the members of the small writing groups that our co-authors have formed with each other, is in great measure determined by their support of and caring for each other.

Also, as Fox and Faver (1984) showed in their study, and as some of the writers in our study confirmed, scholars feel safer taking risks when they co-author. Junior faculty in Verrier's study (1994) took on "short-term, conservative research projects, often not central to their current research interests nor tapping into their more creative energies" (116) because they were more concerned, with good reason, with being rewarded than with being innovative. It seems to us that opportunities abound for scholars to write with other scholars in their disciplines who might have a fresh take on an old issue, or to write with scholars in other disciplines who can help them see their ideas in a new light. Thomas B. Jones and Chet Meyers, two professors in different disciplines who decided to co-author, concluded at the end of their first co-authoring experience (as did Johnson and Bonacci in our study), that "mutual writing encouraged a higher level of intellectual discipline in terms of clarifying concepts, making connections, and considering alternatives than individual writing because the two of us were thinking together" (1994, 9). Instead of looking askance at a colleague who appears to belong in another discipline, scholars might co-author with that colleague to enrich their own understandings of their field. Marilyn Nahrwol (1997) sums up this view eloquently:

Collaboration is an important part of the scholarly work we do . . . it leads to better departments with broader understandings of research, scholarship, and knowledge-building. Collaborative scholars and departments realize that an "ivory tower," monologic, competitive view of the work that they do cuts them off from the society in which they live—a society that offers multiple perspectives calling to be pulled together in an ongoing process of knowledge-building. (Online)

The co-authors in our study chose to work with each other—whether their status was equal in the eyes of the institution or not—and that work has led to published works that have enhanced the careers of the co-authors.

They benefit cognitively, professionally, and socially from their writing together, and other scholars can and should choose to do the same for their students and colleagues.

We're not sure what more we can say that we haven't already said about the implications in our research for co-authored dissertations. As Boyer (1990) says, it's time to redefine scholarship, and we contend that the redefinition should extend to dissertations. Collaborative dissertations are not a radically new concept, anyway; they are only unheard of in the humanities. The most recent collaborative dissertation of which we're aware is the one we mentioned earlier, which was completed by two graduate students in the field of Human and Organizational Systems at the Fielding Institute, Lynne Valek and Toni Knott (see note nine, chapter two). When we began this study, we were told the UMI system was set up to search for single authors only, but in a more recent telephone conversation with Dr. Bill Savage, director of dissertations publishing for UMI (a division of Bell & Howell Information and Learning), we learned that out of 1.7 million dissertations and theses written in the last hundred years, about 166 are catalogued as co-authored. Savage mentioned that most of these, however, are master's theses in nursing and were supervised by the same female professor at an east coast institution. He knew of a 1998 collaborative doctoral dissertation coming out of the California Institute of Integral Studies, and Knott faxed us the cover sheet of a recently completed co-authored dissertation in psychology at Pepperdine. In addition, the University of Louisville social work program recently introduced the option of writing a collaborative dissertation, and the New Jersey Institute of Technology offers a collaborative doctorate that involves a relationship beyond the traditional committee: the program is designed to build bridges between the workplace and the academy.

Perhaps if academia could look at dissertations not as a hoop to be jumped through, a convention to be mastered, a tradition to be perpetuated, but as an opportunity for innovation, discovery, and real joy that comes with authentic learning—perhaps then co-authored dissertations would make more sense. We think of the sessions with each other as we wrote the proposal and review of literature for what we believed would be a co-authored dissertation. Sometimes long reading silences were punctuated by "Wow—listen to this!" or, "Hey—here's just the support we need." And sometimes there was talk—hours of talk—as we searched for and found the appropriate sources, clearest organization, right words. It was stimulating and fun, the way learning and writing should be and the way they cannot be if the learner and writer always work in isolation. In contrast, a few weeks after we were denied permission to co-author a dissertation, we were in our study, at our separate computers, working on creating two protocols from the joint protocol we had written for the Institutional Review Board for the Protection of Human Subjects. At some point, Michele turned to Kami and said, "Did you know you're sighing?" Kami said, "What?" Michele answered, "Yeah—great big sighs." Kami, the introvert, realized she was missing the intellectual exchanges that had been the staple of our writing together.

One of the courses I took for my doctoral work was a literary criticism class. Because postmodern criticism played a large part in our class discussions, a classmate, Karen Love, and I decided to visit a museum in Pittsburgh which was showcasing the work of a postmodern artist. The first piece we viewed appeared to be a large purple square on the wall. Karen and I walked up to it slowly, trying to take in the significance of the work. We spent a long time contemplating it. Admittedly, I was not impressed, and I assumed I just didn't "get it" as usual. However, just as I was about to move away from the square, I touched the edge of it (yes, broke the rules) and my finger went through the wall! It was a window, made to look one-dimensional with lighting. My friend and I screamed with delight! We were ecstatic to have been so completely surprised, to have our assumptions so thoroughly shattered. We realized later that part of the reason we were so ecstatic was that we were able to share the experience. I would never have reacted with such overt joy if I had been alone, even if I had felt it. We needed to share that experience to fully appreciate it.

Sharing an experience, even an intellectual one like writing a dissertation, enriches and deepens the participants, the process of writing, and the product. Those who appreciate the value of collaboration are convinced their co-authored works are better than their individually written ones. Most graduate students want their dissertations to be the jewel in the crown in their collegiate experience, but dissertation writing has come to be more about jumping though hoops, conforming, and getting hired than about making an original contribution to a field of knowledge. A study conducted by John Bavaro (1995) indicates that, when evaluating scholars, the criteria discussed are used only to "evaluate scholarship for the purpose of reward, rather than [to] evaluate scholarship as an academic pursuit for the purpose of knowledge contributions" (12). If two graduate students who have proven themselves to be serious scholars feel they will do their best work together—produce something innovative and original—that kind of work should be encouraged. Perhaps then the writing would be more about making a contribution, and learning and writing voluntarily and joyfully, than about getting a job, fulfilling requirements, and producing a piece of writing that very few people will ever read.

Co-authored dissertations might take many forms—collaborative research and individual writing, co-authored and individually written sections in the same document (providing the array that Knight advocates), entirely co-written projects from first to last word—but the time for their acceptance in every discipline and every institution has come.

7   LEARNING TO CARE

Good teachers bring students to community with themselves and with each other—not simply for the sake of warm feelings, but to do the difficult things that teaching and learning require.

Parker J. Palmer

Our conclusion that the respect, trust, care, support, sharing, heterarchy, and commitment that characterize the relationships of these co-authors have led to a feminine approach to co-authoring raises fascinating questions for us: How did the authors come to have a feminine approach? What are the implications of this approach? Do their backgrounds give clues about their ability to collaborate? Did they bring to their co-authoring a feminine stance already in place, or did the co-authoring help them develop it?

Furthermore, can this nurturing way of seeing and working with others be taught? And what does it have to do with gains from collaboration that extend beyond the cognitive and measurable? Not all of these questions are answerable based on the data from our study, but in this chapter, we will attempt to begin answering a few of them.

MEN AND A FEMININE SENSIBILITY

Is it just you, or is it your background?

Kami Day

We will admit that, even though we consciously resist associating the terms *masculine* and *feminine* with men and women, we were especially interested in what the men in our study had to say about how they came to adopt a feminine stance, at least where their co-authoring is concerned. After all, masculine and feminine characteristics are so labeled for a reason: competition, hierarchy, autonomy, control, objectivity, and justice are terms often associated (perhaps stereotypically) with western male behavior; and collaboration, mutuality, connectedness, nurturance, subjectivity, and attention to context are terms often associated (again, perhaps stereotypically) with western female behavior because these behaviors are sanctioned and ingrained by western culture. Consequently, the nurturing, caring behavior of the women in our study is more easily explained than that same behavior in the men. However, according to Mary M. Lay (1987), "In assigning cooperation to femininity and competition to masculinity, we fail to recognize that men must have the desire and potential to cooperate—since we witness effective collaboration by both genders" (74). The men in our study, who are all products of western schooling and culture, all display feminine characteristics in their ability to co-author. So how have these characteristics become part of who they are?

Lay (1987) laments that composition theorists' accounts of collaboration in the writing classroom have been mostly descriptive, and she believes gender studies can shed more light on how and why collaboration is possible, and even prescribe ways to learn and teach a more collaborative value system. She draws on Chodorow, Gilligan, and Belenky, Clinchy, Goldberger, and Tarule to show that "the ability to relate comes from the gender distinctions stressed within the family and the subsequent systems of knowledge valued by the female gender" (71). Lay contends furthermore that "if we can discover the causes for these different attitudes, then we can encourage the behavior that supports collaboration. . . . if we discover why collaborators identify with each other's values and needs, then we have a means for 'teaching' collaboration" (71–72). In the following section we will explore possible reasons for the male co-authors' feminine sensibilities and the possibility of learning and teaching such sensibilities.

The idea to call the interviewees' approach feminine dawned on us slowly, and it came partly because of Matthew Oldman's speaking so openly, in what was only the second interview, about resisting the traditional masculine need to dominate. So it was not until the third interview that we asked a direct question concerning gender. Throughout the interview with Gilbert Adams and Julie Knight, we observed that neither of them exhibited traditional masculine traits such as the tendency to control the discussion or avoid talking about feelings and relationships. We were especially interested to see that Adams's manner was even less assertive than Knight's, so toward the end of the third interview, revealing our own discomfort with labeling their approach as feminine, Kami asked (sort of), "When I hear you talking . . . I mean . . . some male-female teams . . . I don't know how to say this . . . I don't see any . . . you have a real feminine approach in a lot of ways . . . I don't see that you're [Adams] in charge here . . . do you think that's one reason you work so well together?" Knight acknowledged a feminine standpoint, but the question about their approach had just occurred to us, and we did not think to ask if they were aware of anything in their backgrounds and natures that made such an approach possible.

However, they did give us some insights into their personalities that shed light on Adams's way of interacting. They both characterize themselves as introverts, but Adams told us his score on the Kirton Adaptive-Innovation

Inventory, a measure he gives his students to help them become more astute about their own personalities, identifies him as "more adaptively oriented than Knight." Their scores reveal that Adams is "more steady, reliable, prudent, . . . better able to fit into teams, . . . sensitive to policy and mores; . . . efficient and orderly" (Kirton 1987, 294). Adaptiveness is certainly compatible with the traits of a feminine ego—flexibility, little urge to master or repress, attention to context, the ability to nurture without the thought of self-promotion—so perhaps Adams's ability to "accommodate" rather than "appropriate" (to use Stuart Brown's terms) other views contributes to his feminine stance. Certainly, Adams's and Knight's personality characteristics as they relate to adaptability complement each other and point to the need for more research into personality types and preferences as they impact the ability to co-author.

In broaching this topic with Alexander Davis, we mentioned what we had read in the research about power and hierarchy issues in male-female co-authoring. We asked him, "Have you adopted a feminine approach? Does that approach feel innate to you . . . or does it have something to do with your education or background?" His response was,

> Well, I'm not sure, but I think it's probably learned . . . my background . . . my mother . . . most based on my relationship with my mother, but I've learned so much about the status of women in society that I can't separate these things out. . . I never had the desire to be the boss in any situation.

It was at this point that Cybil Pike told the story of Davis's caring for his mother when she was dying. Perhaps this nurturing relationship—and it sounds mutually nurturing—with his mother laid the foundation for his feminine sensitivity. Certainly his education and work in sex and gender studies have enriched his understanding and awareness of the characteristics of masculine and feminine stances, and he seems to prefer the feminine one.

As always, we were worried about promoting gender stereotypes when we asked Jim Strickland about his approach to co-authoring. We explained that the men in the teams we had interviewed so far had a feminine way of working with their writing partners, and that we "couldn't make up a gender problem out of this research." Kathleen immediately acknowledged that Jim takes a feminine approach as well, so we asked him, "Is it just *you* or is it your background?" Jim's reply was, "Just me . . . I don't know." He did not know if he co-authors well because he's who he is (keeping in mind our earlier discussion of the various influences on individual development), or if working with people had contributed to his feminine stance. As we mentioned earlier, though, he did not enjoy co-authoring with a partner who took a more masculine approach.

Duane Roen was able to immediately pinpoint one of the reasons for his ability to co-author successfully, which we think he would connect to a feminine consciousness based on the value he places on nurturing, although he did not make the connection specifically here:

> For me, a lot of the collaborative stuff I've done goes back to my upbringing. I grew up on a dairy farm in Wisconsin . . . collaboration was just sort of the way we did *everything* . . . it was a way of life and I just got used to it. I did benefit from that . . . there was no alternative so we became pretty comfortable with it.

Professionally, after working as a graduate student with a faculty member on a project and receiving no recognition for the publication, he vowed to set aside hierarchy and status in future collaborations. Stuart Brown said he had not really thought about whether his background influenced his approach, but he did say collaboration "is not something he has to struggle with."

Mark Bonacci's work with community outreach may have contributed to his feminine sensibility, but neither he nor Oldman could identify anything in their backgrounds that led them to a feminine approach to co-authoring. Of course, both of them, like all the men in our study, are highly educated, reflective scholars who have most likely read feminist theory, so they might have questioned their own attitudes and behaviors and moved toward a more feminine way of being, even a feminist pedagogy. Oldman, for instance, has been teaching for about thirty years, and our guess is that education, experience, and a desire to help his students to develop skills as collaborators and teachers have taught him that a nurturing, nonhierarchical, noncompetitive stance more often leads to successful collaboration.

A great deal of Mark Hurlbert and Michael Blitz's interview was taken up with conversation about their pedagogies, which are decidedly feminist. They are committed to good teaching; they both nurture their students, whom they see as individuals needing their guidance but also their care. And their students often co-author. When we sent them copies of their transcript to review, we attached a few follow-up questions. One of the questions was, "Is there anything in your background that you think makes it possible for you to co-author successfully?" Blitz answered,

> I don't know if I can point to specific things. My sister taught me to read on my fourth birthday, and I've had a love of books and writing ever since. It seems only natural to me to want to include other people in work that I love.

Hurlbert's answer was more poignant:

> No, there is nothing in my background that makes collaboration more possible or that helps me do it successfully; in fact, just the opposite. Nothing in my schooling

or in my upbringing or in the ideology of the country in which I live has prepared me for the level of selfless sharing and cooperation that are the matters of course for co-authoring with Michael. In fact, that the collaboration works so well is to me, still, something just short of miraculous.

Lay (1997) maintains that "collaboration calls for a fundamental change in the self-image of men" (72). Of course, the feminine consciousness of these male co-authors is part of who these men are; some may have been raised in an atmosphere that engendered such a consciousness, but some seem to have changed fundamentally at some point. We are all constructed by the cultures in which we were raised and in which we live, but, clearly, as our study shows, all western men do not fit the stereotypes of western culture, stereotypes which we reject but which admittedly still have the power to influence behavior and create expectations. As Davis's and Roen's and Hurlbert's stories indicate, they learned somewhere and from someone to value a feminine way of interacting in the world, either because they experienced it or they experienced its opposite. And we think we can say that some of them, such as Oldman and Hurlbert, perhaps because of education, unsatisfying experiences with a masculine stance, or other reasons they did not hint at, came to that way of interacting later in their lives. The questions, then, are: If evidence exists that suggests a feminine approach can be learned, can such an approach be taught explicitly? Are there ways to help people come to value and even enact nurturing, nonhierarchical, collaborative behaviors?

IMPLICATIONS FOR PEDAGOGY

> *"Collaboration requires peacemaking"*
>
> Michael Blitz

One of the questions we asked most teams was, "Do you see benefits of co-authoring beyond the cognitive gains?" Most of them answered in the affirmative, often describing these kinds of gains as ineffable or intrinsic. As we mentioned earlier, Hurlbert feels he's "a fuller human being" because of his relationship with Blitz; he values the spiritual element of their work together, and while he did not say he is a fuller human being because of co-authoring specifically, co-authoring is a significant part of their relationship. The respect, trust, and connection they experience as co-authors infuses their friendship, which in turn enriches their co-authoring, and perhaps we can say what they learn from that connection informs their relationships with students, colleagues, family members, and the world at large. Blitz provided this written reply to our follow-up question about the benefits of co-authoring. It characterizes beautifully what we know to be true of all the co-authors in our study:

One of the inevitable outcomes of collaboration is that it prompts people to reconsider their ideas about, and expectations for, cooperation. In effect, a collaboration—even between just two people—is a community effort. The tasks have to be divided up; the labor has to be mutually understood; the aim must be common to each collaborator (though there may be some individual aims, as well); and the collaborative "community" will have to live with the results of this labor. Collaboration requires peacemaking, an ongoing process. It's simply not possible, I don't think, to be in perfect harmony through every moment of collaborative effort. So, collaborators have to figure out ways to keep the peace—or to live in conflict, which is far less productive. But keeping the peace cannot mean compromising on the quality of the effort or of the outcome. Keeping the peace, in this context, means placing things like common goals, kindness, civility, creativity in the foreground. It means surrendering a fair amount of ego-requirements, too. So, I guess I would say that one of the greatest values in co-authoring is that it allows for the forging of new bonds of trust and care between and among people.

For Blitz, learning to foreground kindness, civility, and peace are outcomes of collaboration, and these qualities cannot be measured as writing quality might be. Neither can "new bonds of trust and care" be measured, but they also develop in productive collaborative relationships as the writers work to achieve harmony (at least most of the time) in their relationships. We think these qualities may be needed and developed even more when collaboration involves writing together. For one thing, as Mary Beth Debs asserts in a dissertation on collaboration in the computer industry, "The production of any text . . . is a social activity . . . within a team, writers must adapt their individual behaviors to those of the team" (qtd. in Lay 1987, 84). For another thing, and maybe most importantly, writing is, as Adams insightfully pointed out, an "intimate process." A piece of writing is of the author in the same ways a child is of a parent; the writing has the characteristics of the writer, and sharing that writing exposes the writer in some ways. Thoughts are not hidden in the mind or partially obscured by speech that can be immediately revised or hedged; they are there on the paper, subject to scrutiny. Each author must be able to trust a co-author with an intimate part of himself or herself, and each co-author must be kind in receiving, accommodating, revising, or even rejecting the words of their partner. Co-authoring provides experience with this peacemaking.

Peacemaking involves the trust, respect, caring, support, flexibility, appreciation of the strengths of others, and unselfishness about one's own words and ideas that are associated with successful co-authoring; and we don't think we're stretching to assert that the co-authors in our study would agree that their co-authoring has made them more respectful, trusting and trustworthy, caring, supportive, flexible, appreciative, and unselfish. Are there implications that students who co-author can become aware of, learn, and practice those feminine characteristics? We think of J. Elspeth Stuckey's provocative statement: "We promote greater literacy, or we promote greater humanity" (1991, 124). Can co-authoring, in fact, promote greater humanity? Can our students, many of whom have been steeped in a predominantly masculine western culture, learn caring, respectfulness and trustfulness, trustworthiness, commitment, and kindness as they learn to write? Appley and Winder (1977) believe people can change their value systems:

> We must let go of old values . . . in order to embrace the new ones. . . . a capacity for change is inherent in human growth process. . . . This engagement can be nurtured in an environment that supports faith in and hope for the future. Central to the development of such an environment is the presence of human caring. (283)

They go on to say that for people to make the shift from a competitive value system to a collaborative one,

> two important skills that must be learned are 1) participative decision making and participipitative membership, i.e., to learn more about collaboration and how to move from hierarchical to nonhierarchical systems, and 2) the use of human support systems or social networks at work. (287)

If what Appley and Winder say is true, then a feminist classroom, in which students are nurtured and co-authoring is taught and practiced, can be a place where students can learn a nurturing, caring, understanding, appreciative way of interacting with one another.

Bateson (1990) also feels that a feminine standpoint can be learned. Stressing that such a standpoint is not a biological given for all women, she states,

> Attention and empathy are skills, rather than biological givens for all women. Caring can be learned by all human beings, can be worked into the design of every life, meeting an individual need as well as a pervasive need in society. We need attention and empathy in every context where we encounter other living beings. (161)

Caring can be "worked into the design of every life," and we believe it can be worked into the design of every classroom, especially if students are given the opportunity to not only learn cooperatively but to co-author, a more intimate activity and therefore ripe with possibilities for caring and empathy.

Noddings believes people can learn to care; in fact, she believes they must learn to care in order to live ethically. She claims that "the impulse to act in behalf of the present other is itself innate" (1984, 81). For her, that "impulse arises naturally, at least occasionally, in the absence of pathology . . . [and] lies latent in each of us, awaiting gradual development in a succession of caring relations" (81–83). We may reject the initial impulse—"I must do something"—because we feel there is nothing we can do or because we decide someone else should do something, or even because we do not like the person who is in need of our care, but

> if the other toward whom we shall act is capable of responding as cared-for and there are no objective conditions that prevent our receiving this response—if, that is, our caring can be completed in the other—then we must meet that other as one-caring. If we do not care naturally, we must call upon our capacity for ethical caring. When we are in a relation or when the other has addressed us, we must respond as one-caring. The imperative in relation is categorical. (86)

We must reflect upon what we can do and do it, not worrying that what we

> might do would tend to work against the best interests of the cared-for. . . . The test of . . . caring is in an examination of what I considered, how fully I received the other, and whether the free pursuit of his projects is partly a result of the completion of my caring for him. (81)

Furthermore, obligational caring begets natural caring: Noddings insists that the "one-caring" must call on a "sense of duty or special obligation" in order to "stimulate natural caring" (1994, 174).

Thinking about Noddings's ethic of care leads us to reflect on why this project was so important to us and why we plan to continue to study co-authoring. Michele, on one hand, connects readily and enthusiastically with people. She has never doubted the value of these kinds of connections or her ability to make them, and her caring is explicit and generous. But interestingly, Michele is more skeptical than Kami about the possibilities of our field's accepting the connections between composition and care. For Kami, reading Noddings's work was life-changing in some ways. She thinks of herself as a person who has difficulty connecting with people, a person who has difficulty expressing and enacting care. Yet, she knows those kinds of connections make possible spiritual growth and nourishment, fuller participation in the human condition; so, she is drawn to reading and writing about people who can connect, and what she learns from them confirms her belief in the need to care and be cared for, and the possibility that a person who enacts caring behavior will come to care more deeply.

Most of our students have experienced, if not a "succession of caring relationships," at least a few such relationships, so they are not completely unfamiliar with caring. If they have experienced very few, all the more reason to nurture those relationships in our classrooms, to add to the "succession of caring relationships." But can students be taught overtly to care? Probably not; however, as Noddings eloquently maintains with so much faith and optimism in nonpathological human nature, caring is innate. Students can recognize it and experience the urge to enact it, not if they are told to care, but if they are cared for. Composition and literacy scholar Patrick Hartwell (1998) was fond of asking his students to think about the "teacher or teachers who influenced [their] lives in positive ways" (3). He claimed that memorable teachers are memorable not because of what they say but because of what they do. Their students learn from watching them, from being in their presence. We believe students can begin to learn to care and nurture from a teacher who cares for and nurtures them, and if they are given the opportunity to care for and nurture their peers in the class. Noddings feels that teachers must give students "practice in caring" by creating opportunities for students to "support each other," interact, work in small groups, develop a "caring community," and confirm each other (1994, 177). For Noddings, collaboration has the potential to engender ethical acts of caring.

Noddings also insists that "we cannot separate ends and means in education." She goes so far as to point to "the maintenance and enhancement of caring as the primary aim of education" and advises that "intellectual tasks and aesthetic appreciation should be deliberately set aside . . . if their pursuit endangers the ethical ideal" (1984, 174). Noddings does not advocate that a teacher "retreat every time a student shows discomfort or disinterest in a topic," but she says she would

> accept his [the student's—Noddings alternates feminine and masculine pronouns] attitude toward the subject, adjust [her own] requirements in light of his interest and ability, and support his efforts nonjudgmentally. He must be aware always that for [her] he is more important, more valuable, than the subject. (174)

"Ethical behavior," according to Noddings,

> does arise out of psychological deep structures that are partly predispositional (I would prefer to say "natural") and partly the result of nurturance. When we behave ethically as ones-caring, we are not obeying moral principles . . . but we are meeting the other in genuine encounters of caring and being cared for. There is commitment and there is choice. (175)

Can a composition class provide "genuine encounters of caring and being cared for"? Noddings would say "yes," and so would we. The ethic of care is a relational ethic, and students who write together are certainly involved in relationships. Students are in close proximity, capable of caring for one another if their peers are "responding as cared-for and there are no objective conditions that prevent [their] receiving this response" (1984, 86). Students in such a classroom cannot help but think about "whether the free pursuit of [a peer's] projects is partly a result of the completion of [their] caring for him" (81). Students must consider how what they do will affect the work, and the psyches, of their peers. Will their contributions and attitudes hinder or help the writing and even the personal development of a fellow student? A co-author must think about commitment, responsibility, whether they themselves are to be trusted, what in other students makes those students trustworthy, and others' affective responses to their words and actions.

As students write together, their thoughts and feelings are made visible. They come to know each other very well; and in a nurturing environment in which the teacher models caring in class and in conferences, students can learn to nurture. If the teacher responds to student writing kindly, but honestly and helpfully, the students in the class are more likely to do the same. If the teacher rewards students for effective collaboration, might not they come to value it as well (Lay 1987, 72, 74)? If the teacher respects the views of the students, the students may learn to respect each other's views. If a teacher honors her commitments to students, they might follow her example by fulfilling responsibilities to each other. If students believe a teacher truly cares for them, might not the students look at each other in a different light, seeing each other and themselves as worthy of being cared for?

About three weeks into a fall semester, as I (Kami) was in the thick of writing my dissertation and was being strongly influenced by my findings and their implications, the time had come for my students to form permanent groups. They had been moving around from group to group, getting to know each other and practicing writing with their peers for the first few weeks. I spent several hours at home one evening grouping students on paper based on what I knew so far of their strengths and personalities. The next day, I gave the first class of the day the choice of being grouped by me or grouping themselves. First they said, "We want to group ourselves." However, no one moved, but there was some discussion I couldn't make out among some of the students, and a few seconds later, several of them said, "No, no, you group us." The rest agreed unanimously. I was a little puzzled, but I assigned them to groups, and we got to work. When the class was over, I said, "Let me ask you one thing before we go. Why did you change your minds?" They smiled, and one of them said, "We noticed you had a piece of paper with groups already made up, and we didn't want your work to go to waste." They also expressed concern that someone might feel left out or left over if they formed groups on their own.

This class seemed to already be aware that they were creating a caring community, and I'll admit they turned out to be an especially close, cohesive class. Would that have happened if I had not somehow conveyed, with my pedagogy of conferencing, collaboration, and co-authoring, that I cared about them and expected them to treat each other with care? I don't know, but I believe that as students experience and practice feminine traits, they are involved in a succession of caring relationships that teach them more and more about a nurturing way of interacting with their fellow human beings.

Two follow-up stories seem to suggest this possibility: (1) A student from the class mentioned above chose her co-authored paper as one of the pieces for her portfolio, not because she thought it was one of her best papers, but because she wanted me to know how important that group experience had been to her and how much she valued the contributions of her group members; (2) About three weeks into the semester after the one above, I asked the students in my literature course to write a journal entry making suggestions for improving the class; I was feeling pressured to "cover the content" and had neglected community-building and, to some extent, their writing up to that point. One of the students, who had also been in my fall semester class, wrote this: "One suggestion that would help bring the individual group members closer would be to assign a group paper. I remember last semester when we wrote our paper, our group became even closer after we wrote our paper." He seemed to sense that co-authoring can create a site where relationships involving respect, trust, and care have a chance to grow.

Along with caring comes the ability to empathize, which some scholars also believe can be learned. We had always defined empathy as feeling what another is feeling, but as Young (1997) points out in her discussion of asymmetrical reciprocity, we cannot presume to share experiences and emotions with another. However, she does believe empathy on some level is possible, that with hard work and some imagination, we can and must find some small plot of common ground in spite of differences.

Kanpol (1995) moves beyond merely recognizing and appreciating difference to suggest the possibility of finding common ground. He acknowledges that while he can never *be* "black, Puerto Rican, Hispanic, or Asian, the challenge . . .

is . . . to locate those intersections of race, class, and gender where individual and group identities are understood through similarities, despite the celebration of multiple differences." He believes we can and must discover similarities in difference (180). Kanpol finds support in the writing of Fred Yeo (1995), who rejects the notion of incommensurability, insisting that we can move "beyond our isolated experience" to experiences "as and with the Other" (211), and Svi Shapiro (1995), who wonders where the bridges are in a discourse of difference. In an inspiring essay, Shapiro goes so far as to call for education that touches the spiritual and emotional lives of students; for him, education is "about what it means to be human and how people live together" (21, 35).

Students may learn *about* difference and the importance of finding common ground through traditional pedagogy that involves lecture or whole class discussion *about* diverse cultures or *about* the writings of authors from those cultures; but students will not practice finding common ground in such a class. Giroux (1992) feels that schools must be sites of "border crossings" where negotiation between cultures, and even transformation, takes place, and he recommends collaboration as a way to facilitate that transformation: "Creating new forms of knowledge also suggests creating classroom practices that provide students with the opportunity to work collectively and to develop needs and habits in which the social is felt and experienced as emancipatory rather than alienating" (224).

In support of collaboration, Bruffee (1993) criticizes a foundational approach that simply exposes students to the "Other." Even in a class that appears on the surface to be homogeneous, there is a great deal of diversity; in a class of twenty students exist twenty different families and ages; usually two sexes and perhaps a variety of genders; multiple identities; a mix of religions, cultures, ideologies, and races; and twenty ways of positioning a self, of perceiving and incorporating those elements into an individual consciousness. Students must have an opportunity to talk face-to-face, hear each other's stories, and become aware of each other's ideologies and styles and abilities. Such talk is the stuff of a classroom in which students co-author. They don't *learn about* working through differences, finding common ground, and appreciating the strengths of others. They *find* common ground, *work through* differences, and *learn from each other's strengths* as they talk; and through negotiation, they perform the hard work of transforming that talk into writing. Classrooms where students co-author can be "places where students and teachers are able to use language and literacy to give life coherence and meaning, or to facilitate the striving beyond ourselves, widening our identity toward the oneness behind diversity" (McAndrew 1996, 380).

Most of the co-authors in our study agreed that co-authoring provides opportunities to develop skills beyond the cognitive, and they see those skills as outcomes of a collaboration pedagogy. In thinking of these outcomes, Jim Strickland first mentioned "interpersonal skills," and Kathleen added:

> And learning to listen . . . these are all things we have to teach and model. Students learn how to do this very often through our modeling in conferences with them . . . so we always have to keep learning how to get better at this. I don't think it's a natural thing . . . learning when to negotiate . . . it's very much a part of social learning . . . and it's a big responsibility because we have to understand it ourselves before we can help model it and teach it.

Kathleen seems to be saying that if we want our students to learn to negotiate, to make peace and move toward common aims, we must experience and model such negotiation and peacemaking in our own co-authoring and teaching. Her view echoes that of Pike, Ellison, and Davis, who insist that method cannot and should not be separated from substance, and feel it is "good for students to see them working together" through differences in race and gender, creating "unity in diversity."

We asked Kathleen and Jim, admitting our idealistic bent, if co-authoring can make the world a better place, and Kathleen answered:

> That's what keeps us going, isn't it really? Our pedagogy is trying to make the world a better place . . . we have a vision of our world . . . that's why all these ideas about paradigms and so forth are a lot more complicated than people think . . . because we're trying to impact the way people treat one another . . . the way people coexist. You know we can kind of laugh but it isn't really funny. In fifteen weeks I'm not very sure we can expect growth in writing . . . I think if we can change people's attitude . . . or not even change . . . that's too sweeping . . . if we can impact students.

Jim agreed: "You're never sure what kind of difference you make . . . the only thing you're pretty sure of is that you can't measure it statistically." Kathleen mentioned other, more practical benefits of working together. She asks her students who are training to be teachers to work on joint projects, partly because they will have to work with other teachers and partly because she wants to see more collaboration in the field of education. She acknowledges the challenges of such projects but maintains that the students must learn to work as a team, the classroom is an ideal place for them to practice, and it is the teacher's obligation to give them that practice.

We quoted Roen earlier as agreeing that voluntary co-authoring can help students learn to find common ground. He believes that such experiences give students the opportunity to participate "in Rogerian rhetoric . . . you tell me where you're coming from and I'll tell you where I'm coming from." Brown connected the unmeasurable benefits of collaboration with higher education programs that create small cohorts within the freshman class. He wondered if such cohorts would "allow more collaboration simply because people are going to develop a sense of community . . . they are going to be able to establish relationships . . . develop trust." It seems to us that these kinds of cohorts *are* examples of collaboration, and that trust and community are the outcomes of such relationships.

Karen O'Quin feels the students in her social psychology class especially need experiences with group process: "I think they would gain an appreciation of group process . . . the positive aspects of group process and the negative ones . . . especially a new group forming." Susan Besemer related the ineffable benefits of collaboration to her position as a library administrator. She feels "working in groups . . . is extremely important to people . . . to employers at this point . . . if you're a middle manager and you can't get along with people, you're not going to be that successful." She gives her colleagues projects that require collaboration because she thinks they need the experience and because she "won't tolerate people not speaking to each other."

In a follow-up question at the end of the transcript we sent to Lisa Ede, we asked, "Do you think there are benefits of co-authoring beyond the cognitive gains (for all co-authors, but especially for students)?" Her answer was emphatic: "Yes. *Huge.* The most important." In Ede and Lunsford's article "Why Write . . . Together?" (1983) they point out if students are to be successful in most professions—or at least those outside the humanities—they must know how to co-author, and it is our responsibility as their instructors to teach them. However, Lunsford and Ede's commitment to feminism, and by extension, collaboration, would, we think, point to the more important ineffable and affective benefits they would see for students who co-author, benefits they enjoy themselves.

Kent and Oldman did not speak in terms of "promoting greater humanity," but they agreed there are unmeasurable benefits to collaboration that involve students becoming aware of their connections with and responsibility to others. However, Kent believes that one reason collaboration will never be required or widely valued is that its outcomes cannot be measured in traditional ways. She hopes for instruments that will measure more quantitatively the outcomes of collaboration, but Oldman is content with "a feeling that it's working." Oldman said that when his students collaborate, he "can see what they've gotten out of it . . . but they don't see it a lot of times." Oldman, like Ede and Lunsford, O'Quin and Besemer, and Strickland and Strickland, focused in part on real-world skills of collaboration: "You've got to be part of . . . if you work in the 7–Eleven the midnight shift you've got to come in on time because somebody's got to go home . . . and you'd better not slough off your responsibilities . . . we're all interconnected." He also pointed out that his teacher education students, who produce collaborative portfolios, work in teams and have to come to consensus, "so they have to struggle." He cited a study concerning what grades K–12 should prepare students for. The researchers found that 75 percent of the skills needed in business are interpersonal, and Oldman feels it would be unethical to prepare his students to teach elementary and secondary students something they can't do themselves. Also, as teachers they will be evaluated partially on their ability to work well with other people.

In the discussion about collaborative dissertations, we included Knight's observation that aside from a better dissertation, two students would develop other important skills that are "sellable in terms of what folks need when they go out to be employed." We asked Adams and Knight if they thought one of the intrinsic benefits of co-authoring is that the co-authors learn to find common ground, and Adams said he does think it's a benefit. His doctoral advisor was British, and their different cultural and educational backgrounds created a mix that "played out very positively." He added that "when you write well together, you start to cross assumptions and values, and you can't help but develop a good relationship." Knight feels that finding common ground can "absolutely be done" and this is one of the philosophies that drives her and Adams's classes. She admits, "It's very hard, especially once you really get multicultural because you're dealing with layer after layer after layer," but she believes that "collaborative writing as an activity is one way to do that [learn to find common ground] . . . but you have to train for it." It was at this point she included what she called her "real pie in the sky kind of thing to say as a teacher"—her observation that we learn about ourselves from any interaction:

> The skill it takes to work together with other folks so that you can learn about yourself and understand that that adds back to your individuality . . . it's different from the content and the output, but it's a part that I think in teaching and in pedagogy is something to go for.

To wrap up our co-authors' views on the extracognitive benefits of co-authoring, we would like to return to Michael Blitz's statement:

> Collaboration requires peacemaking, an ongoing process. . . . Keeping the peace, in this context, means placing things like common goals, kindness, civility, creativity in the foreground. It means surrendering a fair amount of ego-requirements, too. So, I guess I would say that one of the greatest values in co-authoring is that it allows for the forging of new bonds of trust and care between and among people.

None of the co-authors in our study came together simply because of proximity, as most of the students in our classes do. But some of them began to work together because of proximity and shared interests and continue to work together because they have built a relationship on respect and trust. Some of them, and certainly the teams who were friends before they started writing together, brought respect and trust into the relationship, but we would argue that co-authoring has given them a deeper understanding of respect and trust than they might have had otherwise. They all see that their "completion of caring" contributes positively and productively to their co-author's development professionally and personally. Even if students' only common ground initially is proximity, a caring teacher who uses collaboration pedagogy skillfully might create an environment in which students begin to develop an understanding of relational ethics, begin to understand respect and trust and commitment, begin to see and appreciate others' strengths, and begin to care whether their peers do well inside and outside of the class.

Of course, we may sound naïve and idealistic in such a claim. The creation of better human beings is the grandest hope of co-authoring—the hope that goes beyond the cognitive gains established in studies and acknowledged by the co-authors in our study. And we must take into consideration the work of socialist feminists such as Eileen E. Schell (1998), who critiques "arguments that advocate a feminist pedagogy based on an 'ethic of care'" (74). Schell argues that "feminist pedagogy, although compelling, may reinforce rather than critique or transform patriarchal structures by reinscribing what Magda Lewis calls the 'woman as caretaker ideology.'" She worries that Noddings's ethic of care as applied to writing pedagogy will hinder women's efforts to "improve and transform the working conditions and material realities of writing teachers" (92). We agree that women should not acquiesce to higher education's efforts to relegate them to roles which reproduce patriarchal structures and provide only psychic and perhaps emotional rewards for the teacher, but for us the global issues of labor conditions for women are illuminated by, not undermined by, collaboration. With Doane and Hodges, we see "collaborative writing is both shaped by and subversive of a broader cultural matrix—the conditions of women's work" (1995, 56): shaped by the culture in that scholars who take a feminine approach to both teaching and writing have felt a need to come together to provide the support not offered by the traditional patriarchal structures of the academy; subversive of the culture in that collaborative writing has the ability to disable the well-oiled machinery that drives the engines of static, recidivist, conservative institutions.

More importantly, we are disturbed by the absence of student needs in Schell's argument. Should we abandon a nurturing pedagogy which gives students experience in caring relationships because that pedagogy is not as likely to provide the material benefits we deserve? Jarratt (1998), drawing on the work of Worth, Anderson, and others, points out that unfortunately "the discourses of pedagogy speak themselves almost entirely in the absence of students" (8), and Schell's discourse seems to be making such an omission.

Having said that, we are compelled to admit here that we often think we as teachers assign too much importance to ourselves. We believe we can effect life changes in our students. However, we have come to feel with Cy Knoblauch and Lil Brannon (1984), Kathleen and Jim Strickland, and others that we can expect to accomplish very little with our students—measurable or otherwise—in a fifteen-week semester or ten-week quarter; we can perhaps facilitate more reflection, or a few steps in the move along the continuum from a dichotomous epistemology to a dialectic one, or a dawning awareness of an identity as a competent writer, or a small shift from autonomy to connectedness, or a barely perceptible turning from viewing others as competitors to "cared-for." Susan McLeod (1997) tells a story of a young man whose strong Christian beliefs made it impossible for him to consider or write about other beliefs he saw as "wrong." McLeod did not perceive any opening up of his view during the semester—he seemed to leave even more determined to defend and convince others of his position. On the other hand, a young woman who began her research paper as a treatise on why other beliefs were unacceptable turned in a final draft that had become a comparison of other beliefs and her own, minus the strident preaching of the first draft (83–84).

We take to heart, and take heart from, the warnings of feminist pedagogues such as Elizabeth Ellsworth (1992) and Jennifer Gore (1992), who caution teachers that they need to guard against thinking of themselves as crucially important in students' lives, against thinking of themselves as possessing extraordinary abilities. We as teachers are somewhat arrogant in asking students the question, "What can I do for you," and it's possible for feminine pedagogues to be just as repressive and oppressive as traditional, masculine ones. Ellsworth asks teachers to be more humble and reflective, to problematize their own stances. There are some things we will never know about our students, and the classroom is not necessarily a safe place to practice trust and respect and caring just because we say it is; but we can work toward establishing high levels of trust by helping students know us and each other better. What better way for them to come to know each other than in the intimate activity of writing together?

We hope for a change in the academy so that all of us, students and academicians, can help each other live more meaningful lives. What we have presented here might be what Kenneth J. Gergen (1992) calls "generative theory," theory designed to unseat conventional thought and thereby to open new alternatives for thought and action. Through such theorizing scholars contribute to the forms of cultural intelligibility, to the symbolic resources available to people to carry out their lives together. . . . Each reconstitutes our conception of human action in ways that open new cultural potentials. (27–28)

So, we join our voices with the voices of those theoreticians and practitioners who are attempting to "reconstitute our conception of human action" and "unseat conventional thought." As Blitz says, if a greater number of academicians perceive the need for a paradigmatic change in academia, and are willing to voice such a perception, that change will likely take place.

Still, theorizing and speaking out are not enough. Parker J. Palmer, in a conference talk entitled "The Grace of Great Things: Recovering the Sacred in Knowing, Teaching, and Learning" (1998), sums up our hope for a change in the academy:

We all know that what will transform education is not another theory or another formula but a transformed way of being in the world. In the midst of familiar trappings of educational competition, intellectual combat, obsession with a narrow range of facts, credits, and credentials we seek a life illumined by spirit and infused with soul. (1)

We believe that *(First Person)²* represents the benefits of co-authoring, allowing for exponential growth in the capacity to care. We believe a feminine sensibility, or a collaborative value system, is the "way of being in the world" that can transform academia into a place that nurtures intellectually, spiritually, and emotionally, and we believe our study shows the potential co-authoring has for playing a part in such a transformation.

APPENDIX
Profiles

Following are profiles of the interviewees, the "main players" in this text. Some chose pseudonyms (indicated with an asterisk in these profiles) and some gave us permission to use their real names.

MICHAEL BLITZ AND C. MARK HURLBERT

Michael Blitz is a professor of English and chair of thematic studies, John Jay College of Criminal Justice of the City University of New York. He has been a college professor for fifteen years. Prior to that, he was Toni Morrison's Research Fellow as well as a professional researcher for William Kennedy. With C. Mark Hurlbert, Blitz has co-authored *Letters for the Living: Teaching Writing in a Violent Age* and co-edited *Composition and Resistance*. Blitz and Hurlbert have also co-authored more than a dozen articles and book chapters. Blitz has also collaborated for over ten years and on a number of articles and projects with Louise Krasniewicz, director of the Digital Archaeology Lab at UCLA. Blitz's scholarship includes work on cultural studies, composition and rhetoric, and poetry and poetics. Currently, Blitz is working with anthropologist Kojo Dei on an article on interdisciplinary studies and writing, and, with C. Mark Hurlbert, on a composition textbook.

C. Mark Hurlbert lives in Pittsburgh, Pennsylvania, and is a professor of English at Indiana University of Pennsylvania. Mark is currently co-editing *Beyond English, Inc.: Disciplinary and Curricular Reform for the 21st Century* with David B. Downing and Paula J. Mathieu. He has also co-written *Letters for the Living* with Michael Blitz and co-edited *Composition and Resistance* with Blitz. In addition, he co-edited *Social Issues in the English Classroom* with Samuel Totten. Mark has also written or co-written articles (mostly with Michael Blitz) for *Changing Classroom Practices, Sharing Pedagogies, Stories from the Center, Cultural Studies in the English Classroom, Works and Days, Pre/Text, The Writing Instructor, English Leadership Quarterly,* and *Composition Studies.*

MARK BONNACI AND KATHERINE JOHNSON

Bonnaci is a professor who teaches in the sociology department of a community college in western New York. He holds a Ph.D. in psychology, and one of his areas of interest is community outreach. He has traveled to Southeast Asia several times and has published a number of books, some on his experiences there, and a sociology text with Johnson. Johnson, also a professor, teaches in the same department as Bonacci, and they share an office. One of her areas of interest is social psychology. She had not published anything prior to the text she wrote with Bonacci.

LISA EDE AND ANDREA A. LUNSFORD

Lisa Ede is professor of English and director of the Center for Writing and Learning at Oregon State University, where she has taught since 1980. She has published a number of books and articles collaboratively with Andrea A. Lunsford, including *Singular Texts/Plural Authors: Perspectives on Collaborative Writing* and "Audience Addressed/Audience Invoked: The Role of Audience in Composition Theory and Pedagogy," which won the CCCC Braddock Award in 1985. In 1985, Ede, Lunsford, and Robert Connors received the MLA's Shaughnessy Award for editing *Essays on Classical Rhetoric and Modern Discourse*. In addition, Ede is the editor of *On Writing Research: The Braddock Essays, 1975–1998*.

Currently professor of English and director of the Stanford Program in Writing and Rhetoric, Andrea A. Lunsford has designed and taught undergraduate and graduate courses in writing history and theory, rhetoric, literacy, and intellectual property. Before joining the Stanford faculty, she was Distinguished Professor of English and director of the Center for the Study and Teaching of Writing at Ohio State University. Currently also a member of the Bread Loaf School of English faculty, Professor Lunsford earned her B.A. and M.A. degrees from the University of Florida, and she completed her Ph.D. in English at Ohio State University in 1977. Professor Lunsford's interests include rhetorical theory, gender and rhetoric, collaboration, cultures of writing, style, and technologies of writing. She has written or co-authored thirteen books, including *The Everyday Writer; Essays on Classical Rhetoric and Modern Discourse; Singular Texts/Plural Authors;* and *Reclaiming Rhetorica: Women in the History of Rhetoric*, as well as numerous chapters and articles. Her most recent book, written in collaboration with John Ruszkiewicz and Keith Walters, is entitled *Everything's an Argument (with Readings);* recent essays include "Rhetoric, Feminism, and the Politics of Textual Ownership" (*College English* 61, no. 5 [May 1999]: 116) and "Collaboration and Concepts of Authorship" (with Lisa Ede), forthcoming in the May 2001 issue of *PMLA*.

Professor Lunsford has conducted workshops on writing and program reviews at scores of North American universities, served as chair of the Conference on College Composition and Communication and chair of the Modern Language Association Division on Writing, and as a member of the MLA executive council.

ROJA GRANT* AND EMILY HUI*

Grant is an assistant professor of mathematics at an urban comprehensive four-year college. She has a Ph.D. in mathematics education and her area of interest is international and multicultural mathematics education. Grant listed three publications on her curriculum vitae, all of which are co-authored, and one of which was co-authored with Hui. She also wrote two grants with Hui and one with other co-authors. Hui is a mathematics instructor at a rural comprehensive four-year college. She also has a Ph.D. in mathematics education and her areas of interest include the social context of teaching and learning, and learners with special needs. Hui listed four publications, all of which are co-authored.

ELIZABETH KENT* AND MATTHEW OLDMAN*

Kent teaches at a four-year comprehensive private university. She has a Ph.D. in psychology and was hired by the education department for her expertise in learning theory. Two of her publications were co-authored with Oldman. Oldman teaches in the education department at the same institution as Kent. He holds an Ed.D. and teaches primarily pre-service teachers; his area of expertise is cooperative learning. He has published a textbook and several articles, three of which were co-authored.

JULIE KNIGHT* AND GILBERT ADAMS*

Knight is an associate professor at a mid-sized urban comprehensive four-year college. She has an Ed.D. in educational psychology, and has published thirty books, chapters, and articles. Twenty of those were co-authored, and of those, three (a text and proceedings that became chapters in books) were co-authored with Adams. Adams is chair of the department in which he and Knight work together. He has a Ph.D. in organizational psychology and has publised twenty-eight books, articles, and chapters; twenty of those were co-authored.

KAREN O'QUIN AND SUSAN P. BESEMER

O'Quin is a professor in the Department of Psychology at a mid-sized urban comprehensive four-year college. She has a Ph.D. in social psychology and is particularly interested in gifted education. She lists twenty-three publications, twenty-two of which were co-authored, and four of which were written with Besemer. At the time of this study, she and Besemer were working on an article which they had been invited to write for the *Encyclopedia of Creativity*. Besemer was the director of libraries at a small four-year comprehensive college (a different institution from O'Quin) at that time, and she was working on a Ph.D. from a Norwegian university. Her area of interest is creativity assessment. She lists twenty-seven publications, fourteen of which were co-authored (one with her daughter).

CYBIL PIKE*, ALEXANDER DAVIS*, AND BEN ELLISON*

Pike is a professor in the history department of a large comprehensive university. She is especially interested in issues of gender and race. She had published numerous books and articles, both singly and collaboratively, before she began to work with Davis and Ellison. Davis is a professor in the same department as Pike. He, too, focuses on gender and race. He had singly published a couple of articles before he began his work with Pike and Ellison. In addition to their scholarly work, he and Pike are both published poets. Ellison was a graduate student in the department in which Pike and Davis teach. His scholarly foci are community and ecological issues. He had not published before he began the co-authored project with Davis and Pike.

DUANE ROEN AND STUART BROWN

Duane Roen is professor of English at Arizona State University, where he currently directs the Center for Learning and Teaching Excellence. After teaching in a Wisconsin high school for five years, he began university teaching in 1977. All six of his books and approximately seventy percent of his 140 or so chapters, articles, and conference papers have been collaborative projects. His current projects—all collaborative—focus on gender in the classroom, the scholarship of teaching, and the scholarship of writing program administration.

Stuart C. Brown is associate professor of rhetoric and professional communication in the English department at New Mexico State University, where he teaches history and theory of rhetoric, communication ethics, rhetorical criticism, and environmental rhetoric. He is currently the writing program director and associate department head. Publications include *Defining the New Rhetorics* (1993) and *Professing the New Rhetorics* (1994), both co-edited with Theresa Enos; reports on doctoral programs in rhetoric and composition for *Rhetoric Review* (spring 1994, spring 2000); *Green Culture: Rhetorical Analyses of Environmental Discourse* (1996), co-edited with Carl Herndl; and the advanced composition textbook *The Writer's Toolbox* (with Robert Mittan and

Duane Roen, 1997). His latest project is the co-edited (with Duane Roen and Theresa Enos) collection of essays *Living Rhetoric and Composition: Stories from the Discipline* (1999). He is currently editing (with Theresa Enos) *The Writing Program Administrator's Handbook* for Lawrence Erlbaum.

JAMES AND KATHLEEN STRICKLAND

Kathleen and James Strickland teach undergraduate and graduate students at Slippery Rock University of Pennsylvania, a mid-sized comprehensive four-year university in the northeast. Kathleen, a veteran of twenty-two years of teaching, is currently a professor in the College of Education and teaches reading and language arts. Jim, a professor in the English department, has taught first-year college composition in addition to courses focusing on rhetoric and the teaching of writing and literature for thirty-one years. Together, they have co-authored several books and articles on literacy in a transactional classroom, including their well-received books about assessment and evaluation, *Reflections on Assessment* (1998) and *Making Assessment Elementary* (2000). In addition, they are currently working on a major revision of their 1993 work, *Un-covering the Curriculum*, which will appear in 2002 as *Engaged in Learning*. Individually, Jim published *From Disk to Hard Copy* in 1997, a resource for teachers interested in using computers in the teaching of writing, and Kathleen published *Literacy Not Labels* in 1995, the story of how special education students became readers and writers, each of whom had been given an educational label, ranging from "learning disabled" to "educably mentally retarded." Both hold Ph.D. degrees in rhetoric and linguistics from Indiana University of Pennsylvania.

REFERENCES

Adams, Hazard, and Leroy Searle, eds. 1992. *Critical theory since 1965*. Tallahassee, FL: Florida State University Press.

Addison, Joanne, and Sharon James McGee, eds. 1999. *Feminist empirical research: Emerging perspectives on qualitative and teacher research*. Portsmouth, NH: Boynton/Cook.

———. 1999. Introduction. Addison and McGee: 1–7.

Allen, Nancy, Dianne Atkinson, Meg Morgan, Teresa Moore, and Craig Snow. 1987.What experienced collaborators say about collaborative writing. *JBTE* 1:71–90.

Alm, Mary. 1998. The role of talk in the writing process of intimate collaboration. In *Common ground*, ed. Elizabeth G. Peck and JoAnna Stephens Mink. Albany, NY: State University of New York Press, 123–40.

Appley, Dee G., and Alvin E. Winder. 1977. An evolving definition of collaboration and some implications for the world of work. *The Journal of Applied Behavioral Science* 13:279–91.

Arendt, Hannah. 1998. *The human condition*. 2d ed. Chicago: University of Chicago Press.

Armstrong, Robert Plant. 1981. *The power of presence: Consciousness, myth, and affecting presence*. Philadelphia: University of Pennsylvania Press.

Ashton-Jones, Evelyn, and Dene Kay Thomas. 1995. Composition, collaboration, and women's ways of knowing; A conversation with Mary Belenky. In *Women writing culture*, ed. Gary A. Olson and Elizabeth Hirsh. Albany: State University of New York Press, 81–101.

Austin, Anne E., and Roger G. Baldwin. 1991. *Faculty collaboration: Enhancing the quality of scholarship and teaching*. ASHE-ERIC Higher Education Report No. 7. Washington: George Washington University, School of Education and Human Development.

Bakhtin, Mikhail. 1981. *The dialogic imagination: Four essays by M. M. Bakhtin*. Ed. Michael Holquist. Trans. Caryl Emerson and Michael Holquist. Austin: University of Texas Press.

Ballif, Michelle, D. Diane Davis, and Roxanne Mountford. 2000. Negotiating the differend: A feminist trilogue. *Journal of Advanced Composition* 20:583–625.

Baron, Naomi S. 2000. *Alphabet to email: How written English evolved and where it's heading*. London: Routledge.

Bateson, Mary Catherine. 1990. *Composing a life*. New York: The Atlantic Monthly Press, 1989. Reprint, New York: Plume.

Bavaro, John A. 1995. Faculty perceptions of scholarship and its measures at one school of education. ERIC Document Reproduction Service, no. ED 381 063.

Belenky, Mary Field, Blythe McVicker Clinchy, Nancy Rule Goldberger, and Jill Mattuck Tarule. 1986. *Women's ways of knowing: The development of self, voice, and mind*. New York: Basic Books.

Benhabib, Seyla. 1992. *Situating the self: Gender, community, and postmodernism in contemporary ethics*. New York: Routledge.

Bernstein, Charles. 1998. *Frame lock*. Available at http://wings.buffalo.edu/epc/ authors/bernstein/frame.lock.html.

Bishop, Wendy. 1995. Co-authoring changes the writing classroom: Authorizing the self, authoring together. *Composition Studies* 23:55–61.

Blitz, Michael, and C. Mark Hurlbert. 1998. *Letters for the living: Teaching writing in a violent age*. Urbana, IL: National Council of Teachers of English.

Boice, Robert. 1993. New faculty involvement for women and minorities. *Research in Higher Education* 34:291–341.

Borden, Carla M., ed. 1992. Edited excepts from a Smithsonian seminar series. *Knowledge* 14, no. 1:110–32.

Boyer, Ernest L. 1990. Scholarship reconsidered: Priorities of the professoriate, Princeton, NJ: Carnegie Foundation for the Advancement of Teaching. ERIC Document Reproduction Service, no. ED 326 149.

Boykoff, Susan L. 1989. Coauthorhip: Collaboration without conflict. *American Journal of Nursing* 89:1164.

Brady, Laura A. 1988. Collaborative literary writing: Issues of authorship and authority. Ph.D. diss., University of Minnesota.

Brady, Laura. 1998. The reproduction of othering. Jarratt and Worsham: 21–44.

Brodkey, Linda. 1987. *Academic writing as social practice*. Philadelphia: Temple University Press.

Bronfen, Elisabeth, and Misha Kavka, eds. 2001. *Feminist consequences: Theory for the new century*. New York: Columbia University Press.

Bruffee, Kenneth. 1993. *Collaborative learning: Higher education, interdependence, and the authority of knowledge*. Baltimore, MD: Johns Hopkins University Press.

Buber, Martin. 1965. *Between man and man*. Trans. Ronald Gregor Smith. London: Routledge and Kegan Paul Ltd., 1947. Reprint, New York: Macmillan.

———. 1958. *I and thou*. Translated by Ronald Gregor Smith. Reprint 1987, New York: Collier Books.

Burman, Kenneth D. 1982. Hanging from the masthead: Reflections of authorship. *Annals of Internal Medicine* 97:602–5.

Burnett, Rebecca E. 1994. Productive and unproductive conflict in collaboration. In *Making thinking visible*, ed. Linda Flower, David L. Wallace, Linda Norris, and Rebecca E. Burnett. Urbana, IL: National Council of Teachers of English, 237–42.

Cain, Mary Ann. 1995. *Revisioning writers' talk: Gender and culture in acts of composing.* Albany: State University of New York Press.

Casey, Mara. 1993. The meaning of collaborative writing in a college composition course. Ph.D. diss., University of California, Riverside.

Caughie, Pamela L. 1998. Let it pass: Changing the subject, once again. Jarratt and Worsham: 111–31.

Chapman, Ann D., Judith J. Leonard, and John C. Thomas. 1992. Co-Authoring: A natural form of cooperative learning. *The Clearing House* 66:44–46.

Chodorow, Nancy J. 1978. *The reproduction of mothering: Psychoanalysis and the sociology of gender.* Berkeley: University of California Press.

———. 1989. *Feminism and psychoanalytic theory.* New Haven, CT: Yale University Press.

Cixous, Hélène. 1992. The laugh of the Medusa. In *Critical theory since 1965,* ed. Hazard Adams and Leroy Searle:. Tallahassee: Florida State University Press, 308–20.

Coates, Jennifer. 1993. *Men, women, and language.* 2d ed. London: Longman.

Cohen, Elizabeth. 1994. *Designing groupwork: Strategies for the heterogeneous classroom.* 2d ed. New York: Teachers College Press.

Couture, Barbara. 1998. *Toward a phenomenological rhetoric: Writing, profession, and altruism.* Carbondale: Southern Illinois University Press.

Crase, Darrell, and Frank D. Rosato. 1992. Single versus multiple authorship in professional journals. *The Journal of Physical Education, Recreation and Dance* 63, no. 7:28–32.

Creamer, Elizabeth G. 1999. Knowledge production, publication productivity, and intimate academic partnerships. *Journal of Higher Education* 70:261–276.

Creamer, Elizabeth G., and Catherine McHugh Engstrom. 1996. Institutional factors women academics perceive to be associated with their publishing productivity. ERIC Document Reproduction Service, no. ED 405 755.

Cross, Geoffrey A. 1994. *Collaboration and conflict: A contextual exploration of group writing and positive emphasis.* Written Language Series, Marcia Farr, ed. Cresskill, NJ: Hampton Press.

Daiute, Collette, and Brigette Dalton. 1988. "Let's brighten it up a bit": Collaboration and cognition in writing. In *The social construction of written communication,* ed. Bennett A. Rafoth and Donald L. Rubin. Norwood, NJ: Ablex Publishing, 249–72.

Dale, Helen. 1997. *Co-authoring in the classroom: Creating an environment for effective collaboration.* Urbana, IL: National Council of Teachers of English.

Damrosh, David. 2000. Mentors and tormentors in doctoral education. *The Chronicle of Higher Education,* 17 November.

Davydov, Vasily V. 1995. The influence of L. S. Vygotsky on education, theory, research, and practice. Trans. Stephen T. Kerr. *Educational Researcher* 24:12–21.

Dickens, Cynthia Sullivan, and Mary Ann D. Sagaria. 1997. Feminists at work: Collaborative relationships among women faculty. *The Review of Higher Education* 21:78–101.

Doane, Janice, and Devon Hodges. 1995. Writing from the trenches: Women's work and collaborative writing. *Tulsa Studies in Women's Literature* 14:51–58.

Dralus, Darlene, and Jen Shelton. 1995. What is the subject? Speaking, silencing, (self)censorship. *Tulsa Studies in Women's Literature* 14:19–38.

Durst, Russel, and S. C. Stanforth. 1996. "Everything's negotiable": Collaboration and conflict in composition research. In *Ethics and representation in qualitative studies of literacy*, ed. Peter Mortensen and Gesa Kirsch. Urbana, IL: National Council of Teachers of English, 58–76.

Ede, Lisa, and Andrea Lunsford. 1983. Why write . . . together? *Rhetoric Review* 1:150–57.

———. 1990. *Singular texts/plural authors: Perspectives on collaborative writing.* Carbondale: Southern Illinois University Press.

———. 1998. Writing Back. Jarratt and Worsham :313–320.

Ellsworth, Elizabeth. 1994. Why doesn't this feel empowering? Working through the repressive myths of critical pedagogy. In *The education feminism reader*, ed. Lynda Stone. New York: Routledge, 300–327.

Endersby, James W. 1996. Collaborative research in the social sciences: Multiple authorship and publication credit. *Social Science Quarterly* 77:375–93.

Engers, Maxim, Joshua S. Gans, Simon Grant, and Stephen P. King. 1999. First-author conditions. *Journal of Political Economy* 107:859.

Entes, Judith. 1994. The right to write a co-authored manuscript. Reagan, Fox, and Bleich: 47–60.

Eodice, Michele Ann. 1999. Barn-raising and barn-burning: A study of co-authoring in a developmental writing classroom. Ph.D. diss., Indiana University of Pennsylvania.

Faigley, Lester. 1992. *Fragments of rationality: Postmodernity and the subject of composition.* Pittsburgh: University of Pittsburgh Press.

Farber, Stephen, and Marc Green. 2001. The genius of creative collaboration. The *Chronicle of Higher Education*, 16 February: B17.

Fine, Mark A., and Lawrence A. Kurdek. 1993. Reflections on determining authorship credit and authorship order. *American Psychologist* 48:1141–47.

Follo, Eric J., Sarah L. Gibson, Dyanne M. Tracy, and Joyce A. Eckart. 1995. Creating peer support groups to achieve tenure and promotion: One institution's successful STARS and WRITE programs. *CUPA Journal* 46.1:15–19.

Forman, Janis, ed. 1992 *New visions of collaborative writing.* Portsmouth, NH: Heinemann.

Foucault, Michel. 1992. The order of discourse. Adams and Searle: 138–148

Fox, Mary Frank, and Catherine A. Faver. 1984. Independence and cooperation in research: The motivations and costs of collaboration. *Journal of Higher Education* 55:347–59.

Gainen, Joanne. 1993. A writing support program for junior women faculty. *New Directions for Teaching and Learning* 53:91–100.

Gale, Xin Liu, and Frederic G. Gale, eds. 1999. *(Re)visioning composition textbooks: Conflicts of culture, ideology, and pedagogy.* Albany: State University of New York.

Gearhart, Sally Miller. 1979. The womanization of rhetoric. *Women's Studies International Quarterly* 2:195–201.

Gere, Anne Ruggles. 1987. *Writing groups: History, theory, and implications.* Carbondale: Southern Illinois University Press.

Gergen, Kenneth J. 1992. Toward a postmodern psychology. In *Psychology and postmodernism*, ed. Steinar Kvale. Newbury Park, CA: Sage.

Gergits, Julia M., and James J. Schramer. 1994. The collaborative classroom as a site of difference. *Journal of Advanced Composition* 14:188–201.

Gilligan, Carol. 1982. *In a different voice: Psychological theory and women's development.* Cambridge, MA: Harvard University Press.

Giroux, Henry. A. 1992. *Border crossings: Cultural workers and the politics of education.* New York: Routledge.

Goldstein, Richard. 2000. Ed Linn, 77, magazine writer and author of baseball books. *New York Times*, 5 February: 16C.

Golub, Jeff. 1988. *Focus on collaborative learning*, ed. Jeff Golub and the Committee on Classroom Practices. Urbana, IL: National Council of Teachers of English.

Goodburn, Amy, and Beth Ina. 1994. Collaboration, critical pedagogy, and struggles over difference. *Journal of Advanced Composition* 14:133–47.

Gore, Jennifer. 1992. What we can do for you! What can "we" do for "you"? Struggling over empowerment in critical and feminist pedagogy. In *Feminisms and critical pedagogy*, ed. Carmen Luke and Jennifer Gore. New York: Routledge, 54–73.

Gottlieb, Alma. 1995. Beyond the lonely anthropologist: Collaboration in research and writing. *American Anthropologist* 97:21–27.

Harris, Muriel. 1992. Collaboration is not collaboration is not collaboration: Writing center tutorials vs. peer-response groups. *College Composition and Communication* 43:369–83.

Hartsock, Nancy C. M. 1987. The feminist standpoint: Developing the ground for a specifically feminist historical materialism. In *Feminism and methodology*, ed. Sandra Harding. Bloomington: Indiana University Press, 157–80.

Hartwell, Patrick. 1998. How we learn (and other stories). Paper presented on the occasion of Patrick Hartwell's retirement, Indiana, PA.

Hayes, John R., Richard E. Young, Michelle L. Matchett, Maggie McCaffrey, Cynthia Cochran, and Thomas Hajduk. 1992. *Reading empirical studies: The rhetoric of research.* Hillsdale, NJ: Laurence Erlbaum Associates.

Heath, Stephen. 1987. Male feminism. In *Men in feminism,* ed. Alice Jardine and Paul Smith. New York: Methuen, 2–32.

Hilgers, Thomas. 1986. On learning the skills of collaborative writing. Paper presented at the annual meeting of the Conference on College Composition and Communication, New Orleans, LA.

Hillebrand, Romana P. 1994. Control and cohesion: Collaborative learning and writing. *English Journal* 83:71–74.

Hirsh, Elizabeth, and Gary A. Olson. 1995. Starting with marginalized lives: A conversation with Sandra Harding. Olson and Hirsh: 3–42.

Hord, Shirley M. 1981. Working together: Cooperation or collaboration. Austin: University of Texas at Austin, Research and Development Center for Teacher Education. ERIC Document Reproduction Service, no. ED 226 450.

Horton, Richard. 2000. The imagined author. Jones and McLellan, 30–58.

Howard, Rebecca Moore. 1999. *Standing in the shadow of giants: Plagiarists, authors, collaborators.* Stamford, CT: Ablex Publishing.

———. 2000. Sexuality, textuality: The cultural work of plagiarism. *College English* 62:473–491.

Hurlbert, C. Mark, and Michael Blitz, eds. 1991. *Composition and resistance.* Portsmouth, NH: Heinemann.

Iammarino, Nicholas K., Thomas O'Rourke, R. Morgan Pigg, and Armin D. Weinberg. 1989. Ethical issues in research and publication. *Journal of School Health* 59:101–5.

Isenberg, Joan P., Mary Renck Jalongo, and Karen D'Angelo Bromley. 1987. The role of collaboration in scholarly writing: A national study. Paper presented at the annual meeting of the American Educational Research Association, Washington, D.C. ERIC Document Reproduction Service, no. ED 287 873.

Jarratt, Susan C. 1998. Introduction: As we were saying . . . . Jarratt and Worsham: 1–20.

Jarratt, Susan C., and Lynn Worsham, eds. 1998. *Feminism and composition studies.* New York: Modern Language Association.

Johanek, Cindy. 2000. *Composing research: A contextualist paradigm for rhetoric and composition.* Logan, UT: Utah State University Press.

Jones, Anne Hudson. 2000. Changing traditions of authorship. Jones and McLellan: 3–29.

Jones, Anne Hudson, and Faith McLellan, eds. 2000. *Ethical issues in biomedical publication.* Baltimore, MD: The Johns Hopkins University Press.

Jones, Thomas B., and Chet Meyers. 1994. Collaborative faculty writing: Two heads are better than one. *AAHE Bulletin* 46, no. (6): 7–9.

Kanpol, Barry. 1995. Multiculturalism and empathy: A border pedagogy of solidarity. Kanpol and McLaren: 177–96.

Kanpol, Barry, and Peter McLaren, eds. 1995. *Critical multiculturalism: Uncommon voices in a common struggle*. Westport, CT: Bergin and Garvey.

Kirk, Stuart A., and Kevin J. Corcoran. 1989. The $12,000 question: Does it pay to publish? *Social Work* 34:379–81.

Kirsch, Gesa E. 1999. Reflecting on collaboration in feminist empirical research: Some cautions. Addison and McGee:158–162.

Kirton, Michael J. 1987. Adaptors and innovators: Cognitive style and personality. In *Frontiers of creativity research*, ed. Scott G. Isaksen: Buffalo, NY: Bearly Ltd., 282–304.

Knoblauch, C. H., and Lil Brannon. 1984. *Rhetorical traditions and the teaching of writing*. Upper Montclair, NJ: Boynton/Cook.

Knott, Toni, and Lynne Valek. 1999. Working as one: A narrative study of the collaboration of male-female dyads in the workplace. Ph.D. diss., The Fielding Institute.

Kvale, Steinar. 1996. *Interviews: An introduction to qualitative research interviewing*. Thousand Oaks, CA: Sage.

Laird, Holly A. 2000. *Women coauthors*. Urbana: University of Illinois Press.

Laque, Carol Feiser, and Phyllis A. Sherwood. 1975. A teaching monograph: Co-designed laboratory approach to writing. Ed.D. diss., University of Cincinnati.

Lather, Patti. 1995. Feminist perspectives on empowering research methodologies in debates and issues. In *Feminist Research and Pedagogy*, ed. Janet Holland and Maud Blair. Clevedon, England: Multilingual Matters Ltd., 292–307

Lay, Mary M. 1987. The metaphor of the web: A link between collaborative writing and gender studies. In *Proceedings of the annual meeting of the Council for Programs in Technical and Scientific Communication*, October 7–9, ed. Sam C. Geonetta. ERIC Document Reproduction Service, no. ED 361 778, 68–90.

LeFevre, Karen Burke. 1987. *Invention as a social act*. Carbondale: Southern Illinois University Press.

Leverenz, Carrie S. 1994. Peer response in the multicultural composition classroom: Dissensus—a dream (deferred). *Journal of Advanced Composition* 14:167–85.

Lincoln, Yvonna S., and Egon G. Guba. 1985. *Naturalistic inquiry*. Newbury Park, CA: Sage.

Liptak, Adam. 2000. Author unknown. *The New York Times Book Review*, 29 November 2000: 34.

Lo, Jane-Jane, Kelly Gaddis, and David Henderson. 1996. Building upon student experiences in a college geometry course. *For the Learning of Mathematics* 16, no. 1:34–40.

London, Bette. 1999. *Writing double: Women's literary partnerships*. Ithaca, NY: Cornell University Press.

Louth, Richard, Carole McAllister, and Hunter A. McAllister. 1993. The effects of collaborative writing techniques on freshman writing and attitudes. *Journal of Experimental Education* 61:215–24.

Luke, Carmen, and Jennifer Gore, eds. 1992. *Feminisms and critical pedagogy.* NewYork: Routledge.

Lukovits, I., and P. Vinkler. 1995. Correct credit distribution: A model for sharing credit among coauthors. *Social Indicators Research* 36: 91–99

Lunsford, Andrea A., and Lisa Ede. 2001. Collaboration and concepts of authorship. *Publication of the Modern Language Association* 116: 354–369.

MacNealy, Mary Sue. 1999. *Strategies for empirical research in writing.* Boston, MA: Allyn and Bacon, 1999.

Maher, Frances A., and Mary Kay Thompson Tetreault. 1994. *The feminist classroom.* New York: Basic Books.

Marsh, Jeanne C. 1992. Should scholarly productivity be the primary criterion for tenure decisions? Yes! *Journal of Social Work Education* 28:132–34.

Masten, Jeffrey. 1994. Interpretation of Renaissance drama. In *The construction of authorship,* ed. Martha Woodmansee and Peter Jaszi. Durham, NC: Duke University Press, 361–82.

McAndrew, Donald. 1996. Ecofeminism and teaching literacy. *College Composition and Communication* 47:367–82.

McDermott, R. P., and Henry Tylbor. 1983. On the necessity of collusion in conversation. *Text* 3:277–97.

McLeod, Susan H. 1997. *Notes on the heart: Affective Issues in the Writing Classroom.* Carbondale, IL: Southern Illinois University Press.

Meehan, Johanna. 2000. Feminism and Habermas' discourse ethics. *Philosophy and Social Criticism* 26:39–52.

Morris, Karen. 1998. Text and academic authors: Karen Morris and co-authoring. Available at http://taa.winona.msus.edu/taa/articles/98/06jun/0613morris.html.

Mountford, Roxanne. 2000. Re: Ethics of criticism. Pre/Text listserv. Available at http://pretext@listserv.uta.com (11 December).

Murdock, L. P. 1990. The dynamics of collaboration: An ethnographic study of scientific writing. Ph.D. diss., Indiana University of Pennsylvania.

Myers, Greg. 1986. Reality, consensus, and reform in the rhetoric of composition. *College English* 48:154–74.

Nahrwol, Marilyn. 1997. Practicing what we preach: Valuing collaborative scholarship. Available at http://web.nmsu.edu/~cnahrwol/marilyn.html.

Noddings, Nel. 1984. *Caring: A feminine approach to ethics and moral education.* Berkeley: University of California Press.

———. 1994. An ethic of caring and its implications for instructional arrangements. Stone: 171–83.

Olson, Gary A. 1995. Resisting a discourse of mastery: A conversation with Jean-Francois Lyotard. Olson and Hirsh: 169–192.

Olson, Gary A., and Elizabeth Hirsh, eds. 1995. *Women writing culture*. Albany: State University of New York Press, 1995.

O'Reilley, Mary Rose. 1993. *The peaceable classroom*. Portsmouth, NH: Heinemann.

Owens, Derek. 1994. *Resisting writings (and the boundaries of composition)*. Dallas: Southern Methodist University Press.

Palmer, Parker J. 1993. *To know as we are known: Education as a spiritual journey*. San Francisco: HarperCollins.

———. 1998. The grace of great things: Recovering the sacred in knowing, teaching, and learning. Available at http://csf.colorado.edu/sine/transcripts/palmer.html.

Panitz, Ted. 2000. Yes Virginia there is a big difference between cooperative and collaborative learning paradigms. Available at http://tedscooppage.homestead.com/index.html.

Patton, Michael Quinn. 1980. *Qualitative evaluation methods*. Beverly Hills, CA: Sage.

Peck, Elizabeth G., and JoAnna Stephens Mink, eds. 1998. *Common ground: Feminist collaboration in the academy*. Albany, NY: State University of New York Press.

Phelps, Louise W., and Janet Emig. 1995. Editors' reflections: Vision and interpretation. In *Feminine principles and women's experience in American composition and rhetoric*, ed. Louise W. Phelps and Janet Emig. Pittsburgh: University of Pittsburgh Press, 407–425.

Porter, James. 1986. Intertextuality and the discourse community. *Rhetoric Review* 5:34–47.

Qualley, Donna J., and Elizabeth Chiseri-Strater. 1994. Collaboration as reflexive dialogue: A knowing "deeper than reason." *Journal of Advanced Composition* 14:111–30.

Reagan, Sally Barr, Thomas Fox, and David Bleich, eds. *Writing with: New directions in collaborative teaching, learning, and research*. Albany: State University of New York Press.

Reamer, Frederic G. 1992. From the editor: Publishing and perishing in social work education. *Journal of Social Work Education* 28:129–31.

Reinharz, Shulamit. 1992. *Feminist methods in social research*. Cambridge, MA: Harvard University Press.

Reither, James A., and Douglas Vipond. 1989. Writing as collaboration. *College English* 51:855–67.

Rider, Janine, and Esther Broughton. 1994. Moving out, moving up: Beyond the basement and ivory tower. *Journal of Advanced Composition* 14:239–55.

Ritchie, Joy S. 1989. Beginning writers: Diverse voices and individual identity. *College Composition and Communication* 40:152–74.

Roen, Duane H., and Robert K. Mitten. 1992. Collaborative scholarship in composition: Some issues. In *Methods and methodology in composition research*, eds.

Gesa Kirsch and Patricia A. Sullivan. Carbondale: Southern Illinois University Press, 287–313.

Rogers, Priscilla S., and Marjorie S. Horton. 1992. Exploring the value of face-to-face collaborative writing. Forman: 120–46.

Romaine, Suzanne. 1994. *Language in society*. Oxford: Oxford University Press.

Rule, Rebecca. 1993. Conferences and workshops: Conversations on writing process. In *Nuts and bolts*, ed. Thomas Newkirk. Portsmouth, NH: Heinemann, 43–66.

Samuelson, Paul A. 1996. On collaboration. *American Economist* 40, no. 2:16–22.

Schell, Eileen E. 1998. The costs of caring: "Feminism" and contingent women workers in composition studies. Jarratt and Worsham: 74–93.

Schultz, John. 1978. Story workshop: Writing from start to finish. In *Research on composing*, eds. C. R. Cooper and Lee Odell. Urbana, IL: National Council of Teachers of English, 151–87.

Selden, Raman, and Peter Widdowson. 1993. *A readers' guide to contemporary literary theory*. 3d ed. Lexington: University of Kentucky Press.

Shapiro, Svi. 1995. Educational change and the crisis of the Left: Toward a postmodern educational discourse. Kanpol and McLaren: 19–38.

Spear, Karen. 1988. *Sharing writing: Peer response groups in English classes*. Portsmouth, NH: Heinemann.

Spellmeyer, Kurt. 1994. *Common ground: Dialogue, understanding, and the teaching of composition*. Englewood Cliffs, NJ: Prentice-Hall.

Spiegel, Donald, and Patricia Keith-Spiegel. 1970. Assignment of publication credits: Ethics and practices of psychologists. *American Psychologist* 25:738–47.

Spivey, Nancy. 1997. *The constructivist metaphor: Reading, writing, and the making of meaning*. New York: Academic Press.

Steinmetz, Sol, et al., eds. 1996. *Random house compact unabridged dictionary*. New York: Random House.

Stillinger, Jack. 1991. *Multiple authorship and the myth of solitary genius*. New York: Oxford University Press.

Stone, Lynda, ed. 1994. *The education feminism reader*. New York: Routledge.

Strickland, Kathleen, and James Strickland. 1993. *Un-covering the curriculum: Whole language in secondary and postsecondary classrooms*. Portsmouth, NH: Boynton/Cook.

Stuckey, J. Elspeth 1991. *The violence of literacy*. Portsmouth, NH: Boynton/Cook.

Sullivan, Patricia A. 1994. Revising the myth of the independent scholar. Reagan, Fox, and Bleich: 11–29.

Szenberg, Michael. 1996. Intellectual collaborative experiences. *American Economist* 40:3.

Tannen, Deborah. 1990. *You just don't understand: Women and men in conversation*. New York: William Morrow.

Thorne, Barrie. 1999. *Gender play: Girls and boys in school*. New Brunswick, NJ: Rutgers University Press.

Thralls, Charlotte. 1992. Bakhtin, collaborative partners, and published discourse: A collaborative view of composing. Forman: 63–81.

Tomm, Winnie. 1992. Ethics and self-knowing: The satisfaction of desire. In *Explorations in feminist ethics*, ed. Eve Browning Cole and Susan Coultrap-McQuin. Bloomington: Indiana University Press, 101–10.

Trimbur, John. 1992. Consensus and difference in collaborative learning. In *Becoming political*, ed. Patrick Shannon. Portsmouth, NH: Heinemann, 208–22.

Trimbur, John, and Lundy A. Braun. 1992. *Laboratory life and the determination of authorship.* Forman: 19–36.

Vermette, Paul J. 1998. *Making cooperative learning work: Student teams in K–12 classrooms.* Upper Saddle River, NJ: Prentice Hall.

Verrier, David A. 1994. Perceptions of life on the tenure track. *The NEA Higher Education Journal* 9:95–124.

Vygotsky, L. S. 1978. Mind in society: The development of higher psychological processes. Trans. Michael Cole, Vera John-Steiner, Sylvia Scribner, and Ellen Souberman. Cambridge, MA: Harvard University Press.

Wasser, Judith Davidson, and Laura Bresler. 1996. Working in the interpretive zone: Conceptualizing collaboration in qualitative research teams. *Educational Researcher* 25:5–15.

Wilson, Robin. 2001. A higher bar for earning tenure. *The Chronicle of Higher Education*, 5 January: A12.

Winston, Roger B. 1985. A suggested procedure for determining order of authorship in research publications. *Journal of Counseling and Development* 63:515–18.

Wittgenstein, Ludwig. 1965. Philosophical investigations. Adams and Searle: 767–88.

Wood, Diane R. 1992. Teaching narratives: A source for faculty development and evaluation. *Harvard Educational Review* 62:535–50.

Word, Ron. 2000. Collaborative novel tells story of nation's first serial killer. *Lawrence Journal-World*, 2 July: 10D.

Worsham, Lynn. 1998. After words: A choice of words remains. Jarratt and Worsham: 329–356.

Yancey, Kathleen Blake. 1998. *Reflection in the writing classroom.* Logan: Utah State University Press.

Yancey, Kathleen B., and Michael Spooner. 1998. A single good mind: Collaboration, cooperation, and the writing self. *College Composition and Communication* 49:45–62.

Yeo, Fred. 1995. The conflicts of difference in an inner-city school: Experiencing border crossings in the ghetto. Kanpol and McLaren: 197–216.

Young, Iris Marion. 1997. *Intersecting voices: Dilemmas of gender, political philosophy, and policy.* Princeton, NJ: Princeton University Press.

Zebroski, James. 1994. *Thinking through theory: Vygotskian perspectives on the teaching of writing.* Portsmouth, NH: Heinemann.

INDEX

ABOUT THE AUTHORS

KAMI DAY, Ph.D., is an assistant professor of English at Johnson County Community College in Overland Park, Kansas. In addition to her teaching, she is involved in promoting writing across the curriculum, and is a facilitator in the teacher formation movement based on the work of Parker Palmer.

MICHELE EODICE, Ph.D., is the director of the writing center at the University of Kansas, where she also teaches courses in writing center theory and practice and technical writing. She has leadership roles with the Midwest Writing Centers Association and the National Conference on PeerTutoring in Writing.

Kami and Michele live and write together in Lawrence, Kansas, where theyenjoy gardening, golf, and grandchildren.

.